JN297425

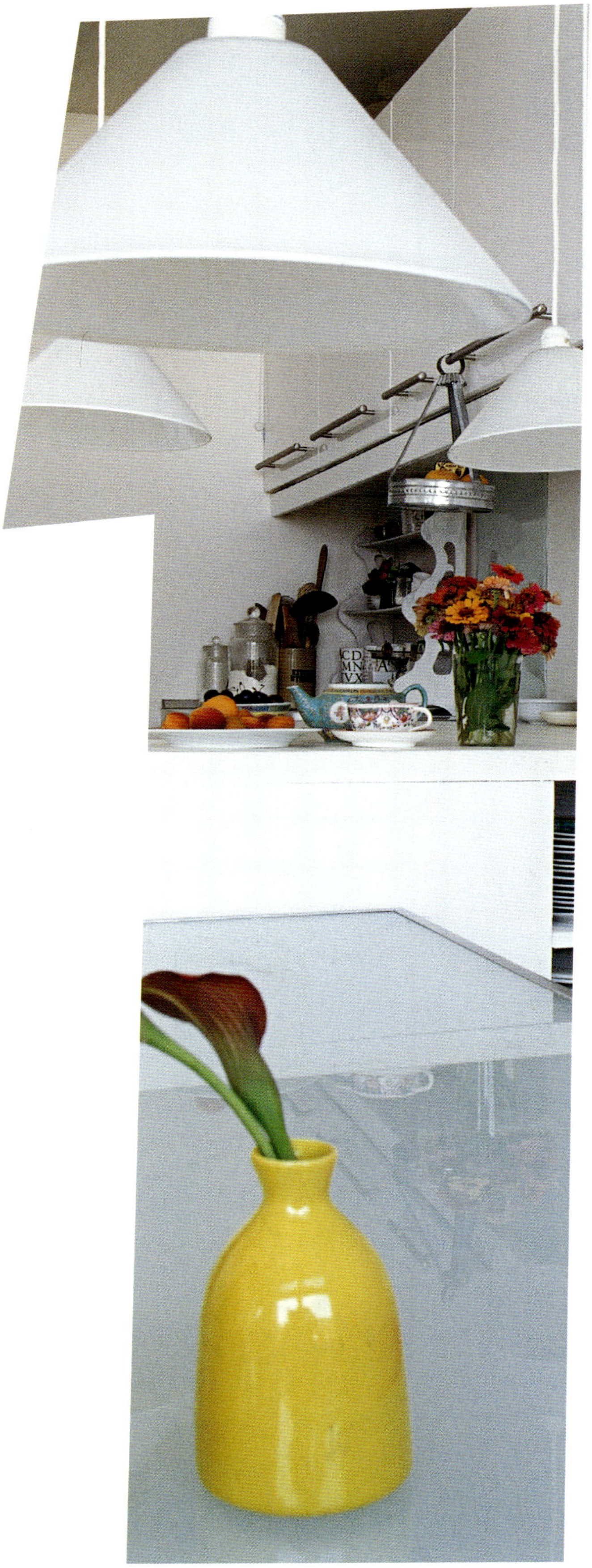

2

3

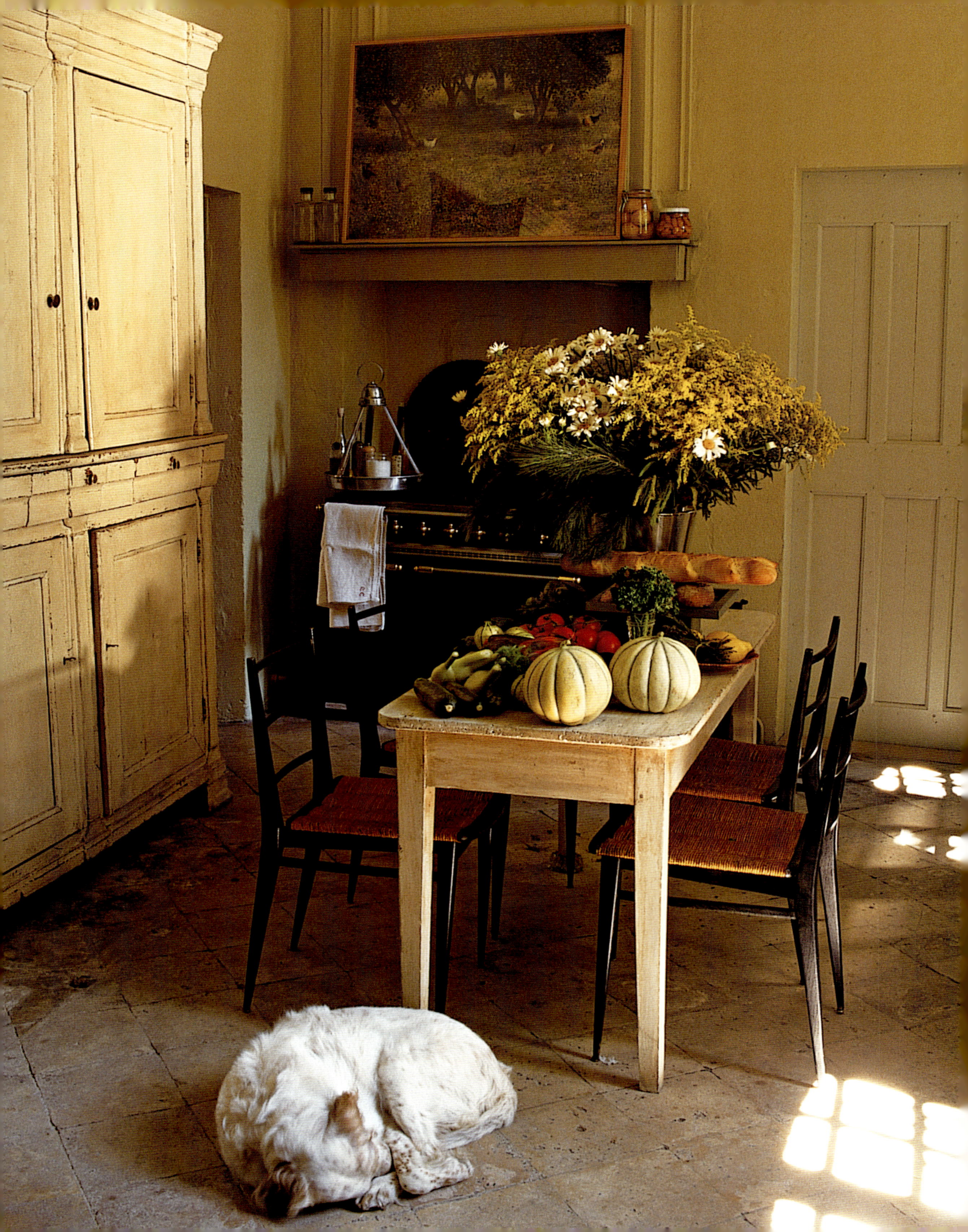

1000
ダイニング
キッチンブック

スタッフォード・クリフ 著
クリスチャン・サラモン 写真
今井 由美子 翻訳

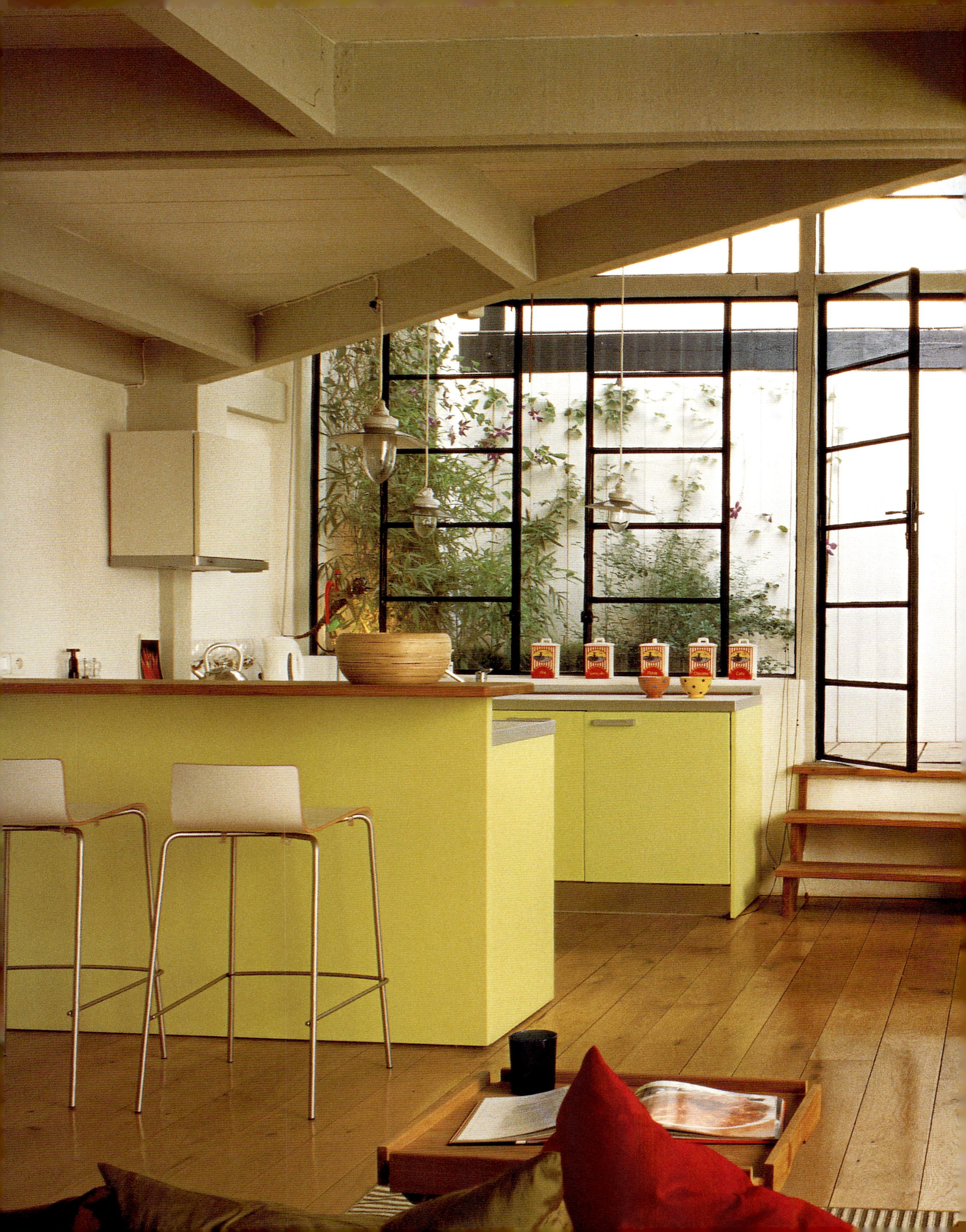

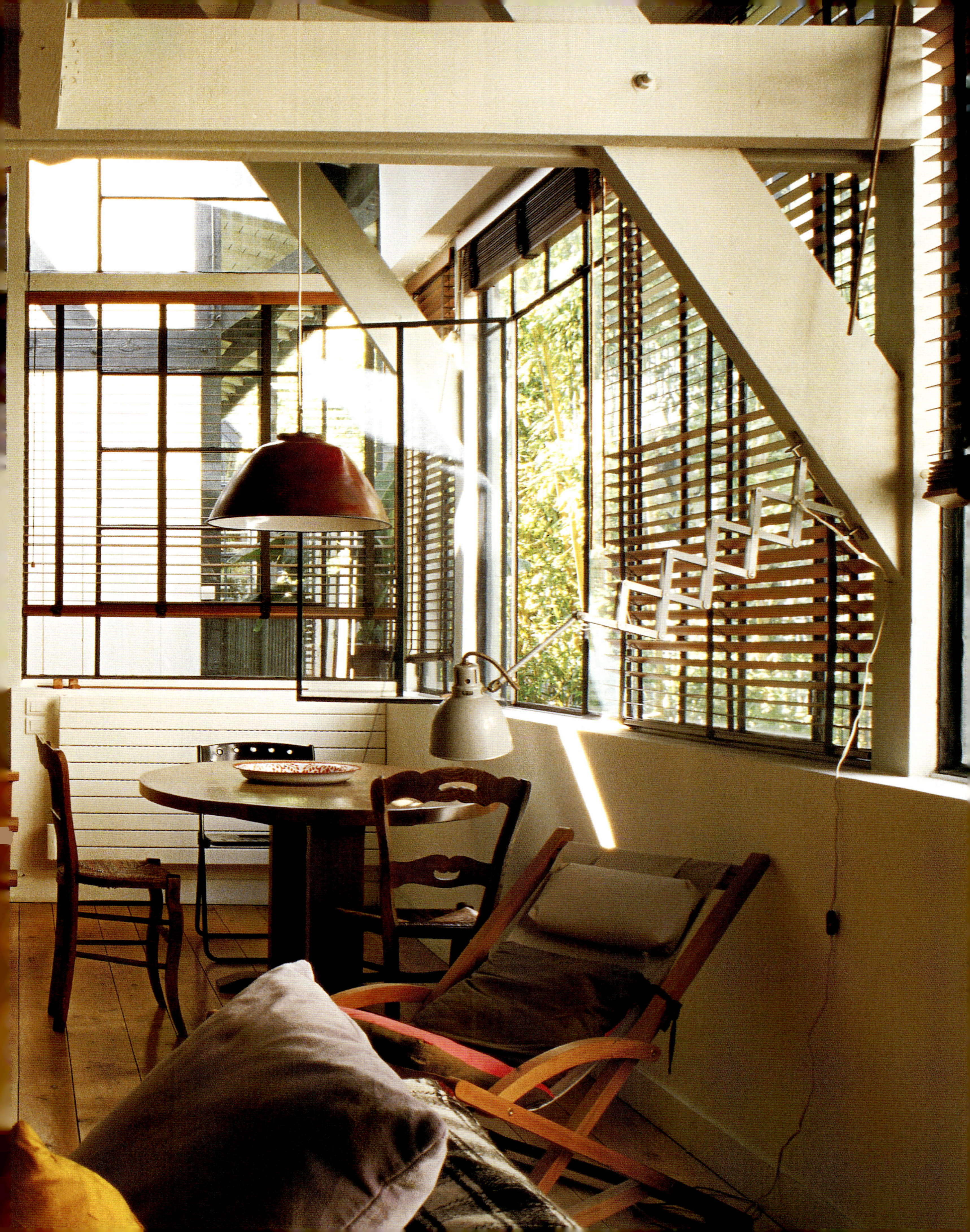

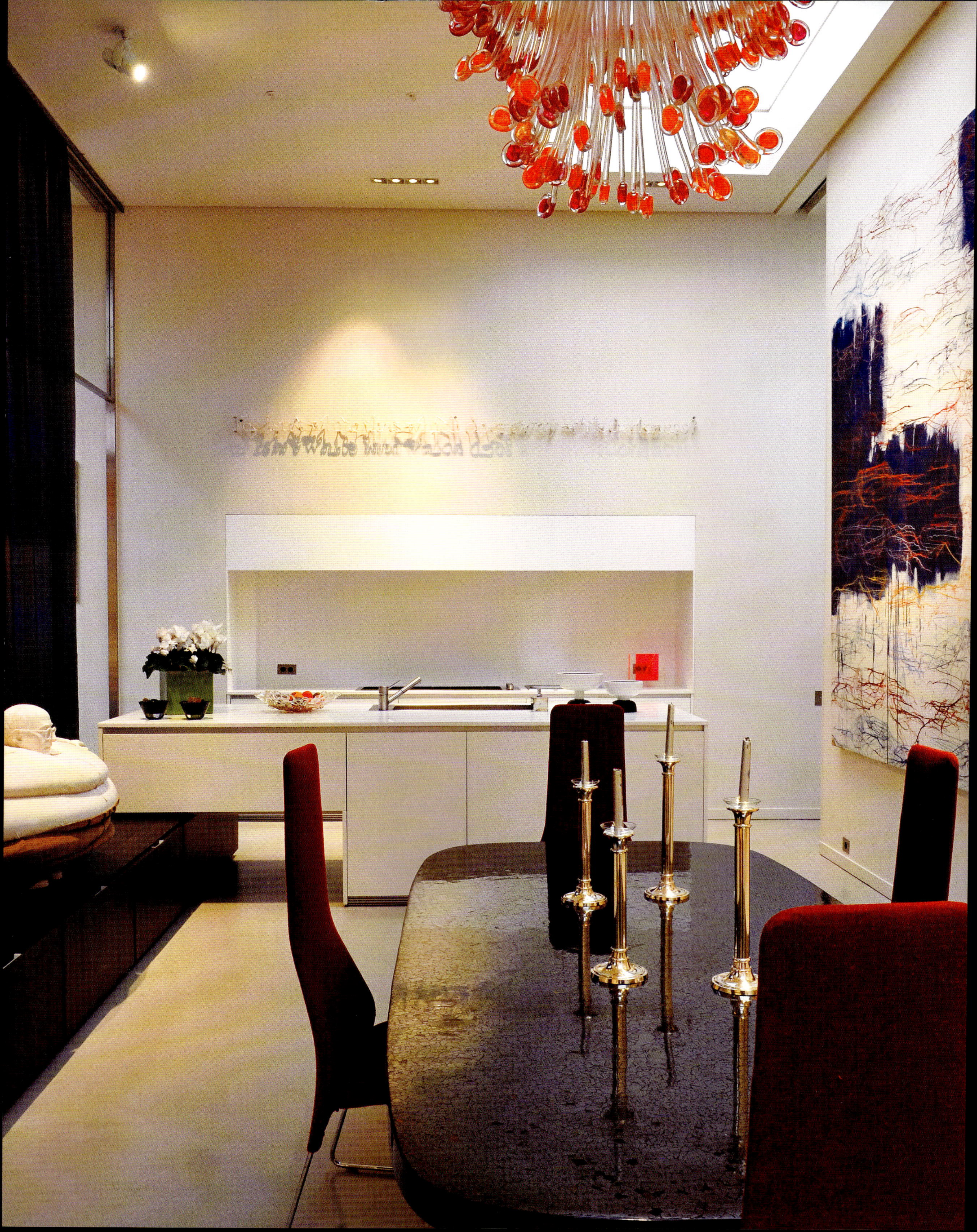

はじめに　10

スタイルと機能　12

調理と食事　26

カントリー・キッチン　46

シティ・キッチン　72

収納スペース　90

照明器具　108

見せる収納　124

床と壁　146

色と素材感　168

調理設備　184

個性的な演出　194

はじめに

今日、キッチンは、"リビングルーム"と呼び方を変えるべきでしょう。キッチンは、食事の支度だけでなく、食事そのものにも使われることが多いからです。キッチンでは調理しかしないという場合でも、食事する部屋が、すぐ隣にあると思います。調理と食事のスペースは、もはや切り離せなくなっているのです。住まいの中で、家具選びを始め、考慮すべき事項が、もっと多い部屋がキッチンです。衛生面、安全性、機能性、実用性、美感、用途…。これらすべてを考えなければなりません。いつも人の集まる、にぎやかなキッチンにしたい場合もあるでしょう。また、忙しい日常生活の中で、静かに料理をしたり、食事をしたりする、安息の場所にしたいキッチンもあるはずです。キッチンをリフォームする場合、現時点での部屋の造りによって、仕上がりの状態は、ある程度決まってきます。たとえ、キッチンをすっかり改装する資金があっても、それは変わりません。部屋の大きさと形。ドア、窓、配管の位置。天井の高さ。これらは簡単には変えられないものだからです。しかし、調理カウンターのドアやワークトップの素材、仕上げ、色には、多くの種類がありますし、今日では、設備のバリエーションも、昔とは比べものにならないほど充実しています。そのため、かえってご自分の美意識や、予算に合う選択をするのが難しいかもしれません。新しいキッチンにする時、ぜひ考えていただきたいことがあります。そのキッチンに、どんな特色をもたせるか、という点です。始めから、一番のポイントを考えておくのです。たとえば、「フレンチ・ドア」とか、「天窓」、「床暖房」と言った具合に。住宅メーカーの個性ではなく、家主の個性が反映されているのが、最良のキッチンです。まず、自分の好みの料理のスタイルから考えてみましょう。ひとりで料理するのが好きですか、それとも誰かと一緒に？ また、料理以外のどんなことに、キッチンを使いたいですか？ 家族が集まる部屋、または友だちと楽しむ部屋として？ それとも、自分のライフスタイルの主張や、ステータス・シンボルとして？ キッチンに詳しいあるライターが、以前、キッチンがどんなことに使われるか、列記していました。その中には、「ペットにエサをやる」、「宿題をする」、「テレビを見る」、「愛を交わす」というものもありました。最後のひとつは考えたこともないと、お思いかもしれません。でも、それほどキッチンが魅惑的な場所になったとしたら、どんなにおいしい料理が、食卓にのぼることでしょう。

The kitchen of today should be renamed the living room. Not only is it the room you prepare and cook food in, but more than likely you eat in it too – or in a space adjacent to it. Cooking and eating can no longer be separated. More than any other room in your house, planning the kitchen involves many considerations in addition to the furniture: hygiene, safety, function, practicality, flexibility and aesthetics. Some kitchens will be constantly full of activity; some will be a singular retreat for quiet cooking or meals on the trot. What you have to begin with will dictate, to an extent, what you end up with – even if you have the luxury and the finances to start completely from scratch. The size and shape of the room, where the doors, windows and plumbing are, the height of the ceiling and so forth will all play a part. Doors and worktops are available in dozens of materials, finishes and colours, and the range of equipment has never been so varied. This probably makes it harder than ever to choose those that will fit your aesthetics and your budget. What you need to think about is how to make your kitchen individual: the finishing touches, even if they might come at the beginning – French doors, for instance, a roof light or under-floor heating. The best kitchens are those that reflect the personality of the owner, not the personality of the manufacturers. Start from the way you like to cook – in company or in private – and the other purposes you want the room to serve. Is it a family room, a place for entertaining friends or a spotless lifestyle statement and status symbol? A professional kitchen writer once provided a list of things that might take place in a kitchen. As well as cooking and eating, she included feeding pets, doing homework, watching TV, and making love. You may not have anticipated the latter, but if your room turns out to be seductive enough, who knows what will be on the menu?

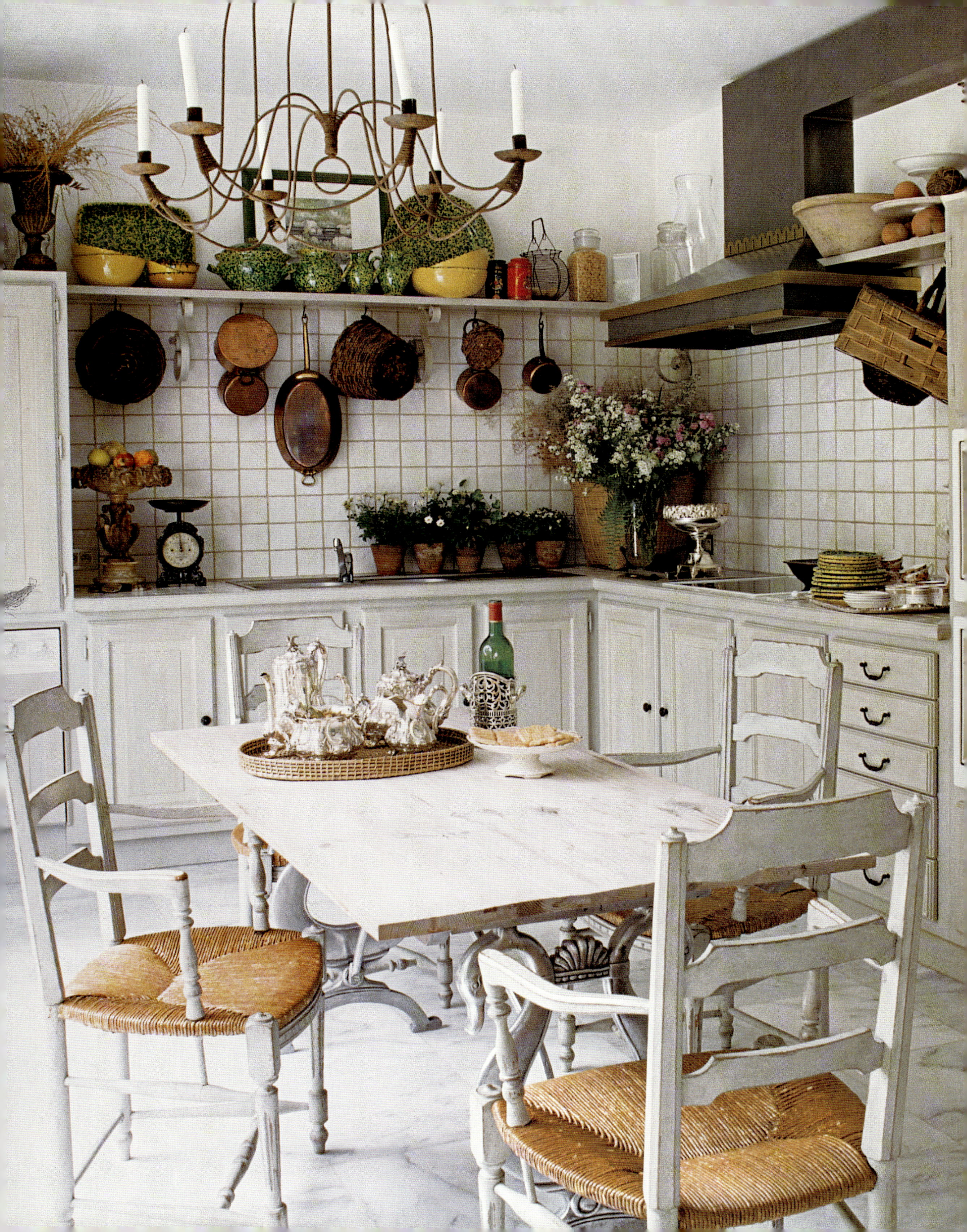

スタイルと機能

Style and Function

引っ越しを考え始めた時、家を選ぶ決め手になることが多いのは、キッチンの大きさとスタイルです。新しい家のキッチンは、サイズ、形、外観が、今使っているキッチンに勝っているでしょうか？　どのくらいの広さのキッチンが必要か、把握していますか？　食事スペースは取れるでしょうか？　気持ちのいい窓や、庭に出られるドア——なおいいのはテラスやバルコニーに続くドア——は、あるでしょうか？　明るくて楽しい気分になれる部屋でしょうか、それとも、暗い部屋でしょうか？　比較的最近、キッチンが交換されている場合、そのスタイルは好みに合っていますか、それともすべて取り外して、いちからリフォームしますか？　もし、配管や配線まで変えるとしたら、手間と費用がかかりますが、そこまでするつもりはありますか？　新しい家に、手持ちの家具を持っていきますか？　しかし、テーブルと椅子、そしておそらく食器棚をのぞいては、キッチン用の家具は、引っ越し先に合わせて揃えることになるでしょう。ですから、夢のキッチンを実現するために、具体的に何を準備すればいいのか、決断することが大切です。もし他の部屋がモダンなら、キッチンもモダンにしたいですか？　そうだとしたら、キッチンの設備も、みな最新にしたいですか？　「どうしたいか」を考えるより、「こうはしたくない」と思うことは何か、と考えるほうが、早道かもしれません。壁、床、天井から着手しましょう。キッチンで食事もしたいと思うなら、何人が、どのくらいの頻度で席に着くか、という点も考慮してください。また、小さいお子さんのいる家庭なら、キッチンでやりたいことが色々と出てくるでしょう。最後に——ご自身に問いかけてみてください。料理は好きですか？　それとも、アメリカの人気舞台俳優のように、調理設備をすべて取り外して、一切使えないようにしてしまいたいタイプですか？

When we start thinking about moving house, the thing that decisions most often hinge on is the size and style of kitchen. Is the new kitchen better than your current one in terms of size, shape and outlook? Do you know what size you want anyway? Does it include space to eat, nice windows, a door to a garden – or better still, a patio or deck? Is it a bright, cheerful space or a gloomy one? If the kitchen has been recently refitted, are the units and the equipment in the style you like, or will you want to rip everything out and start again? If it has what they call 'original fittings', are you up to the task and the cost involved in its transformation? You might be bringing your own furniture, but you are unlikely to move in with new kitchen furniture apart, that is, from a table and chairs and perhaps a kitchen dresser. So it's a good idea to decide what you are prepared to do to realise your dream. If the rest of your rooms are modern, do you want a modern kitchen too? And if so, do you want to fill it with state-of-the-art equipment? Sometimes it's easier to consider what it is you don't want. Start with the walls, floors and ceiling. You will probably want to eat in your kitchen, but if so, how many people do you want to seat, and how often? If you have a young family, they will bring their own demands. Finally – do you want to cook at all? Or are you like one famous NY theatre star who, when she moved into her new apartment, had the cooker removed, along with any temptation to use it.

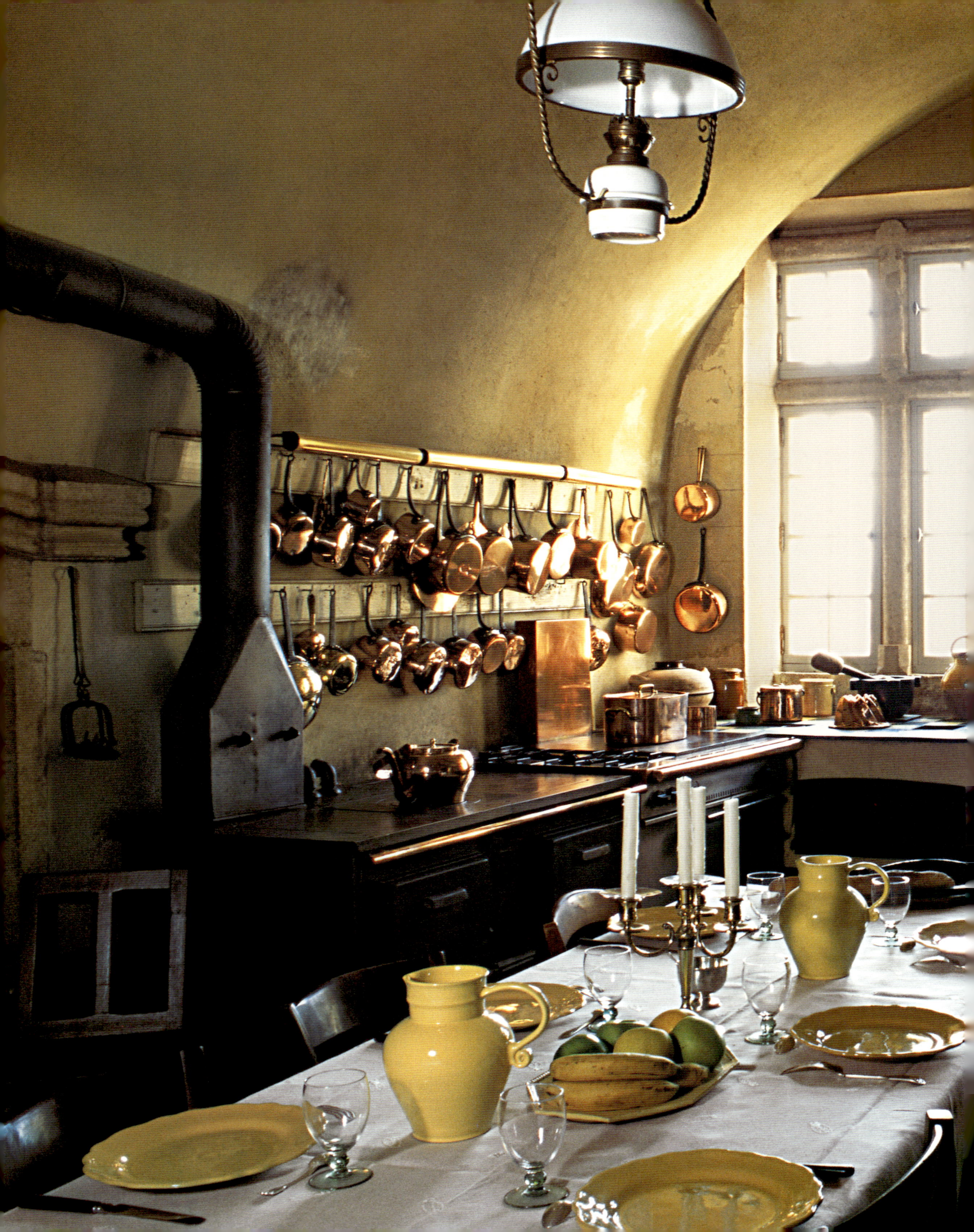

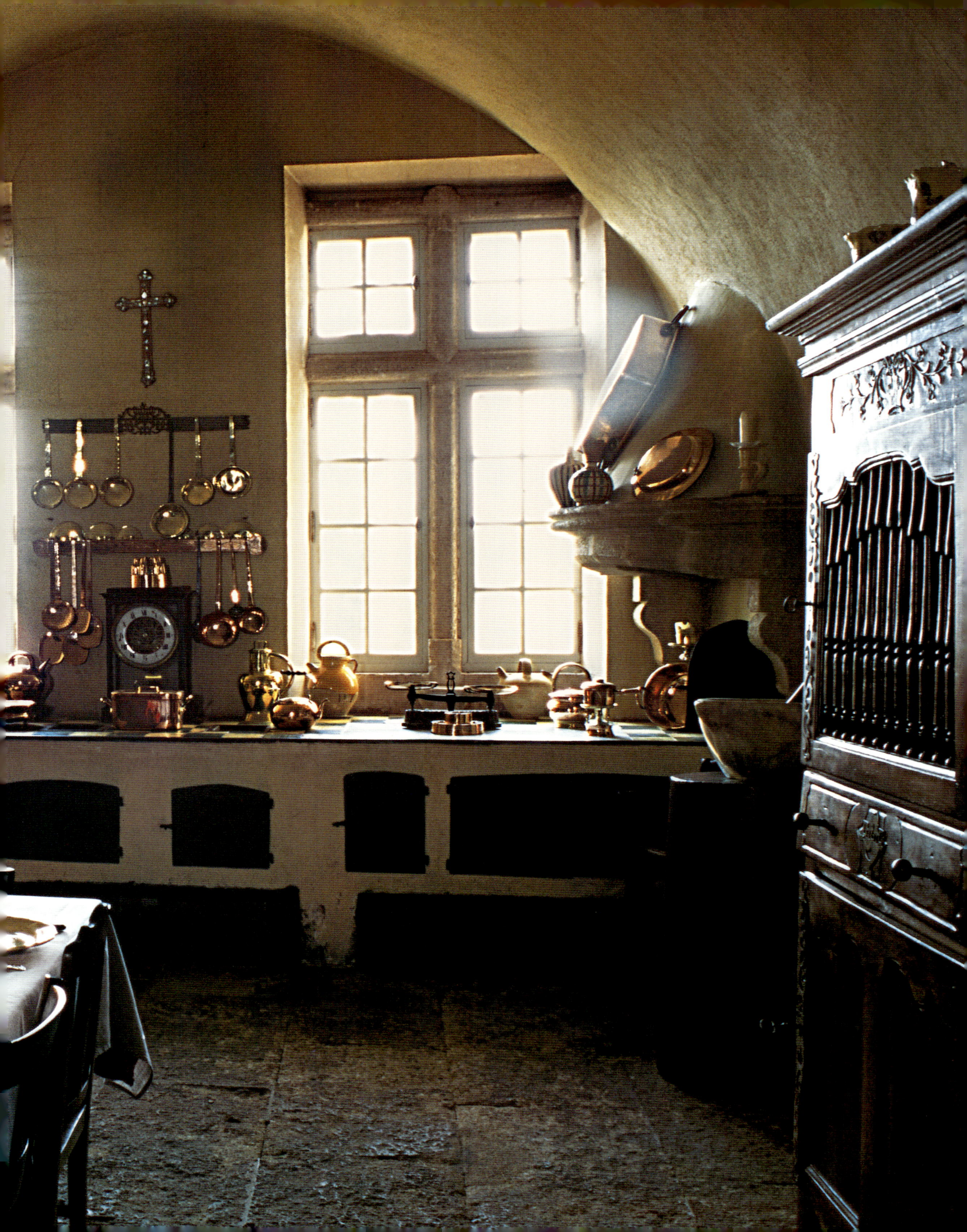

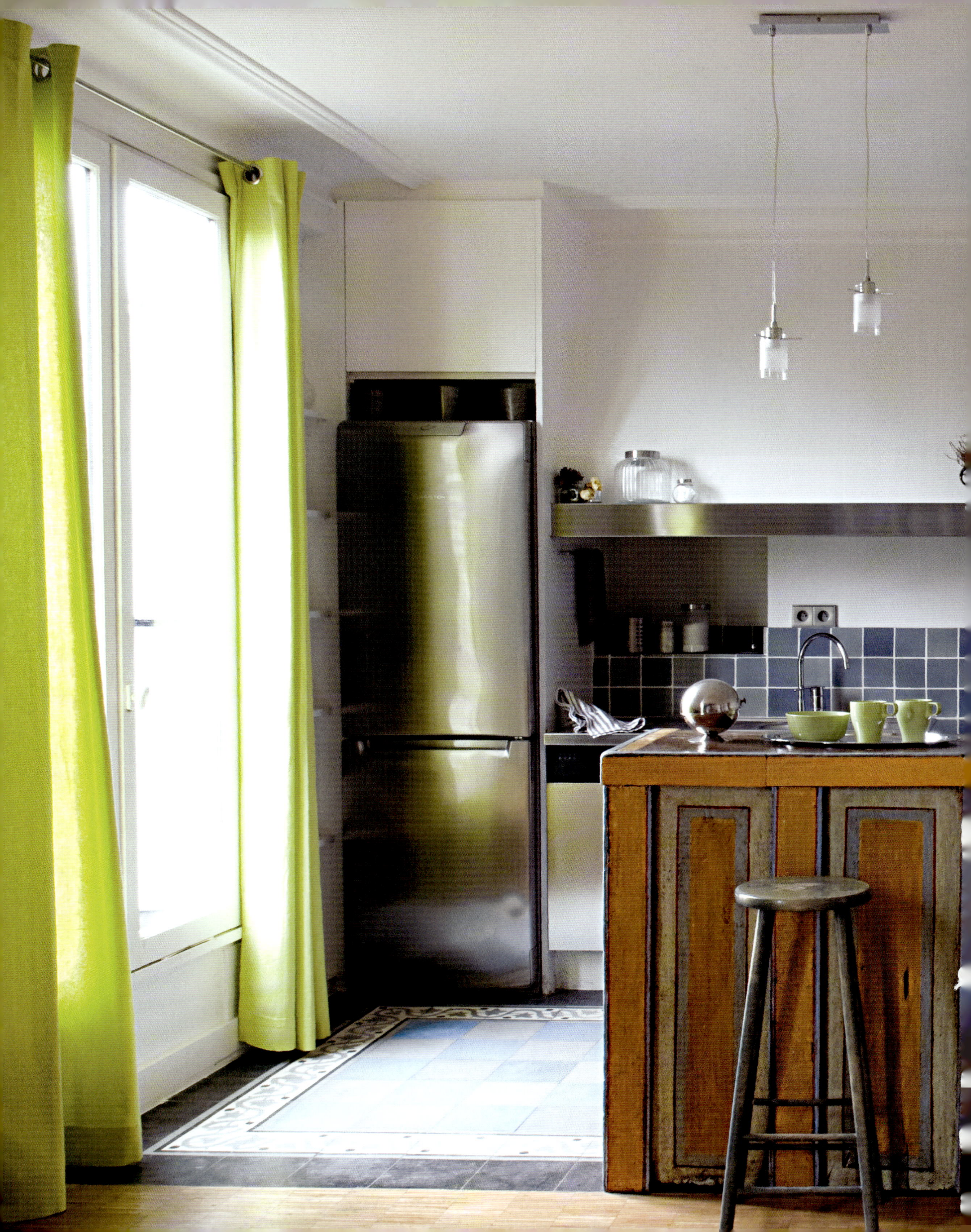

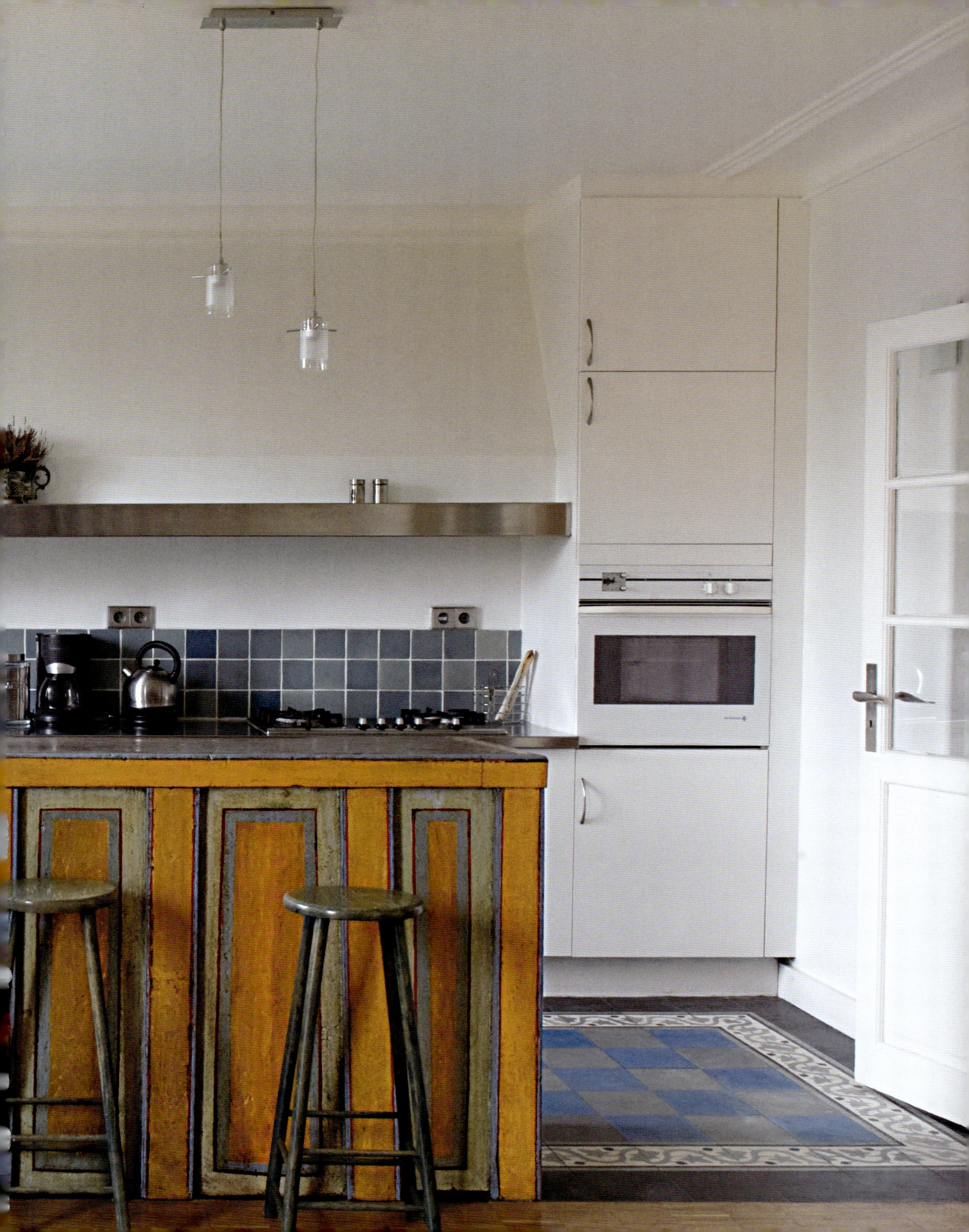

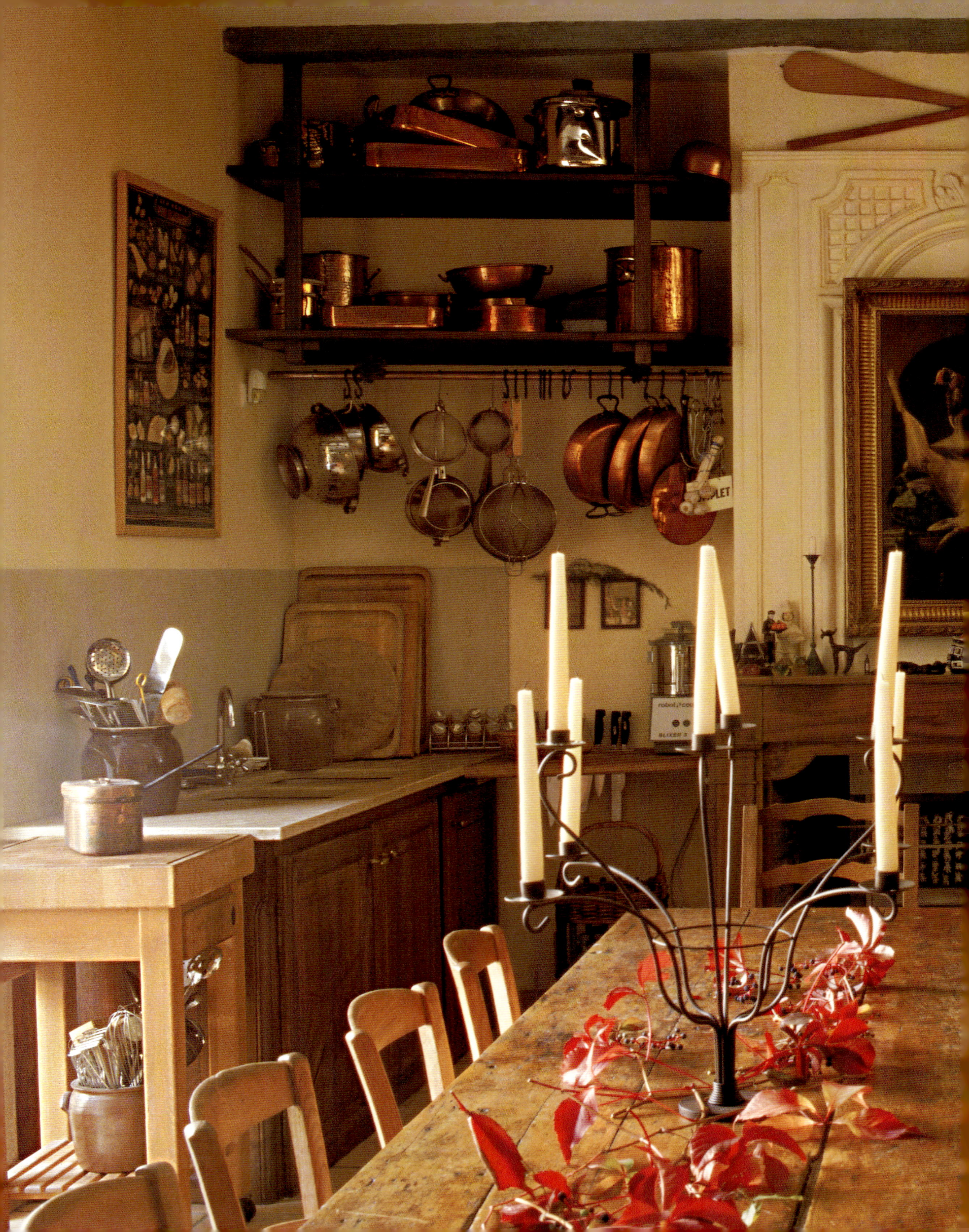

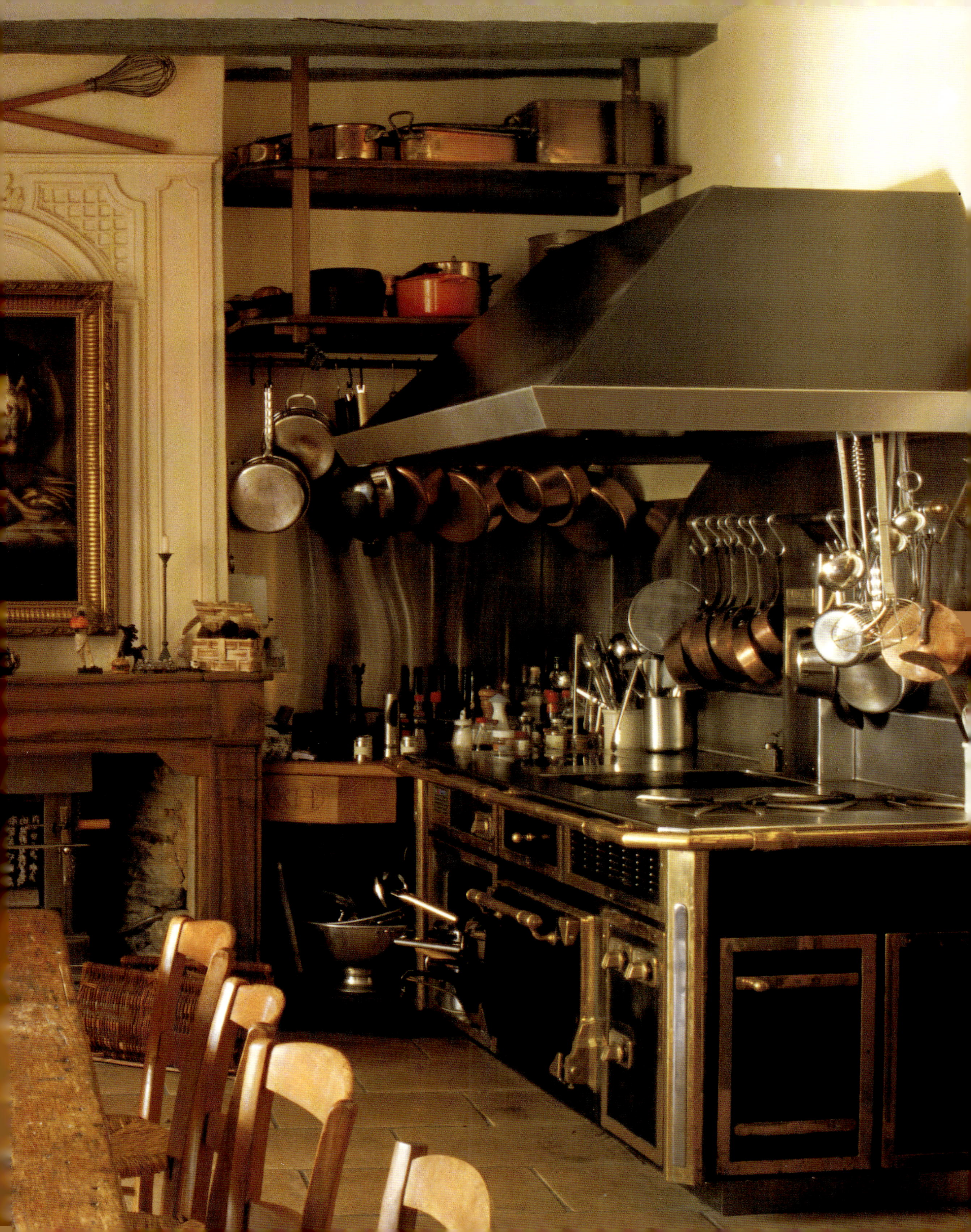

スタイルと機能

スタイルと機能

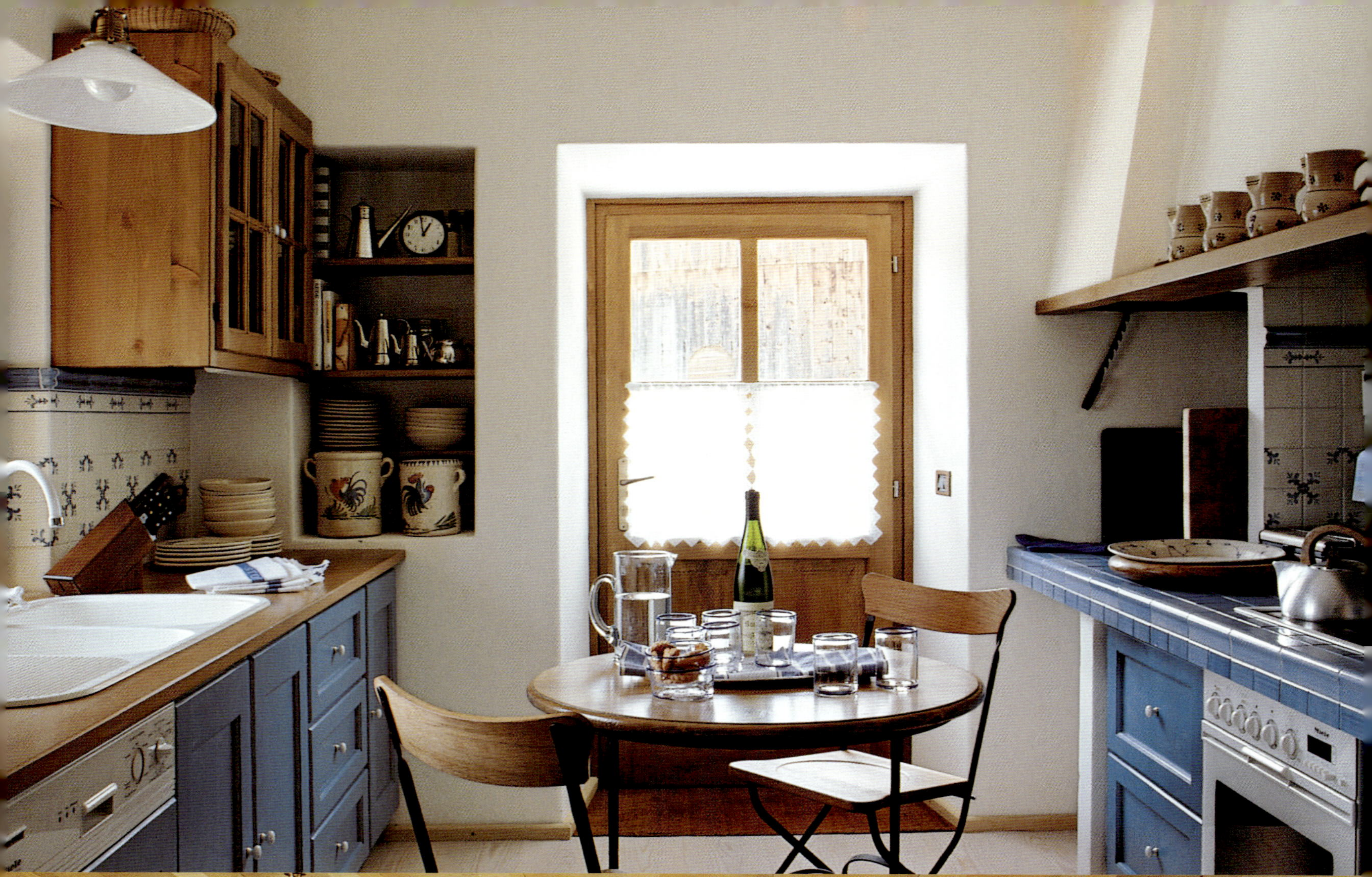

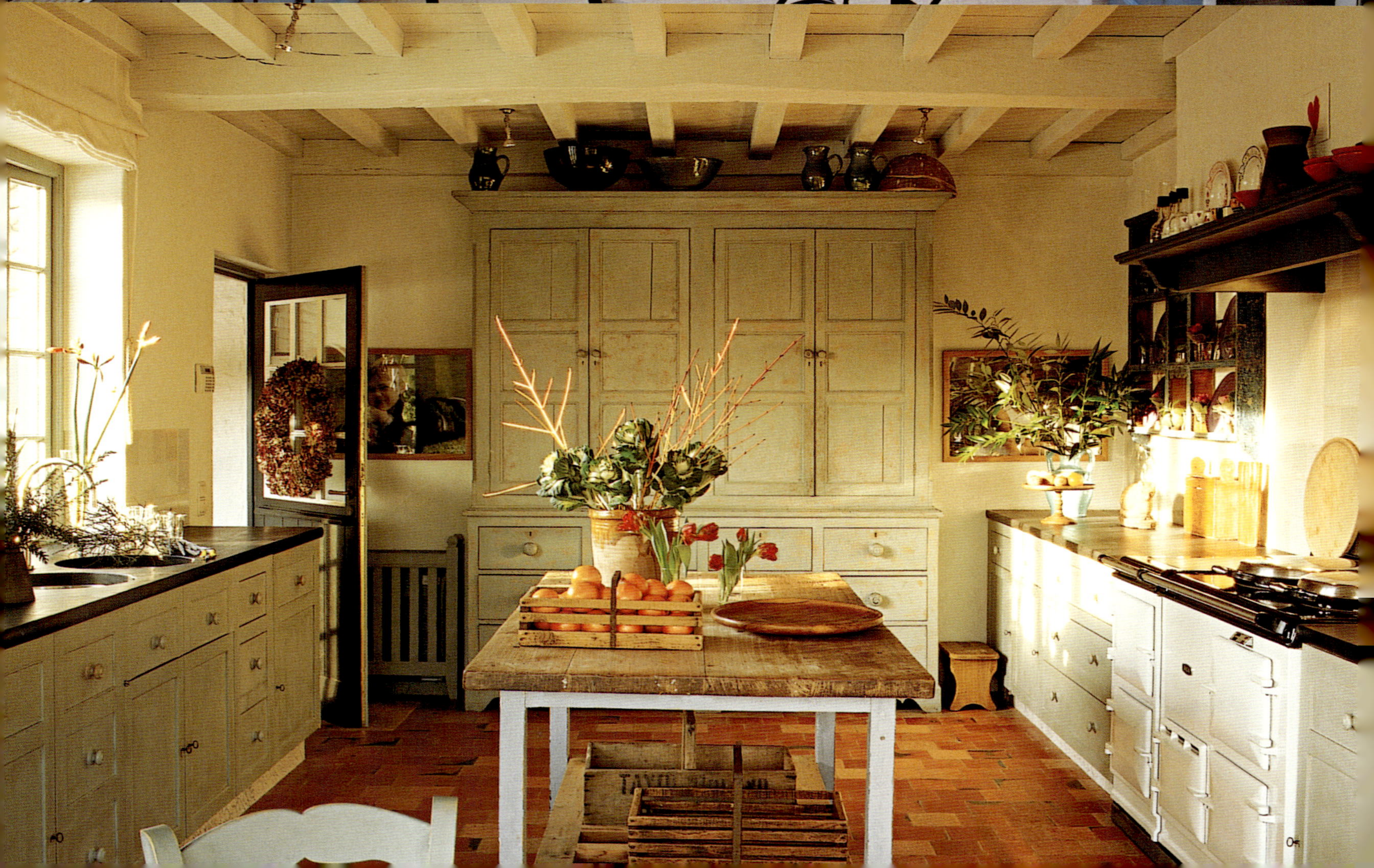

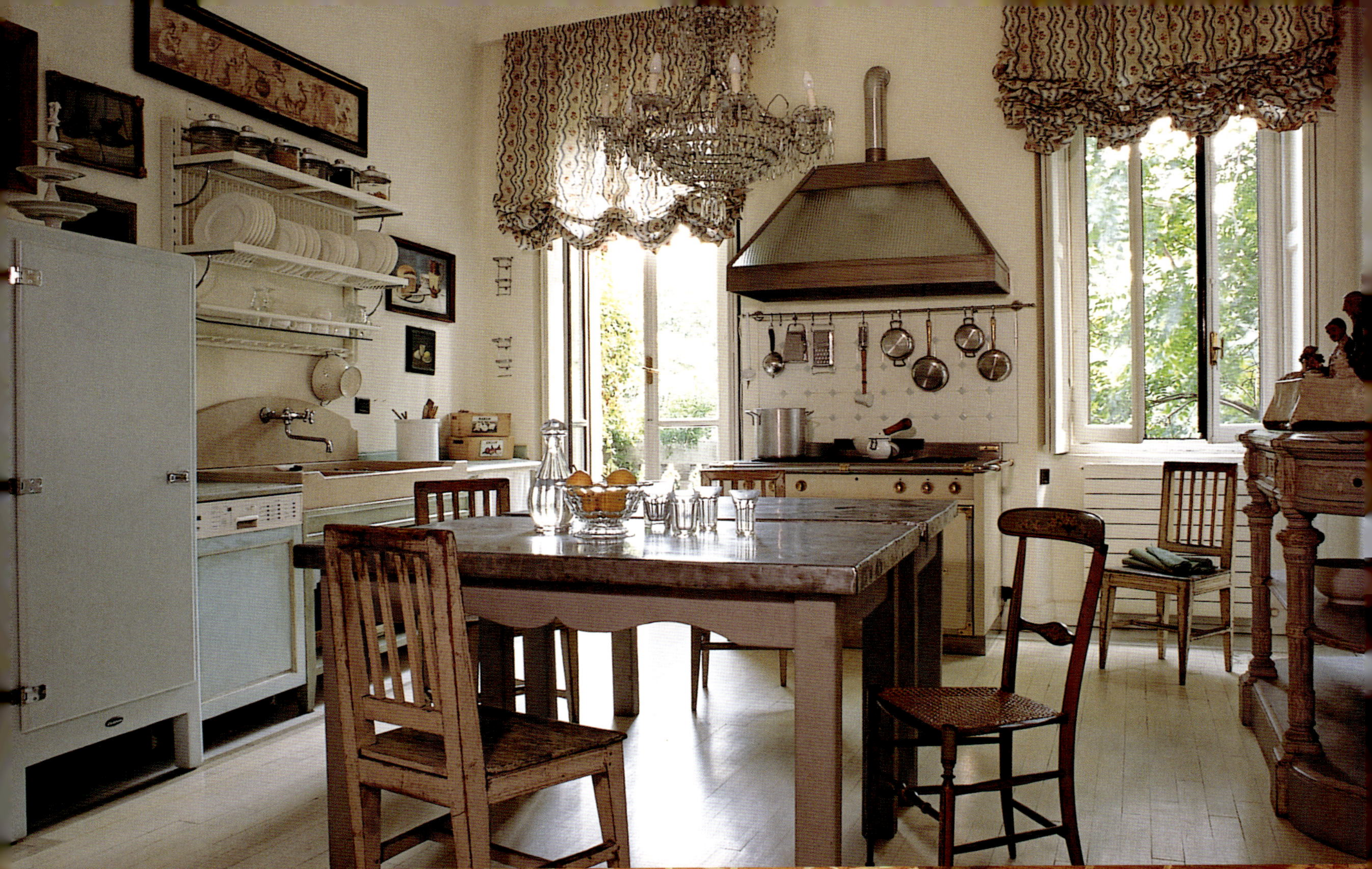

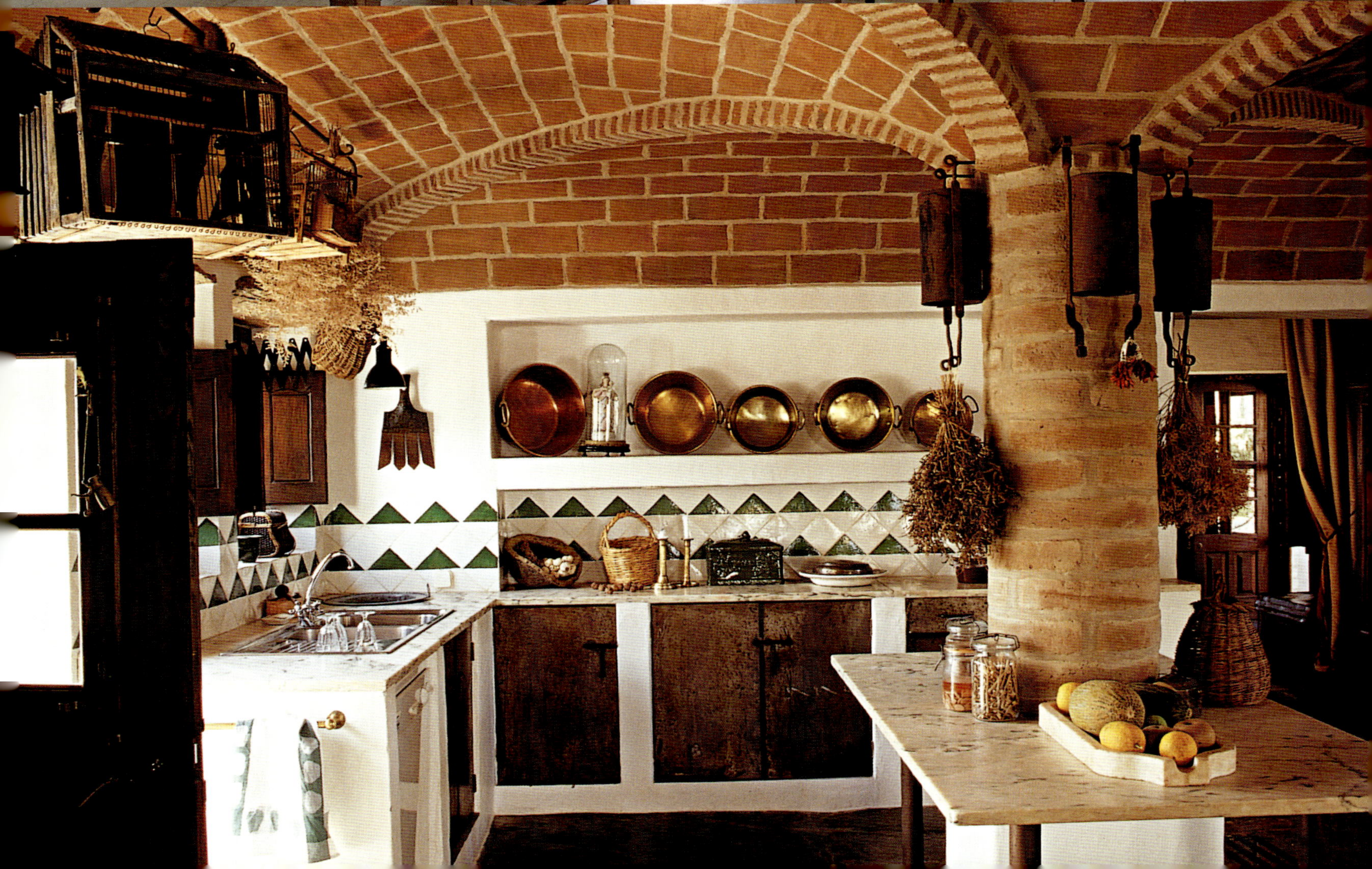

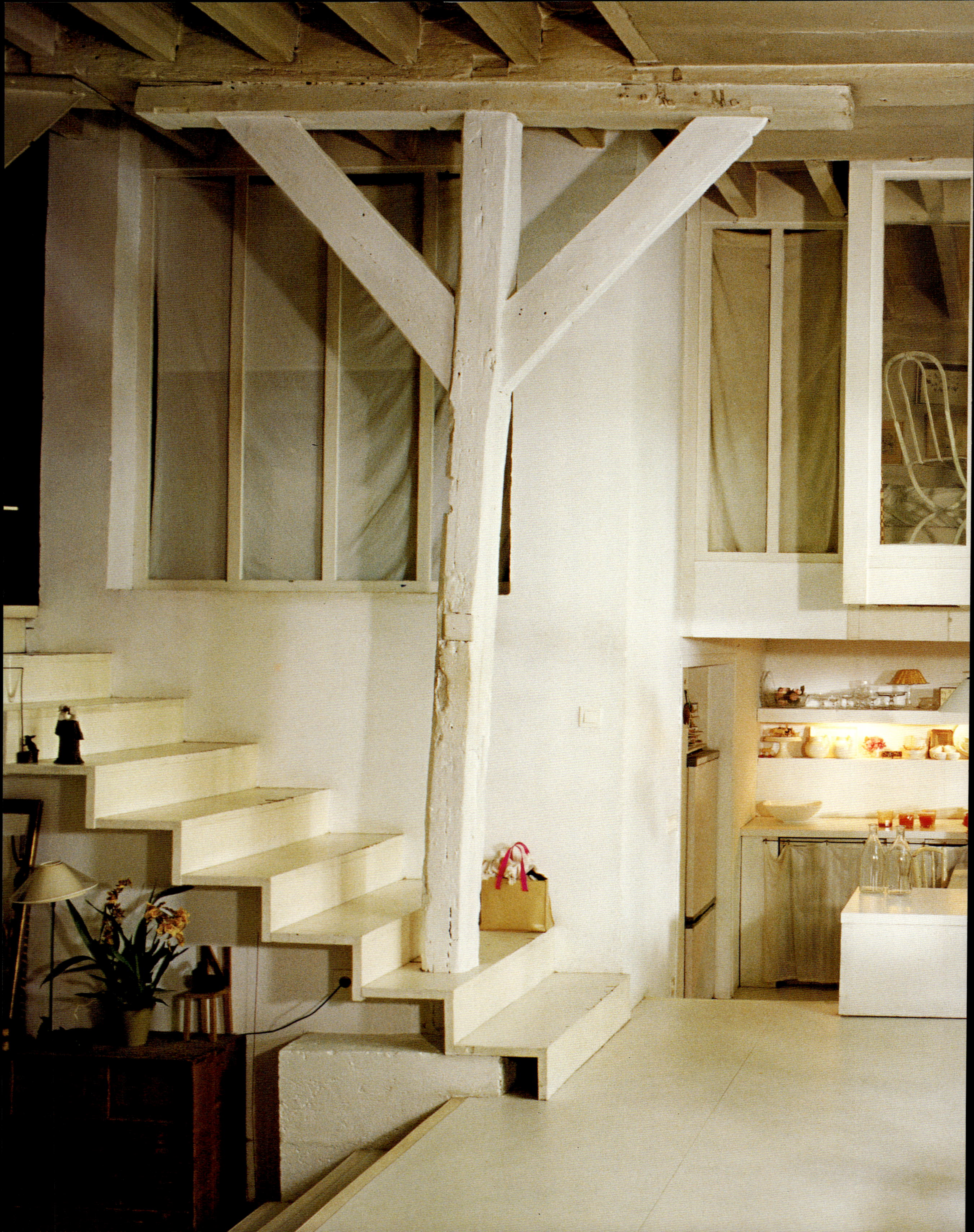

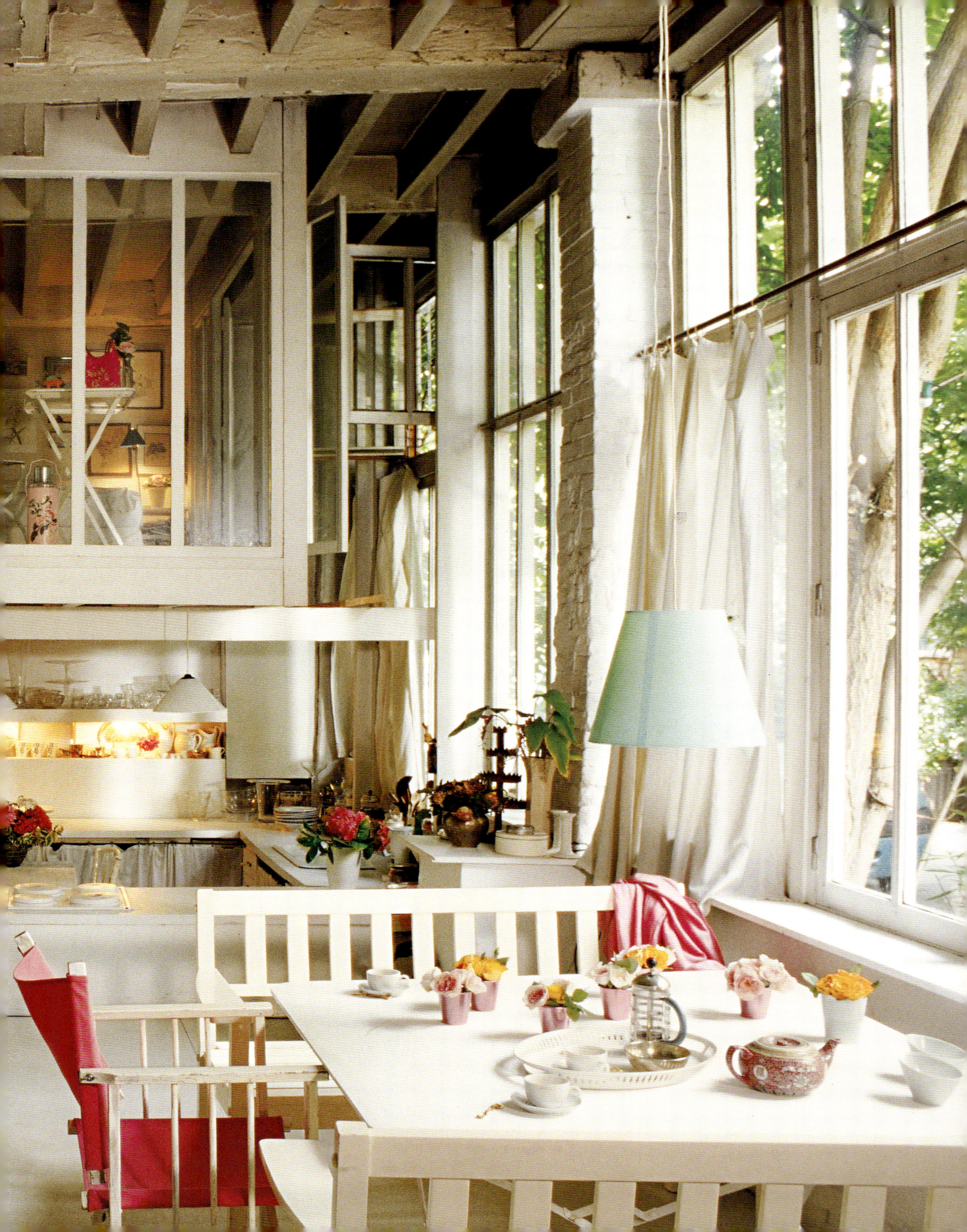

調理と食事

Cooking and Eating

料理を、芸術、趣味、仕事のうちの、いずれと捉えているにしても、食事を作り、供することは、生きていくうえの基本であり、エネルギーを生み出す活動です。ですから、もっとも満足感のある楽しいキッチンとは、調理と食事の、両方が行われる空間でしょう。家族での昼食はもちろん、友だちとのディナーや、何か「特別な」会食であっても、キッチンで食事をするのです。こういう「特別な」機会のために使える部屋があった時代は、終わりました。今では、調理場が見渡せる造りになったレストランが数多くあります——これなら、料理のあらゆる作業を眺め、調理場の臨場感も味わえます。実は、トップクラスのレストランで、もっとも人気のある席は、調理場の中にある席です。壁を取り払うことによって（つまり、壁に隠されていた料理の秘密を明らかにし）、客の期待感を高め、味覚を刺激し、料理をよりおいしく感じさせるのです。自宅のキッチンだって同じです。調理と食事が同じ部屋なら、料理をする人と、家族やその他のお客さんとの間に「壁」がなくなります——いい面でも悪い面でも、互いの関わりが増えるのです。食事用のテーブルと椅子に関しては、数限りない選択肢があります。スツールが引き出せるアイランド型のユニットから、伸長式のテーブルと折りたたみ椅子、また大型の木製テーブルと、革張りでハイバックの肘掛け椅子という組み合わせまで、よりどりみどりです。どんなタイプでも、比較的手頃な値段で手に入ります。もし自宅の「レストラン」がとても居心地よく、くつろいで食事ができるうえに、時間を気にする必要もなく、誰もが楽しい時間を過ごせるなら、これ以上インテリアに望むことが、何かあるでしょうか？

Whether you think of cooking as an art, a hobby, or a chore, there is an energy that is given off by the activity of preparing and serving food that is as primal as life itself. As a result, some of the most satisfying and joyful types of kitchens are those where cooking and eating take place in the same space; whether for a family lunch, friends for dinner, or even what you might call a special occasion. Gone are the days when houses had a room that was used only for such events. Many restaurants now have open views of the kitchen – so that you can watch and share in all the activity – and in some top-class establishments, the most sought after table is one sited in the kitchen itself. Removing the walls (and the secrecy of cooking that goes with them) heightens anticipation, stimulates tastebuds and makes the food taste better. The same is true at home. Doing the cooking and eating in the same space breaks down the barriers between the cook, the rest of the family, and other dinner guests – allowing for plenty of interaction, good and bad. In terms of the furniture, there are countless options for tables and chairs, from the island unit with pull-up stools, to the slide-out table and folding chairs, to the big wooden table with high back leather carvers; all at relatively affordable prices. If your diners feel so comfortable that the meal becomes relaxed and open-ended, and everyone is having a good time, what more can you ask from your décor?

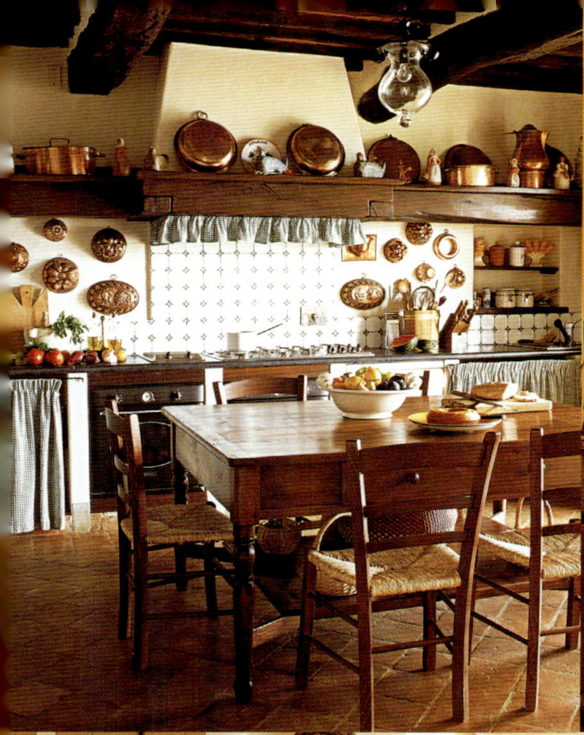
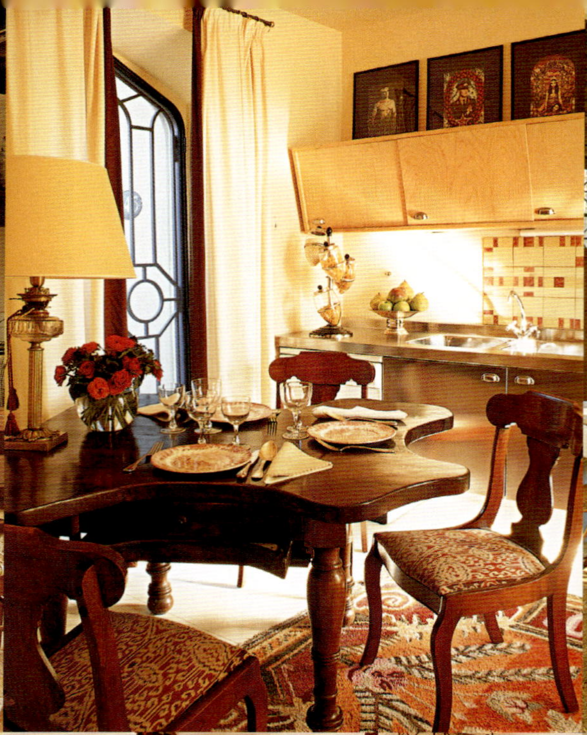
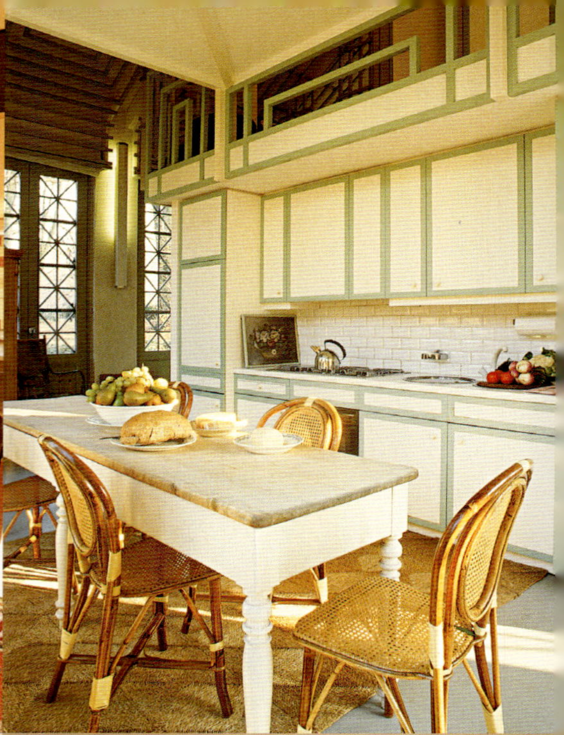
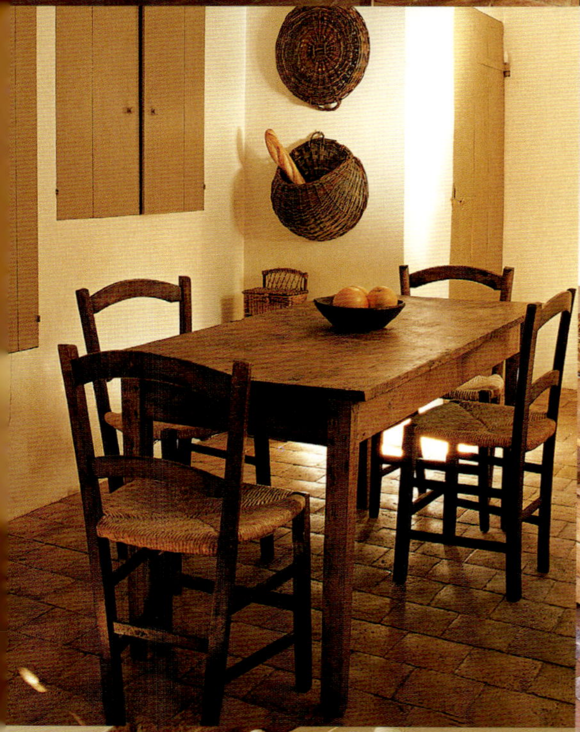
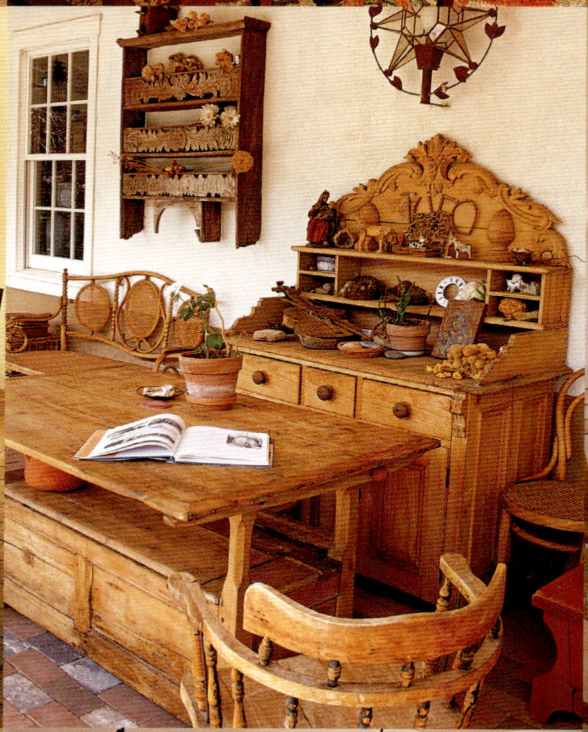
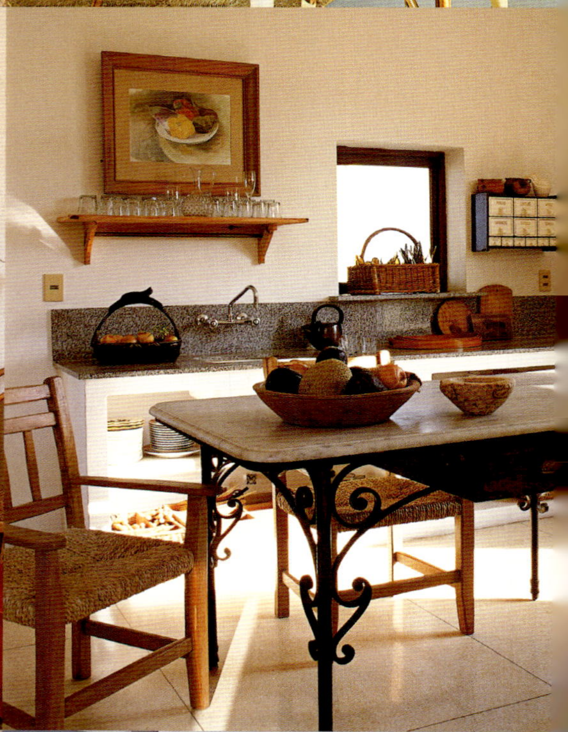
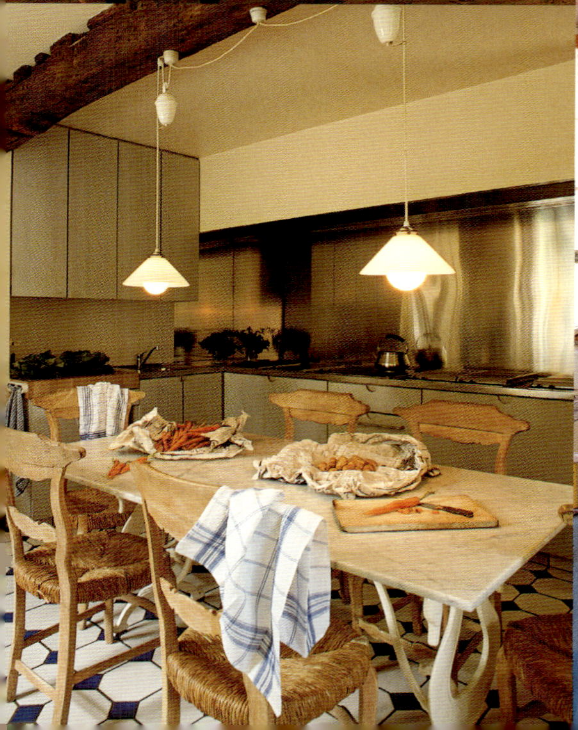
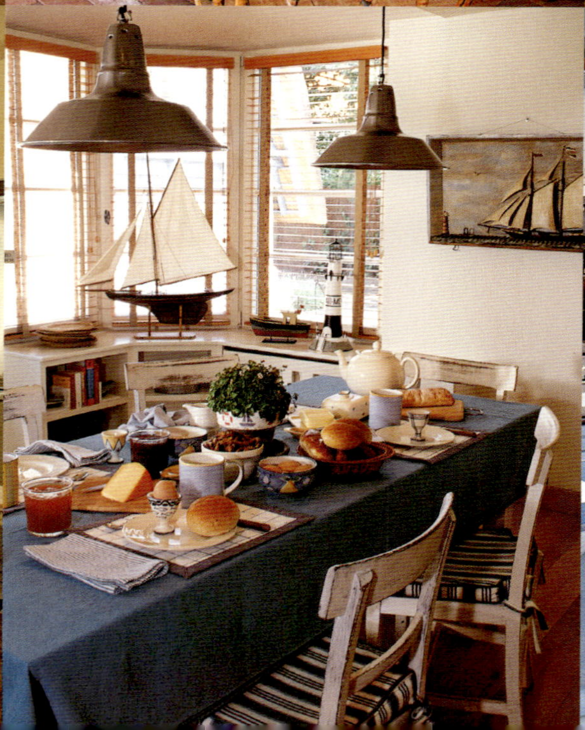
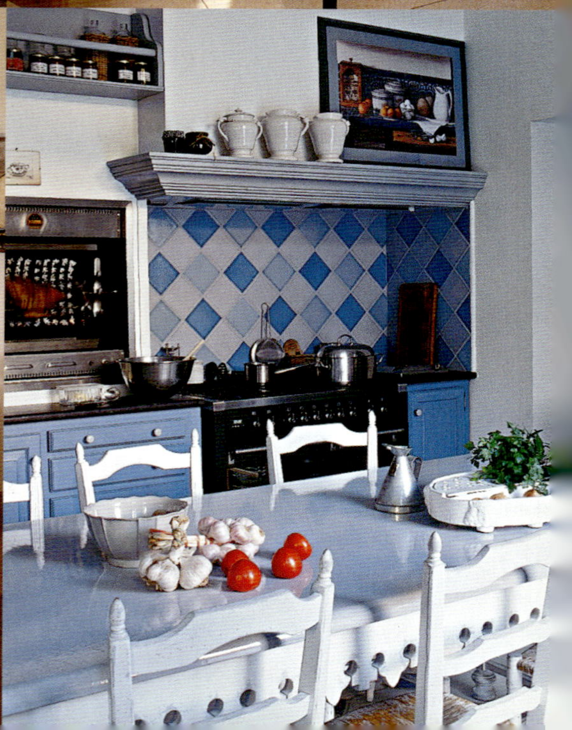

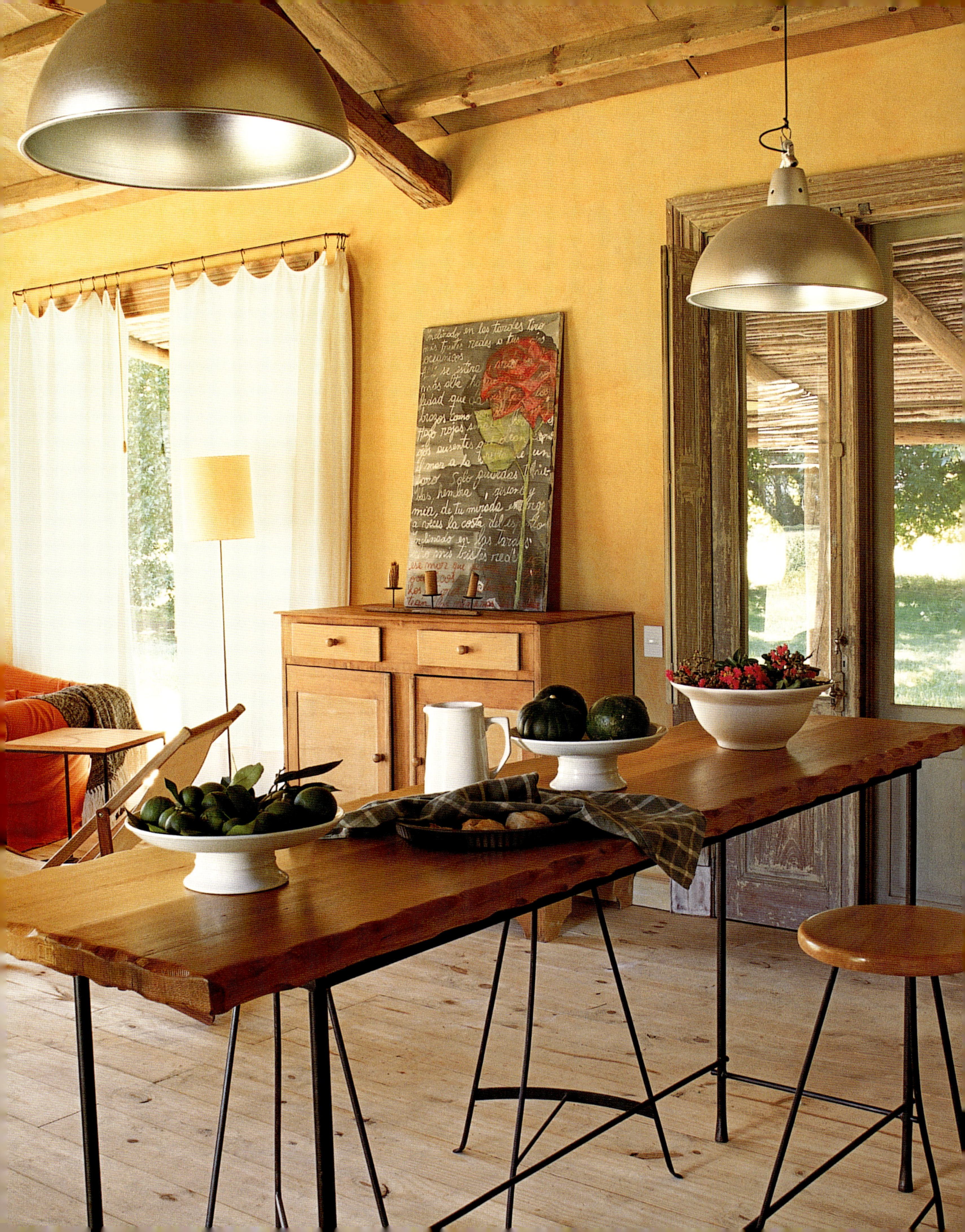

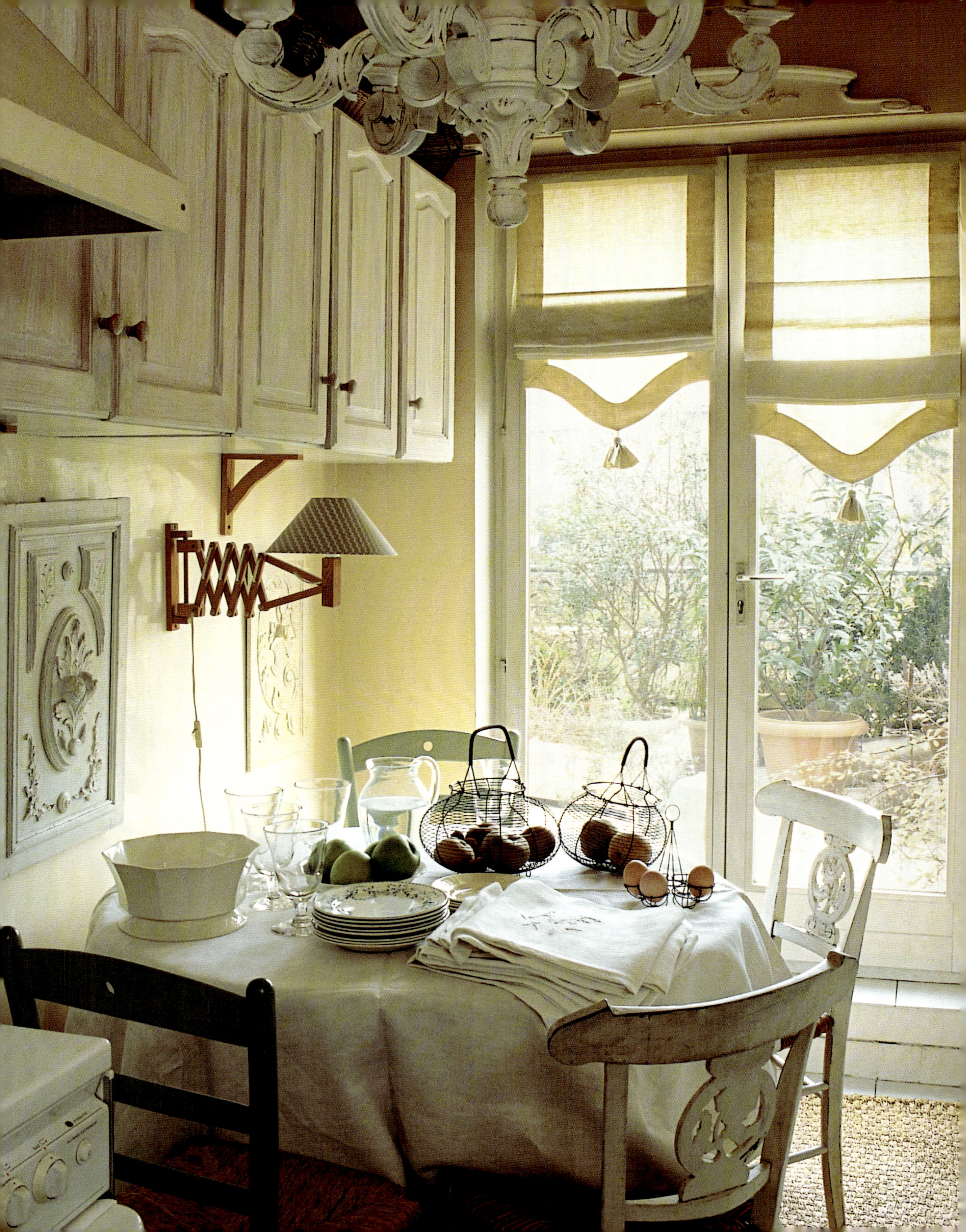

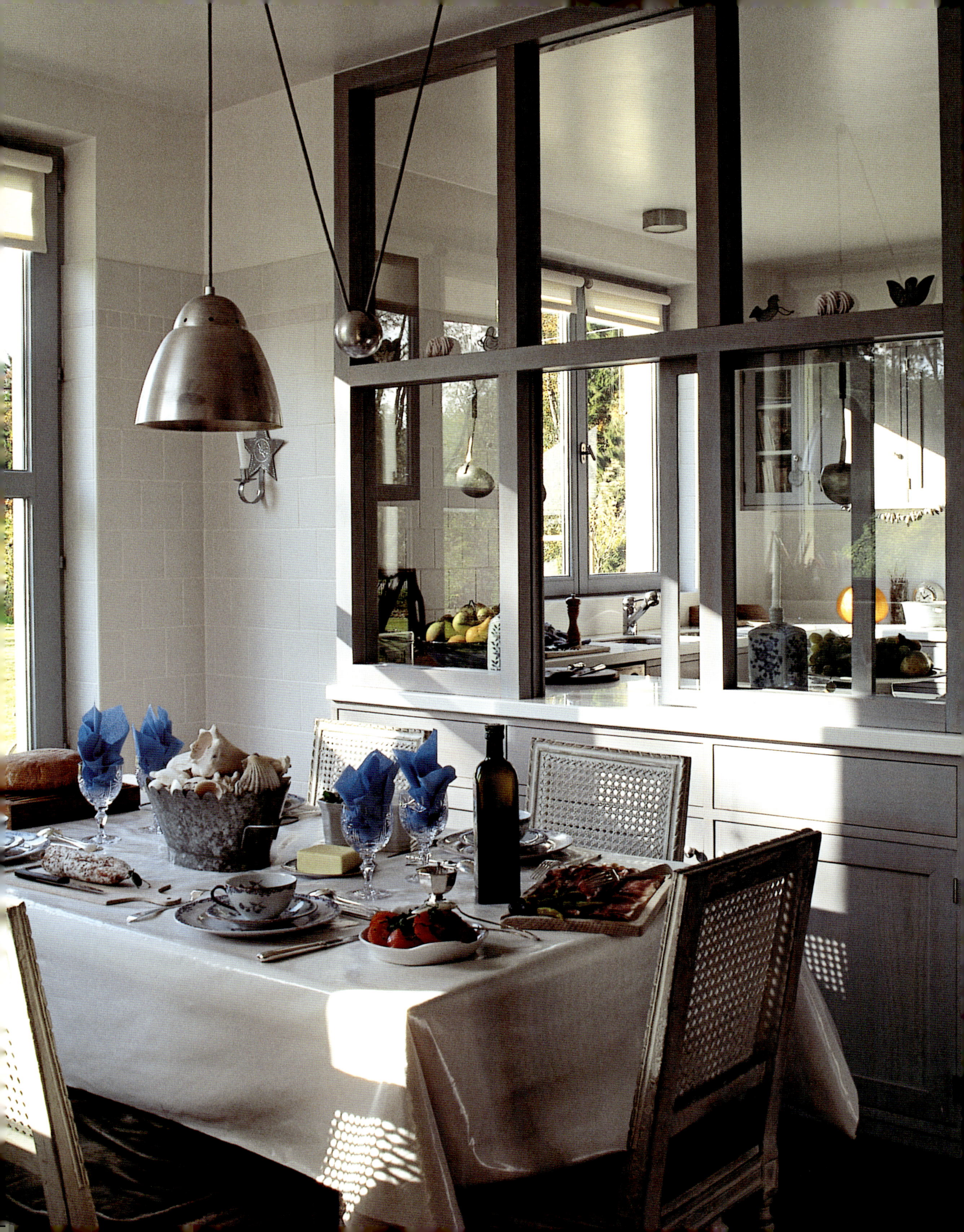

調理と食事

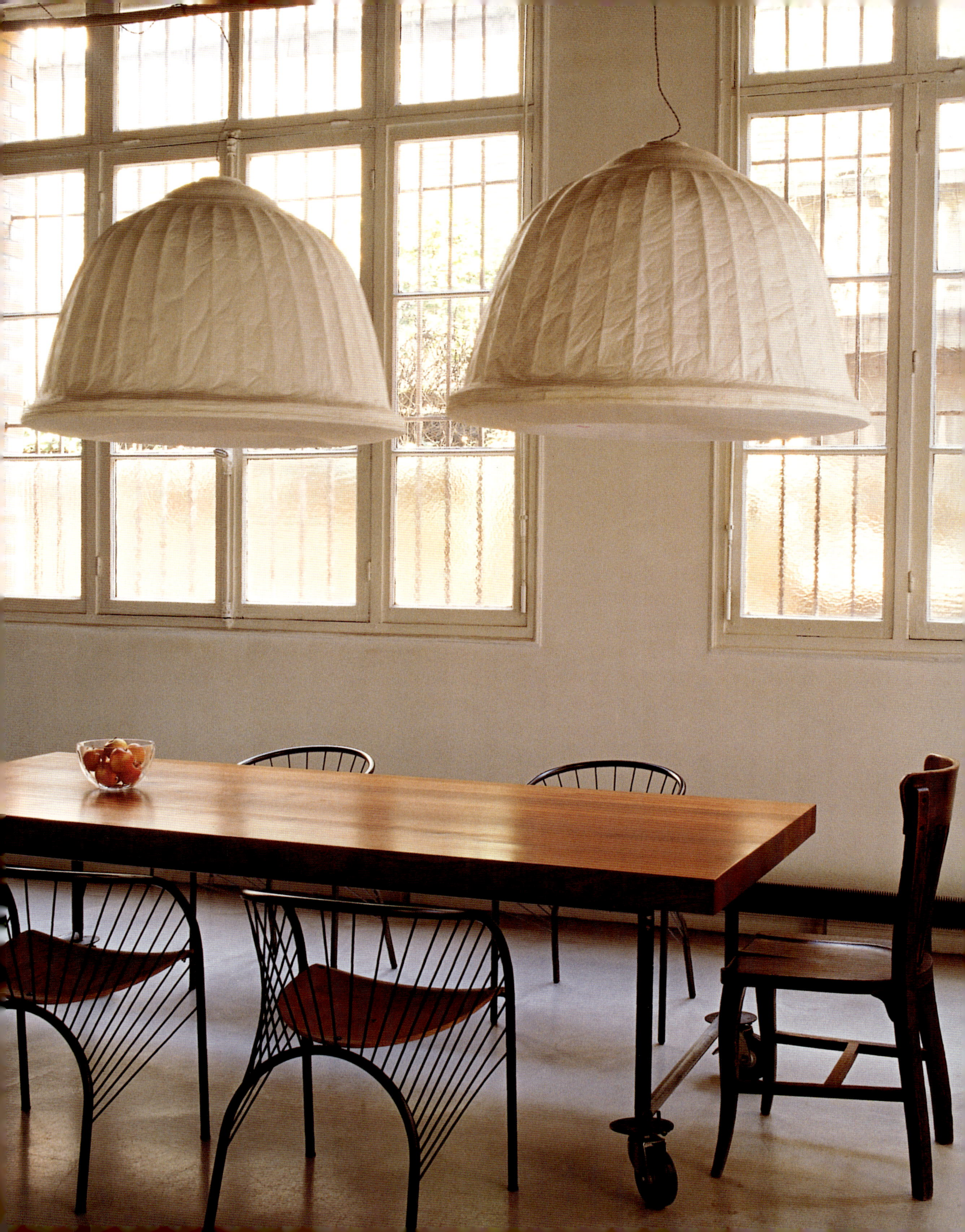

調理と食事

調理と食事

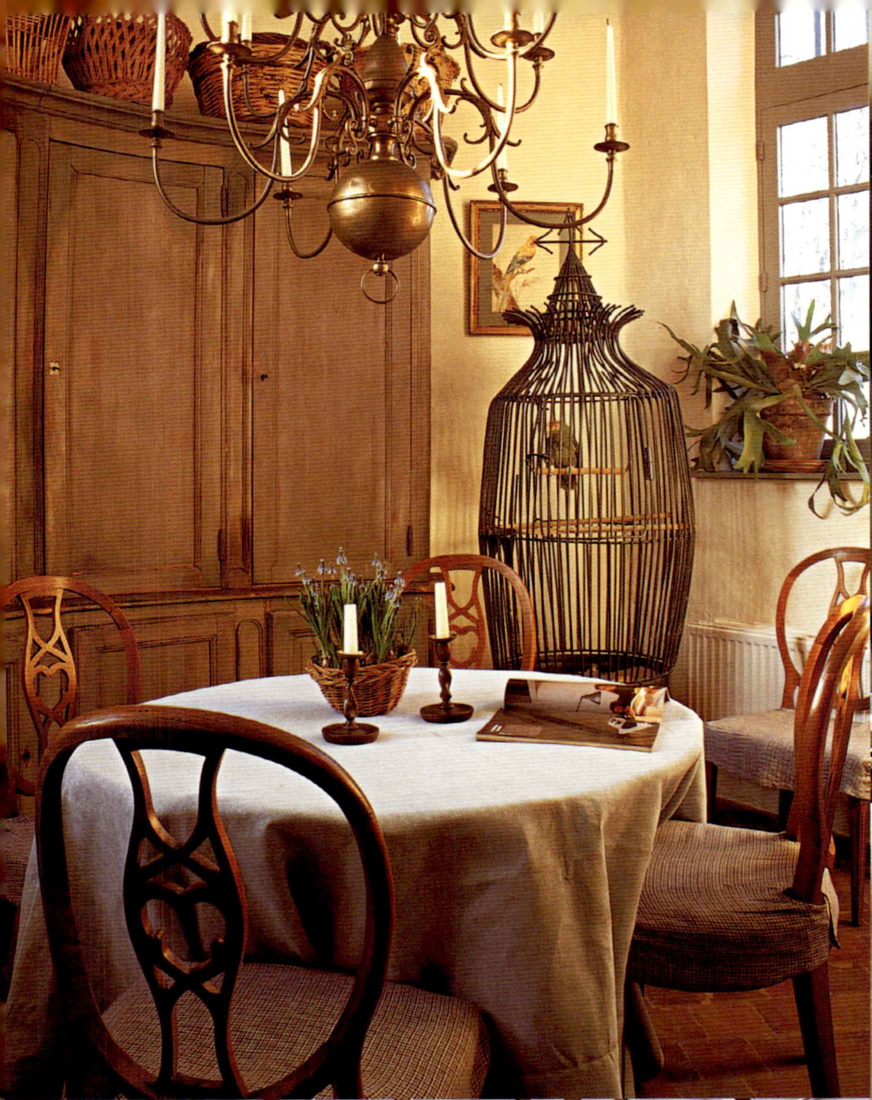

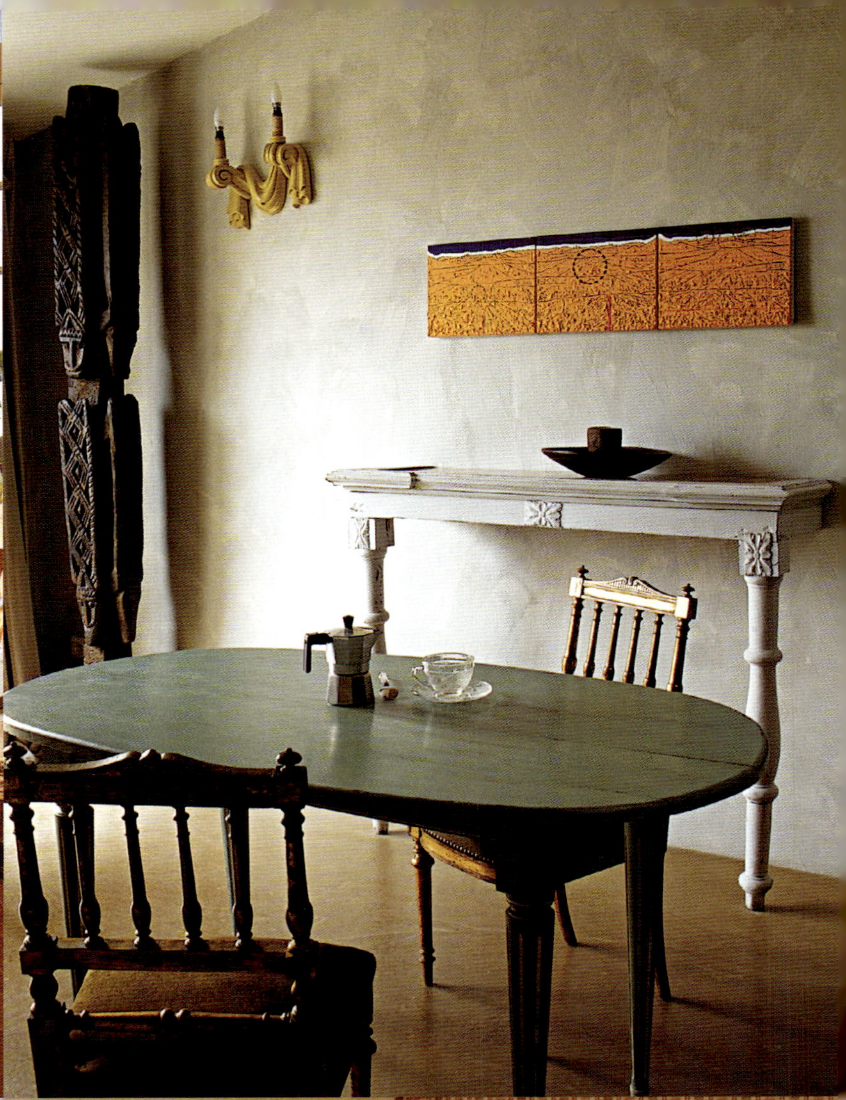

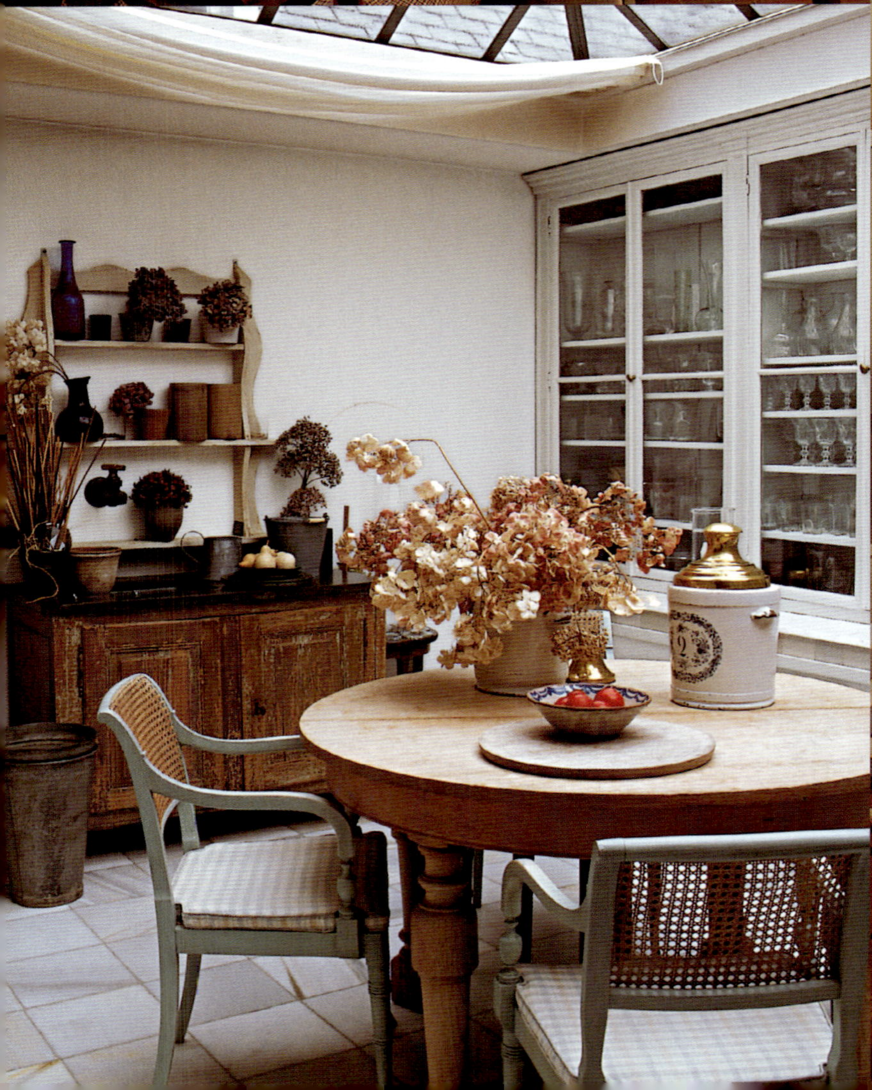

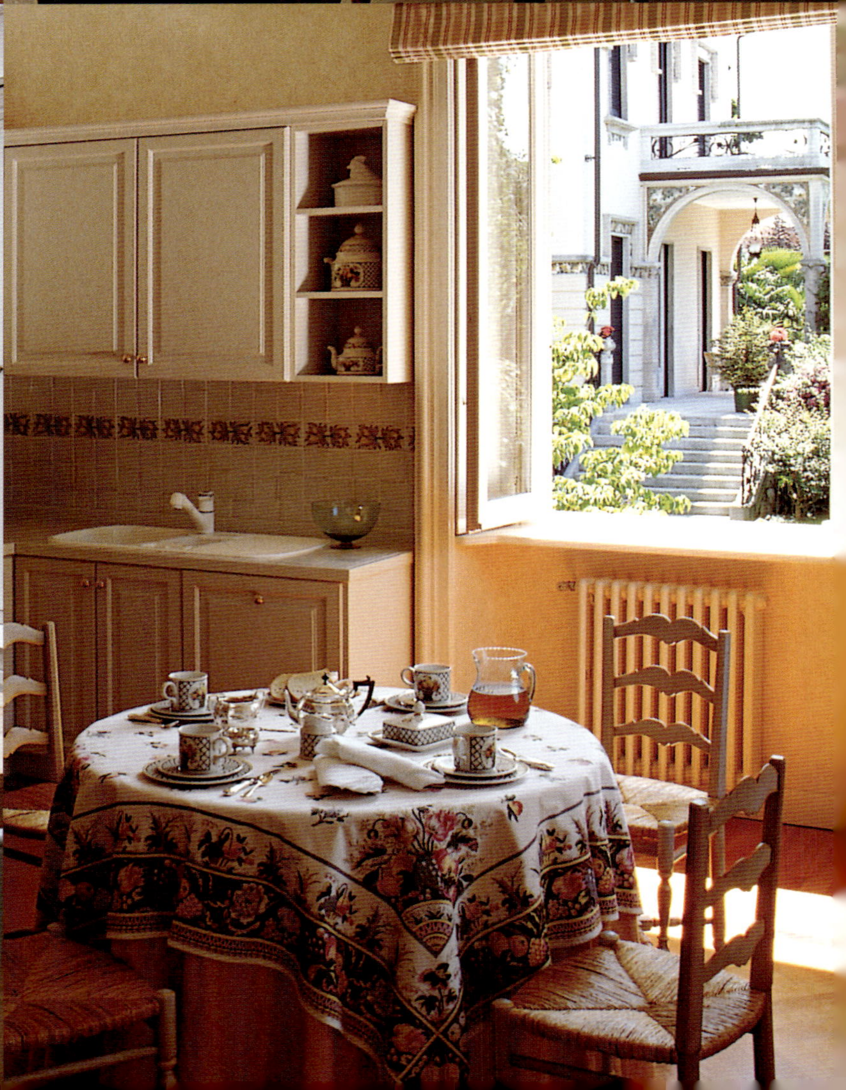

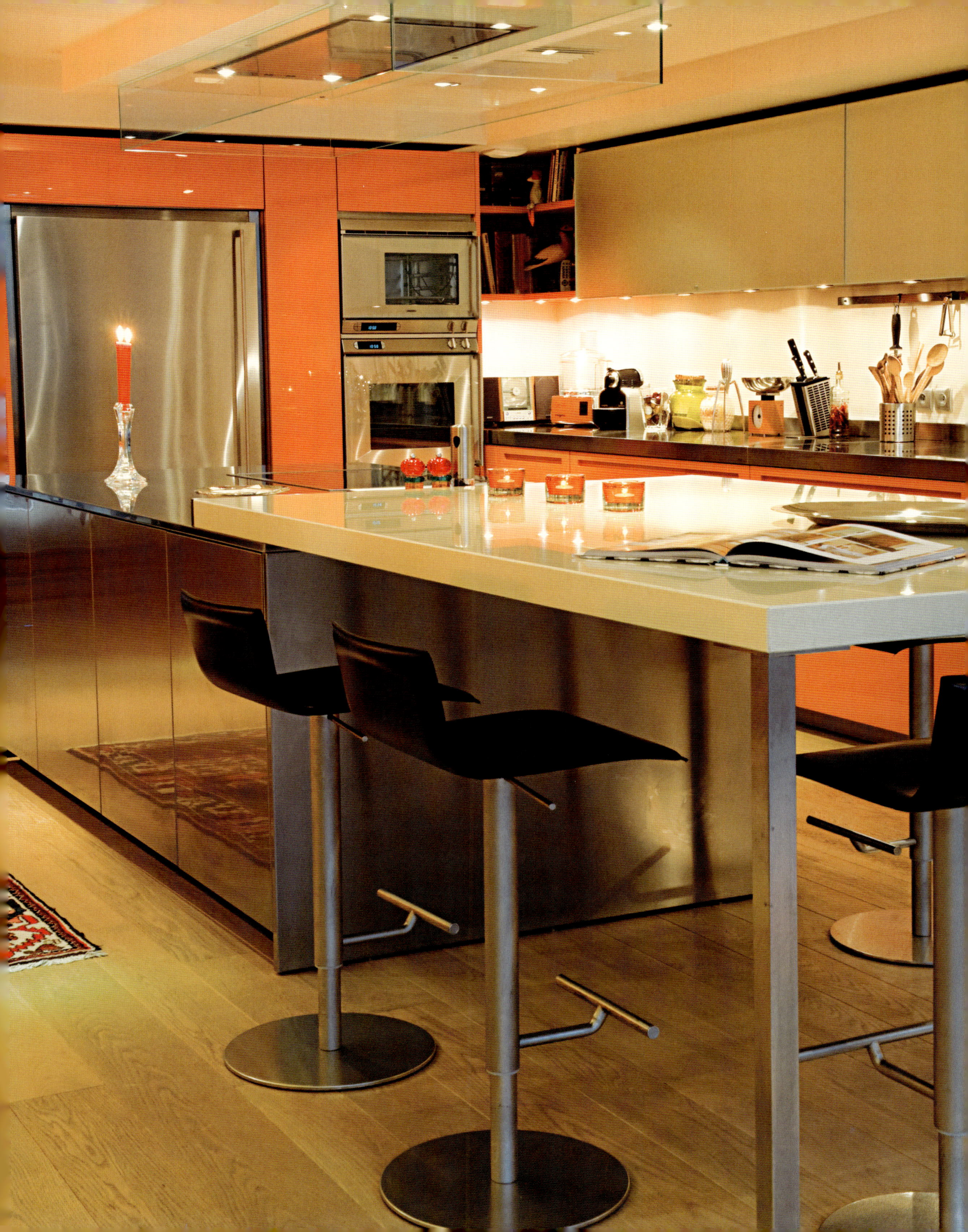

調理と食事

調理と食事

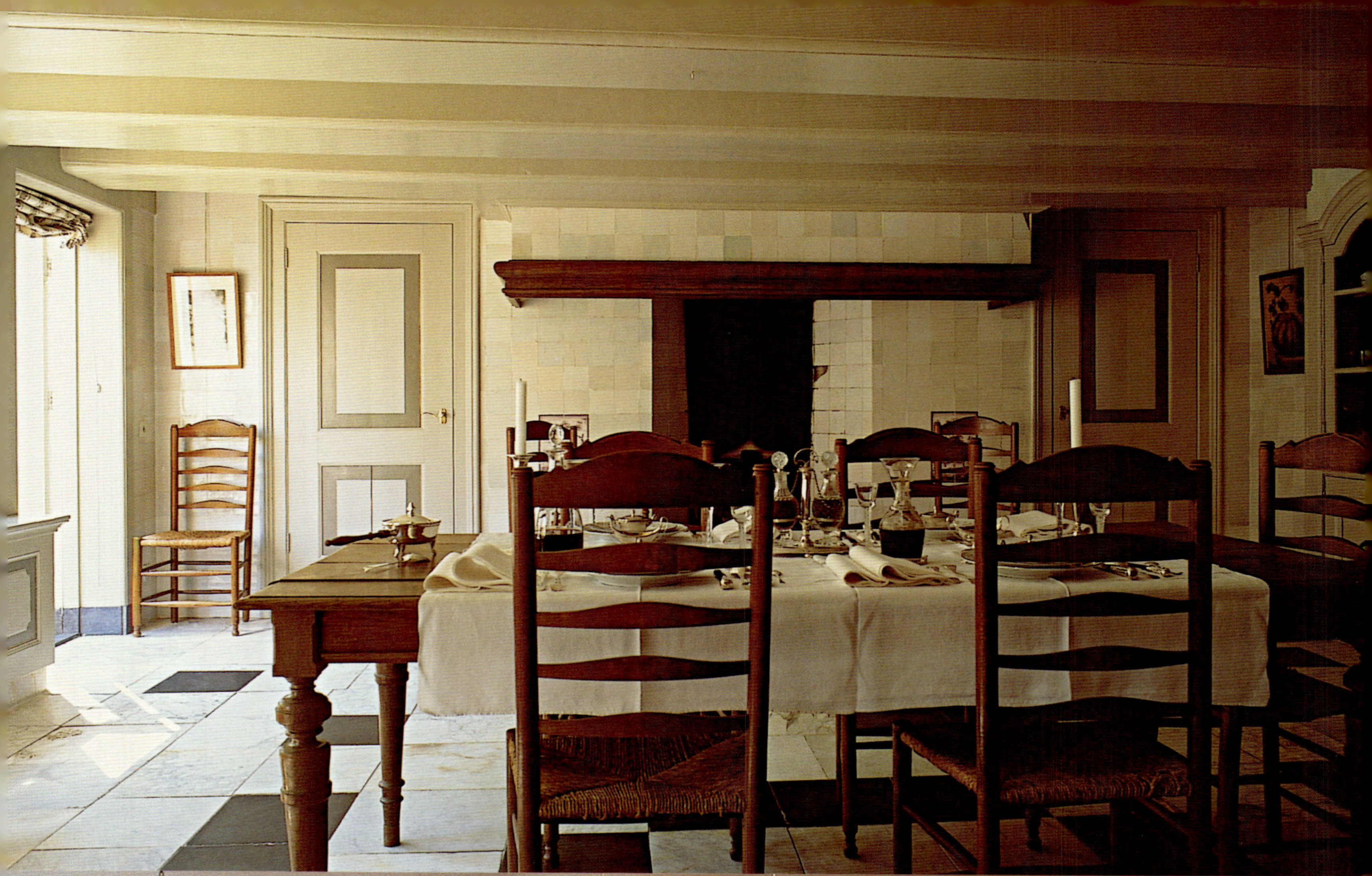

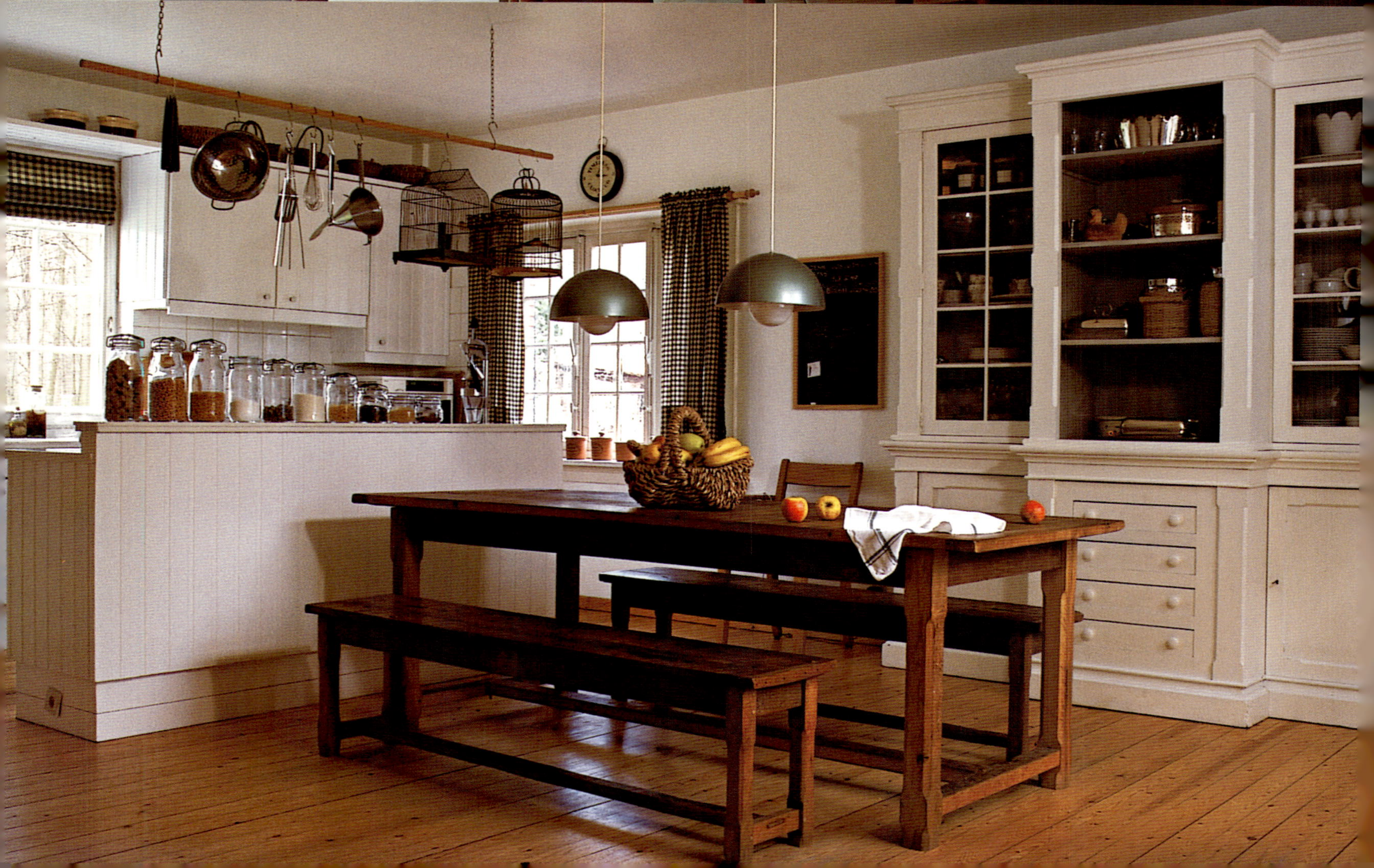

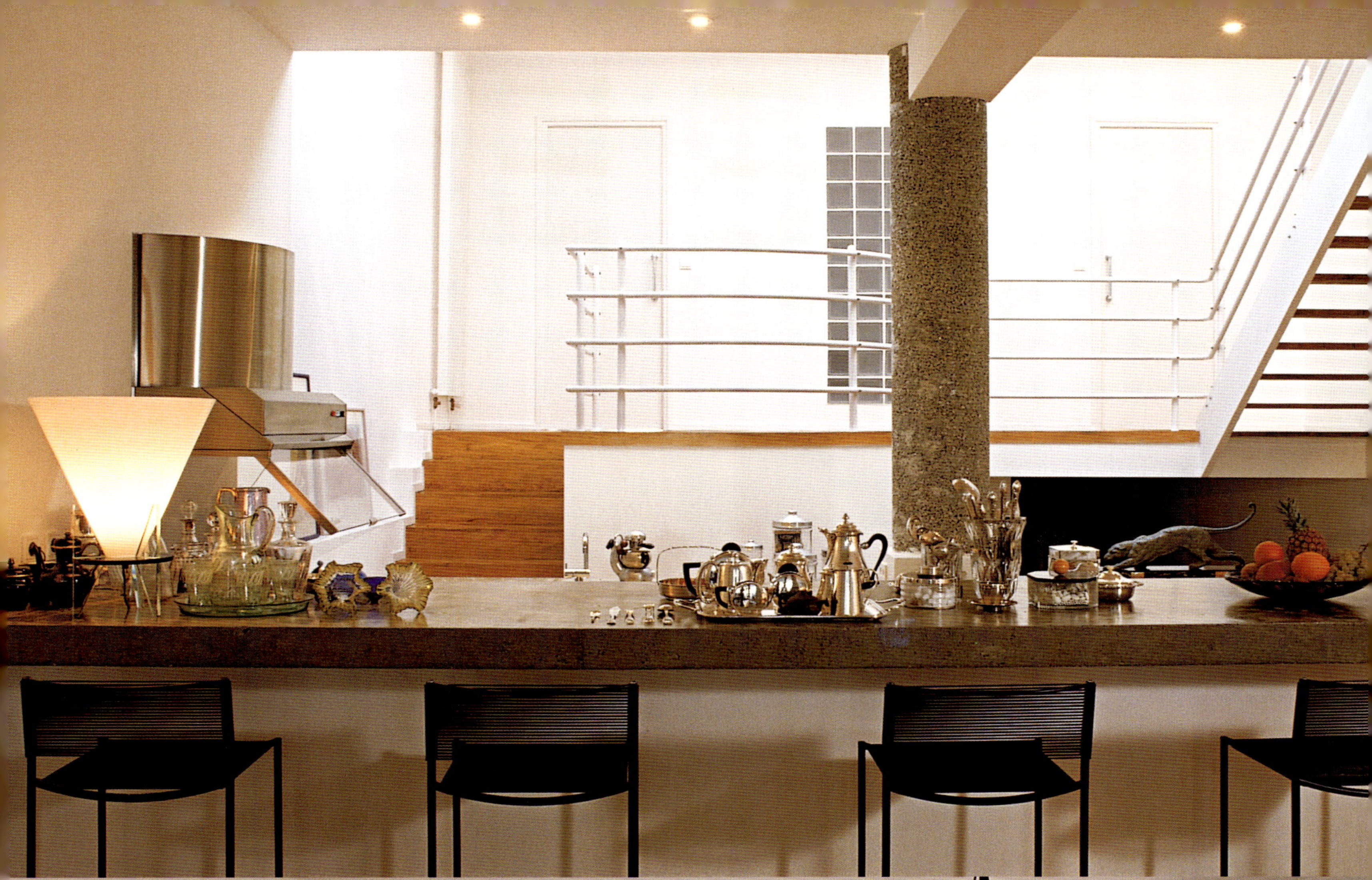

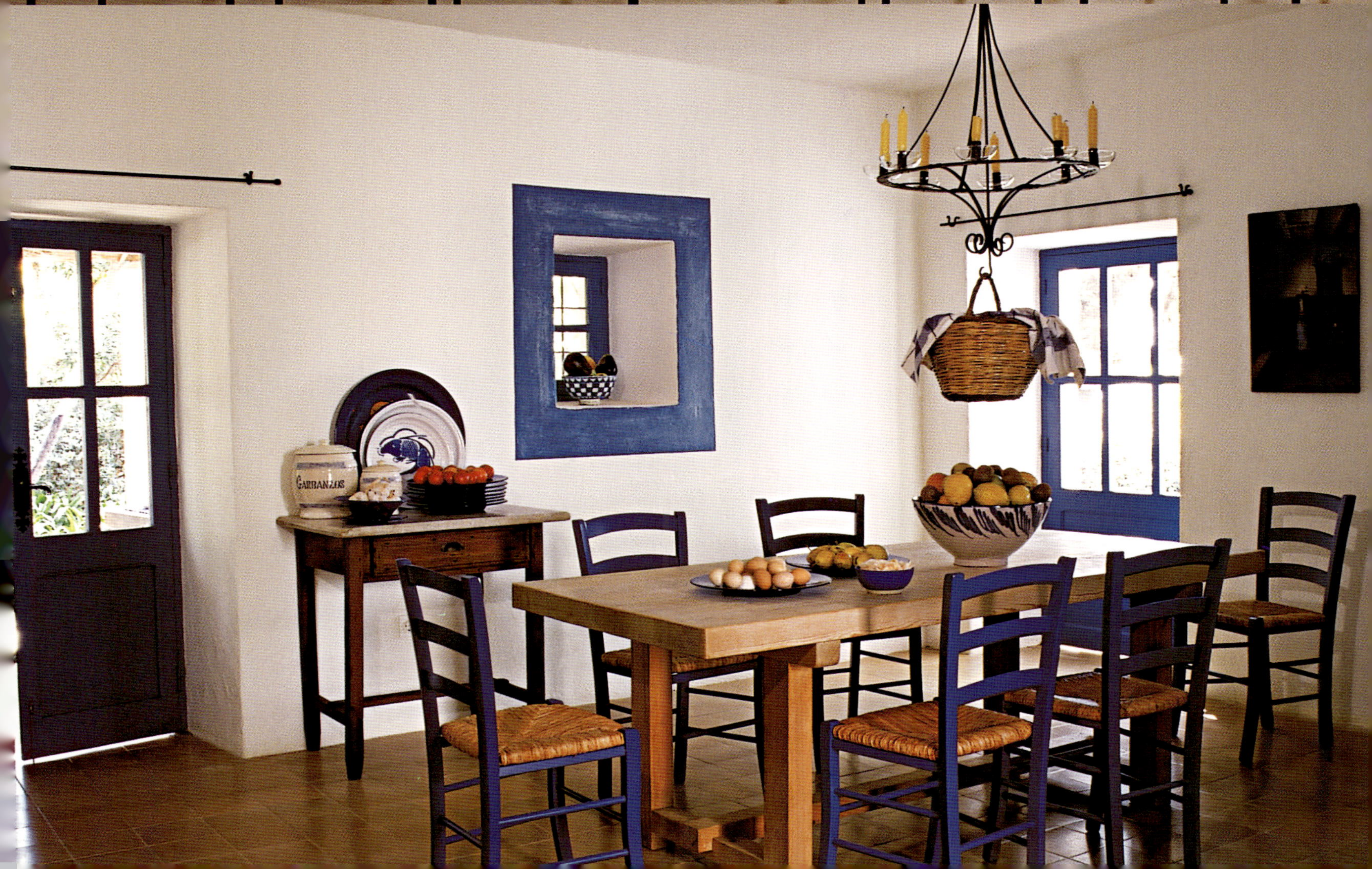
GARBANZOS

調理と食事

調理と食事

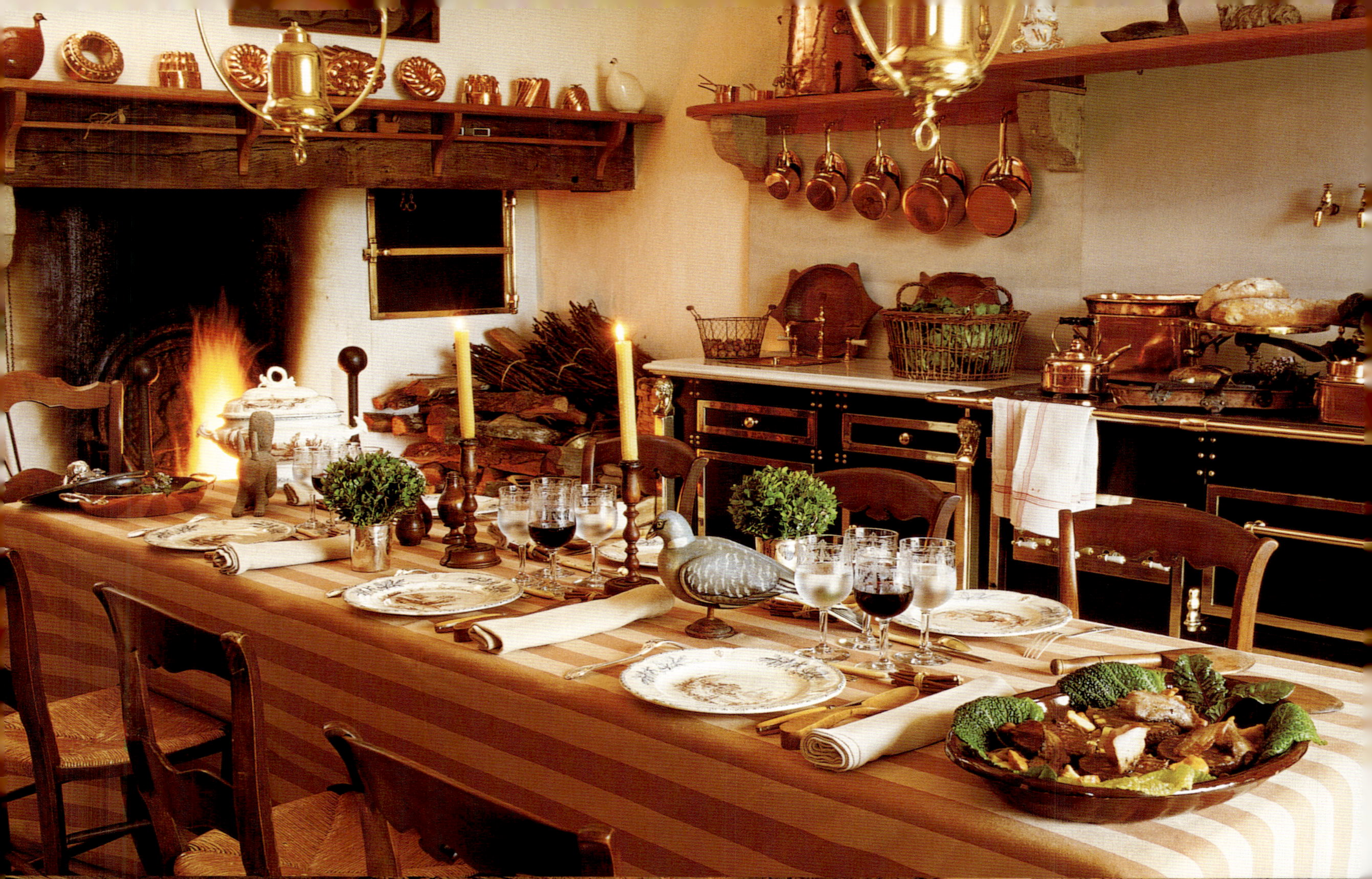

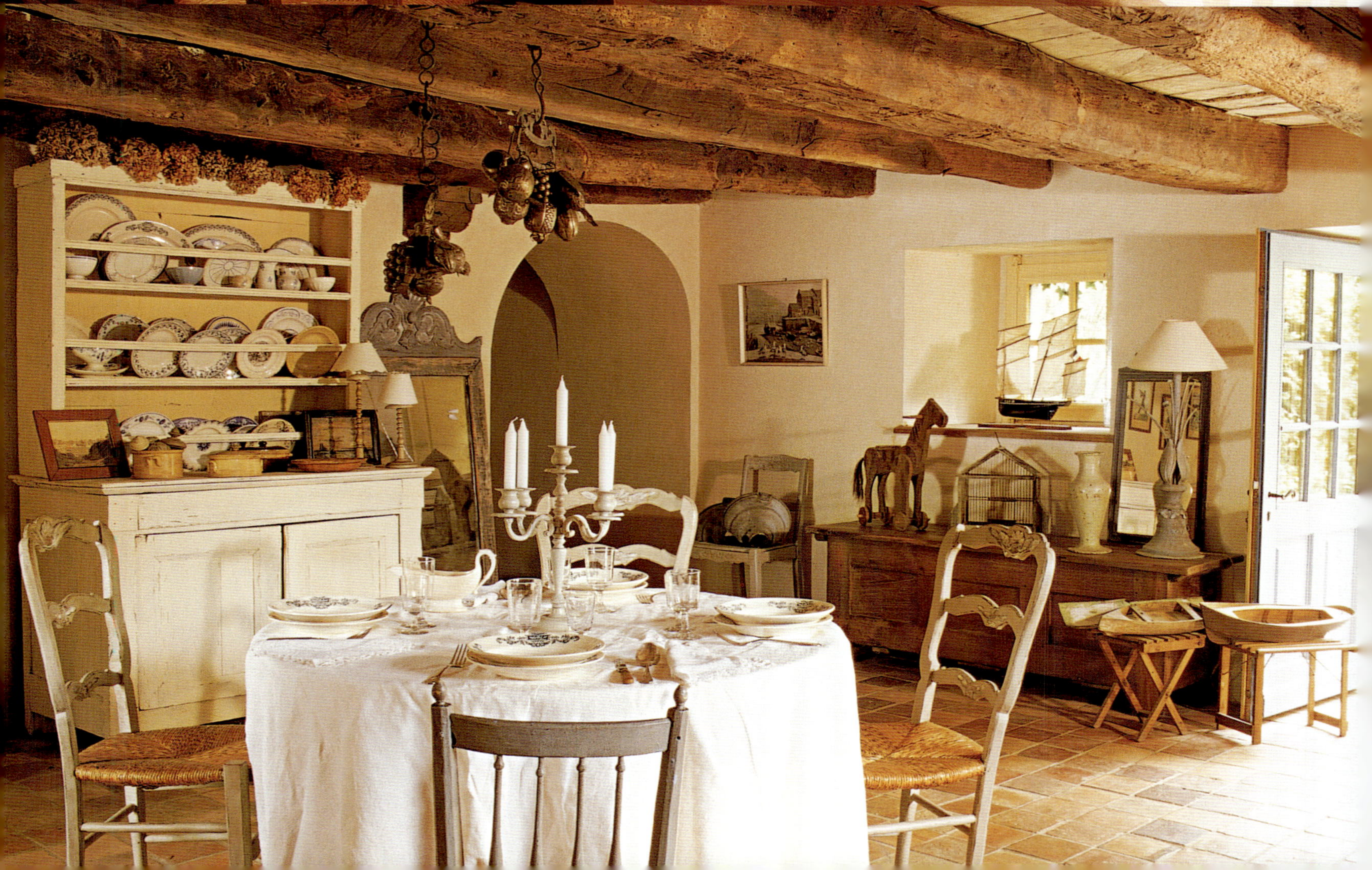

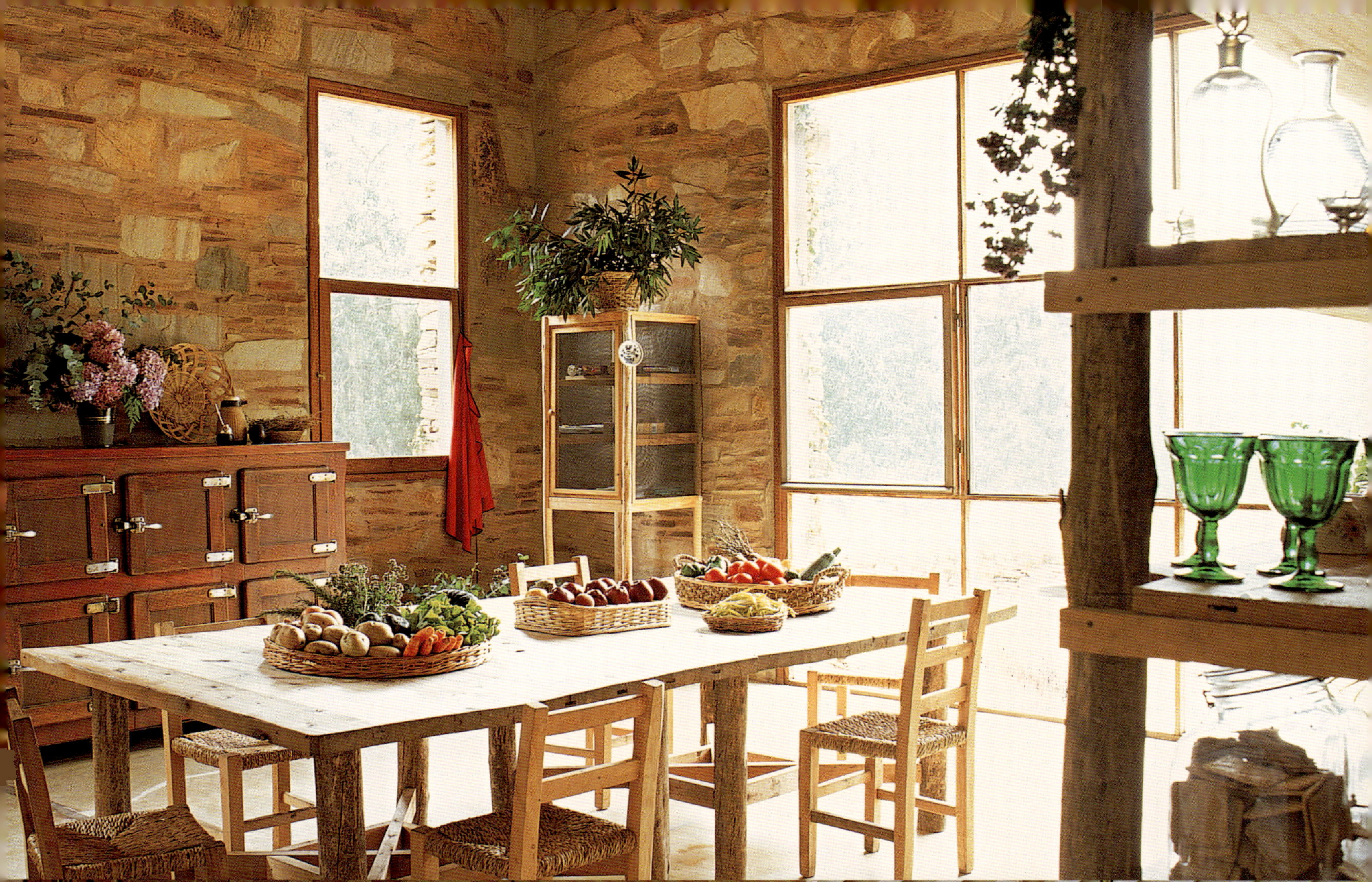
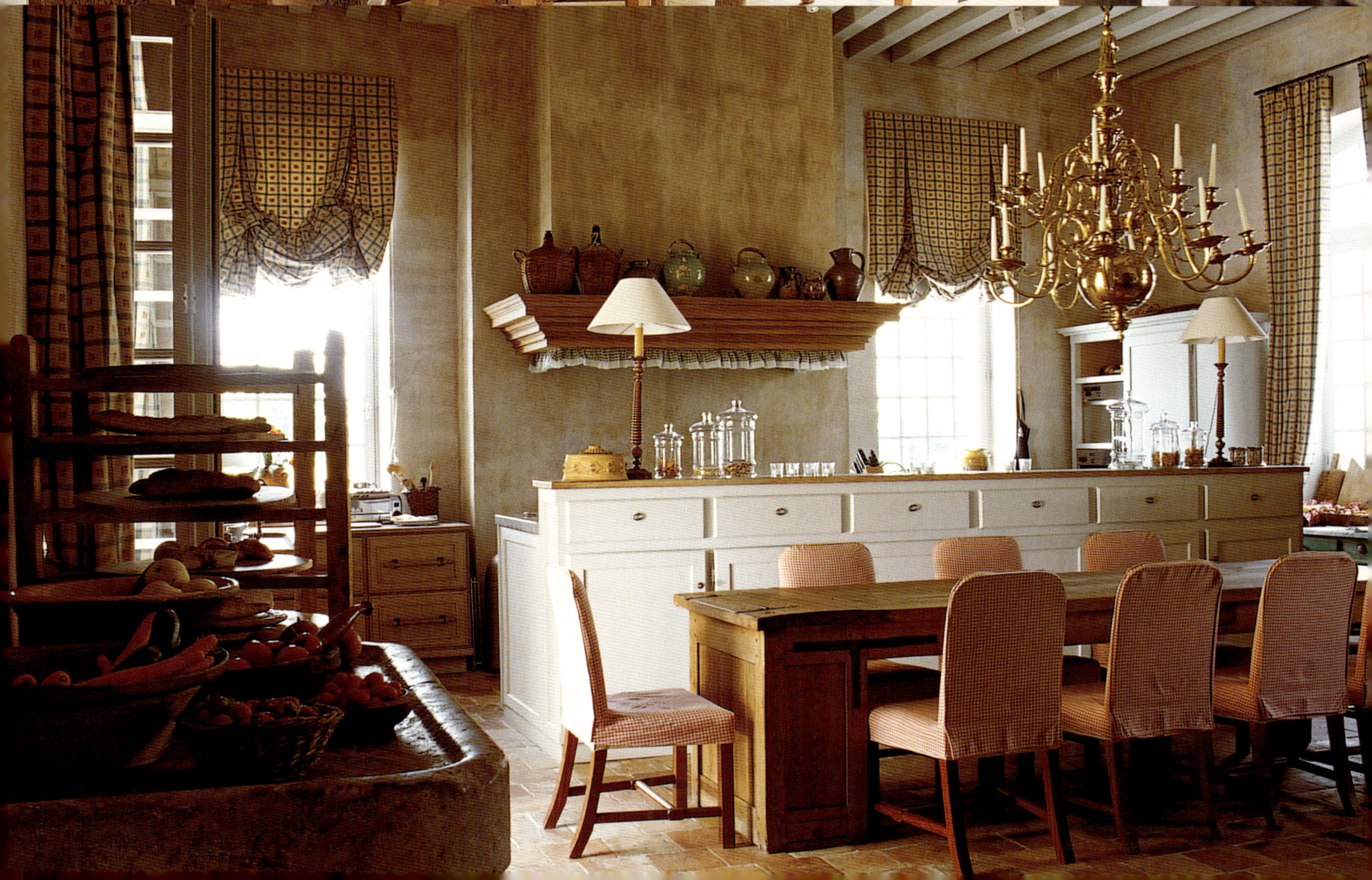

カントリー・キッチン

Country Kitchens

勝手口のそばに、土のついたゴム長靴があり、窓からは、胸のすくような自然の景色が見渡せます。室内にこれほど温かく幸せなムードがあふれ、そこここに歴史と伝統が感じられるのは、カントリー・キッチン以外にありません。農場にある博物館や、保存されたカントリーハウスの中にあるキッチンは、どれも魅力的です。カントリー・キッチンに使われているのは、素朴な天然素材です。床には、石や、レンガ、タイルが敷かれています。天井の梁はむき出しです。木肌を生かす、塗装する、と使い方は様々ですが、木材が多用されていることも特徴です。おそらく暖炉があるか、昔ながらのコンロがはめこまれたチムニー・ブレストがあると思います。キッチンのメーカーも、やはりカントリースタイルを意識した商品を取り揃えています。クラシカルなアガ社のガスレンジや、バトラーズ・シンクがそうですし、飾り縁と、真鍮の取っ手を付け、クリーム色に塗装した食器棚のドアもあります。カントリー・キッチンでは、ありとあらゆる物を飾り付けます。画家の絵、子どもの描いた絵、観葉植物、カゴはもちろん、ガラスの器、お皿、水差しは、オープン棚に飾り、（特に、ステンレス、銅、ホーローの）調理器具も、しまいこみません。食器棚にはガラスのドアがついているか、ドアの代わりに、レースのカーテンがさげてあります。照明器具は、真鍮か、鉄が使われている伝統的なデザインです。そして、犬用のカゴや、猫用のドア、金魚鉢、ハムスターの回し車もあります。この部屋は、動物の住まいでもあるのです。しかし、一番カントリー・キッチンらしさを演出するのは、手作りの品です。カゴに山盛りになった野菜や、摘みたての果物、びんに詰めた手作りジャム、熟成したチーズや、ケーキ、スコーン。そして絶対に欠かせないのは、焼きたてのパンです。

Complete with muddy rubber boots by the back door and, from the windows, views of rolling countryside, no other style of room abounds with so much warmth and well-being, so much sense of history and tradition, as the country kitchen. These are our favourite rooms in farm museums and restored country houses. The materials used here are rustic and natural: stone, brick or tiles on the floor; beams on the ceiling and plenty of wood – either natural or painted. Where possible there may be an open fire, or an old chimney breast in which a traditional-style cooker has been fitted. Kitchen manufacturers see this vision too, and fulfil it with their ranges of Aga cookers, butler's sinks and cream-painted cupboard doors with mouldings and brass handles. In the country kitchen, everything is on display: paintings, children's drawings, plants, baskets, glassware, plates and jugs on open racks, and cooking utensils (especially if stainless steel, copper or enamel). The cupboards here have either glass-fronted doors or none at all, with ruched fabric curtains taking their place instead. Lighting tends to be traditional, with brass or iron fittings, and with its dog baskets, cat flaps, goldfish bowls or hamster wheels, this room is a home for animals too. But the most evocative item here has to be the produce – the baskets of vegetables and fresh-picked fruit, jars of homemade jam, maturing cheeses, cakes, scones, and most important of all, freshly baked bread.

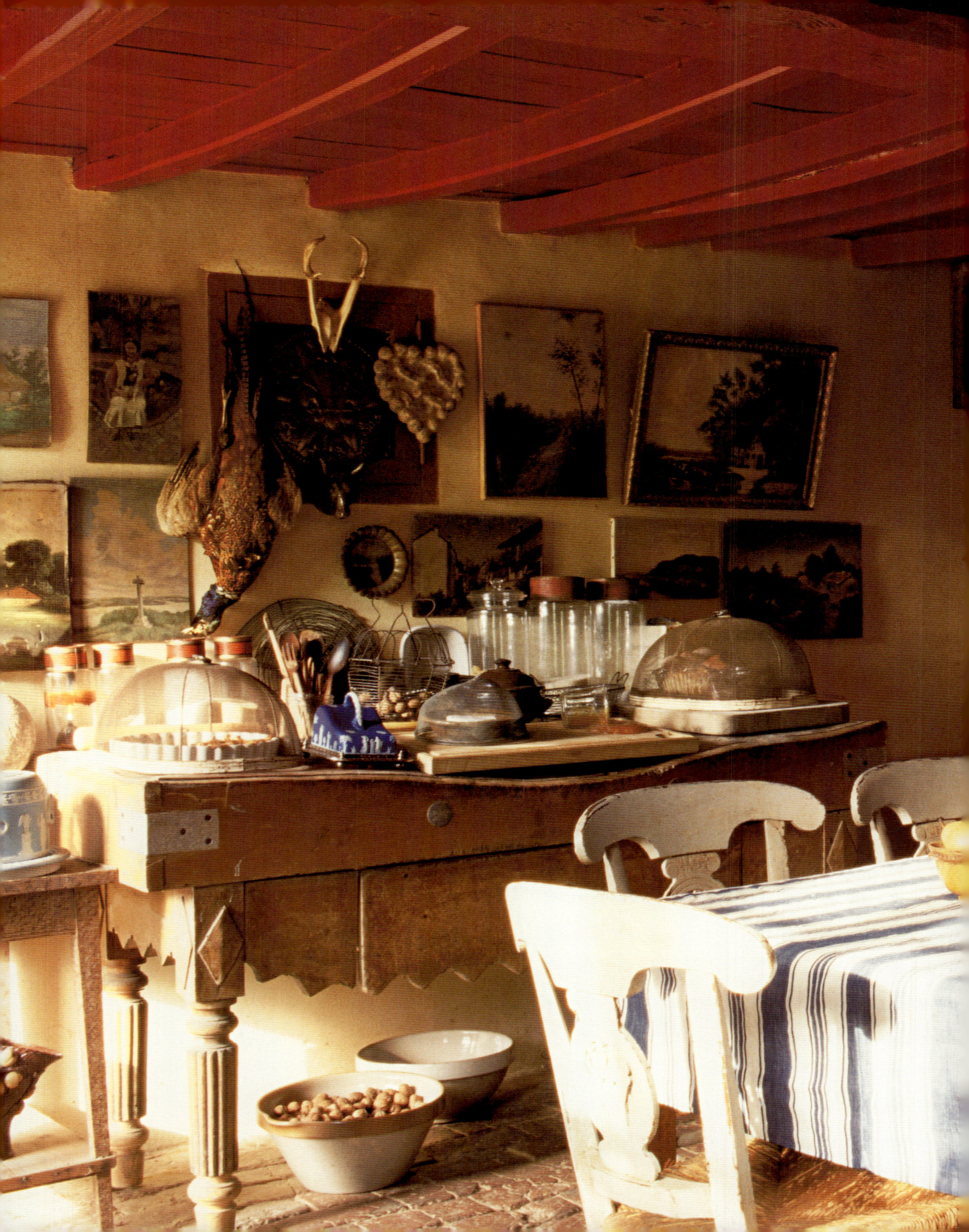

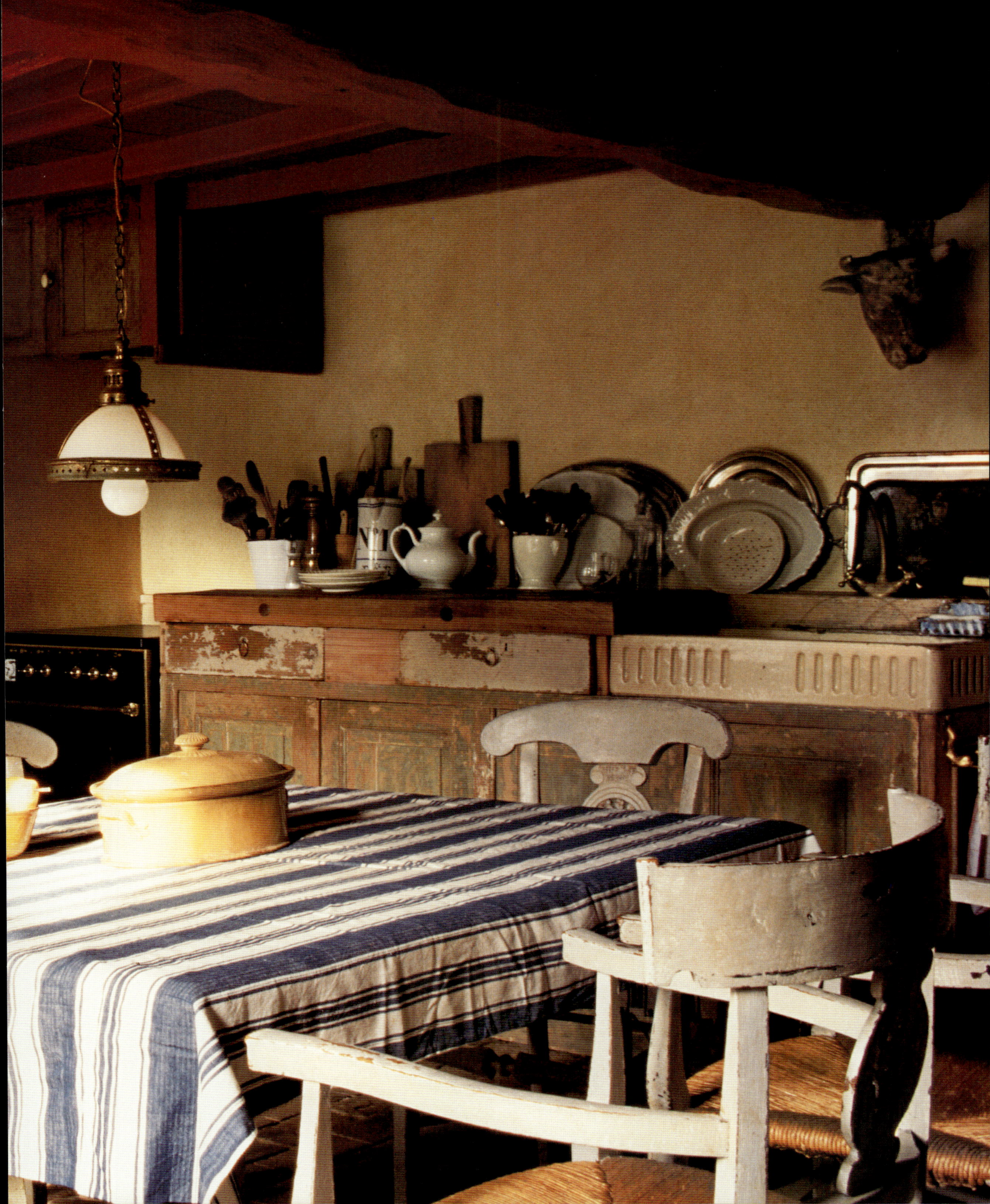

カントリー・キッチン

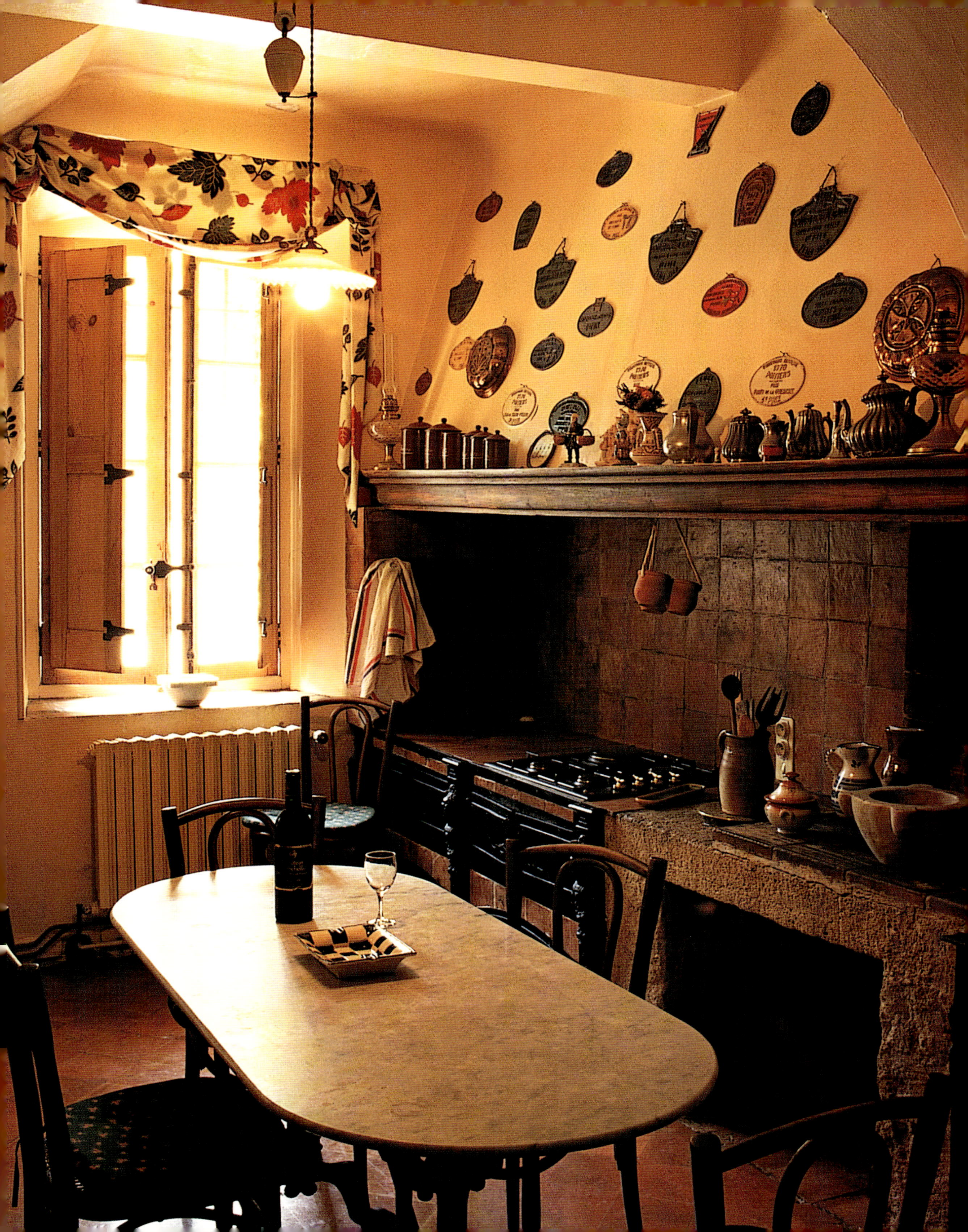

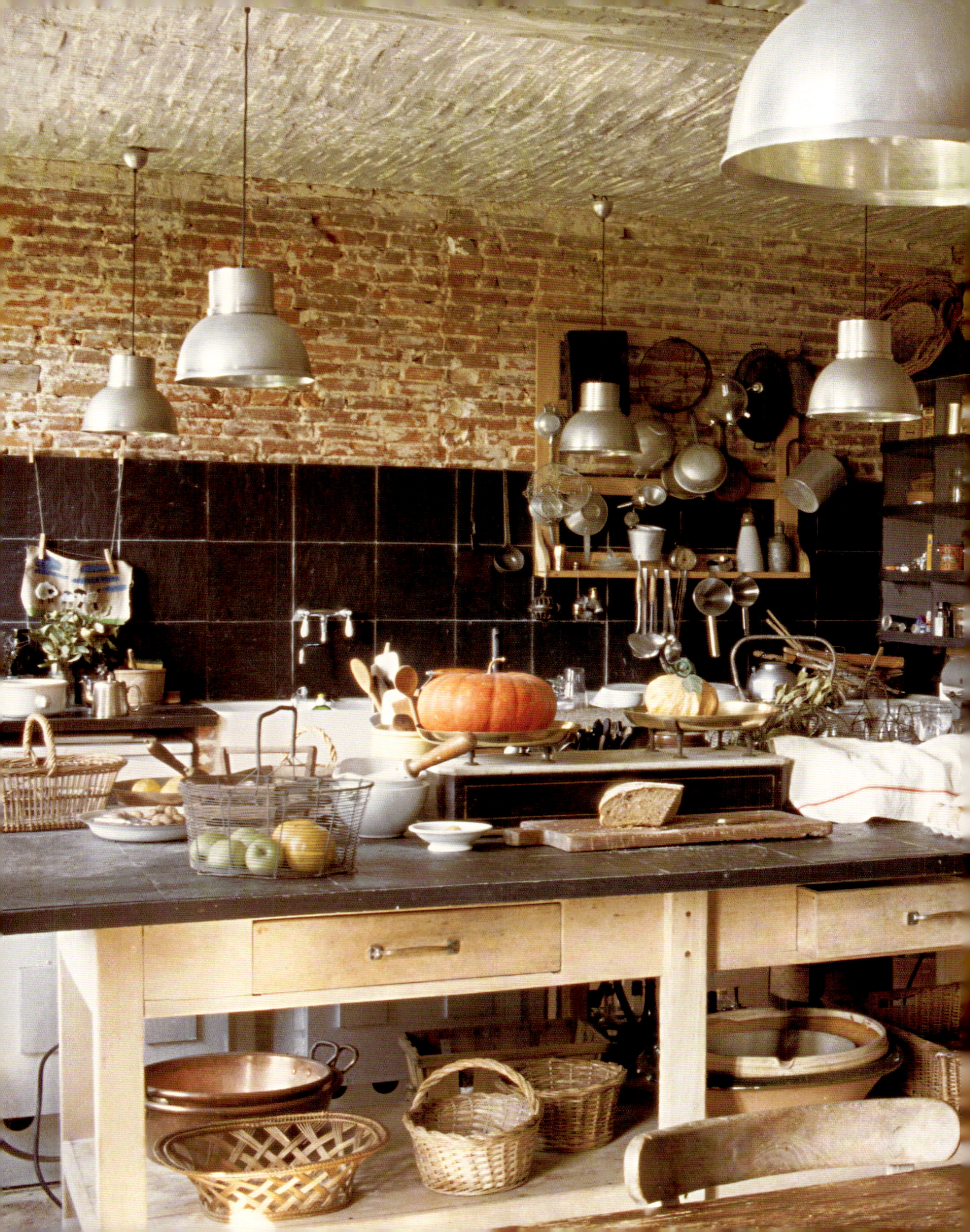

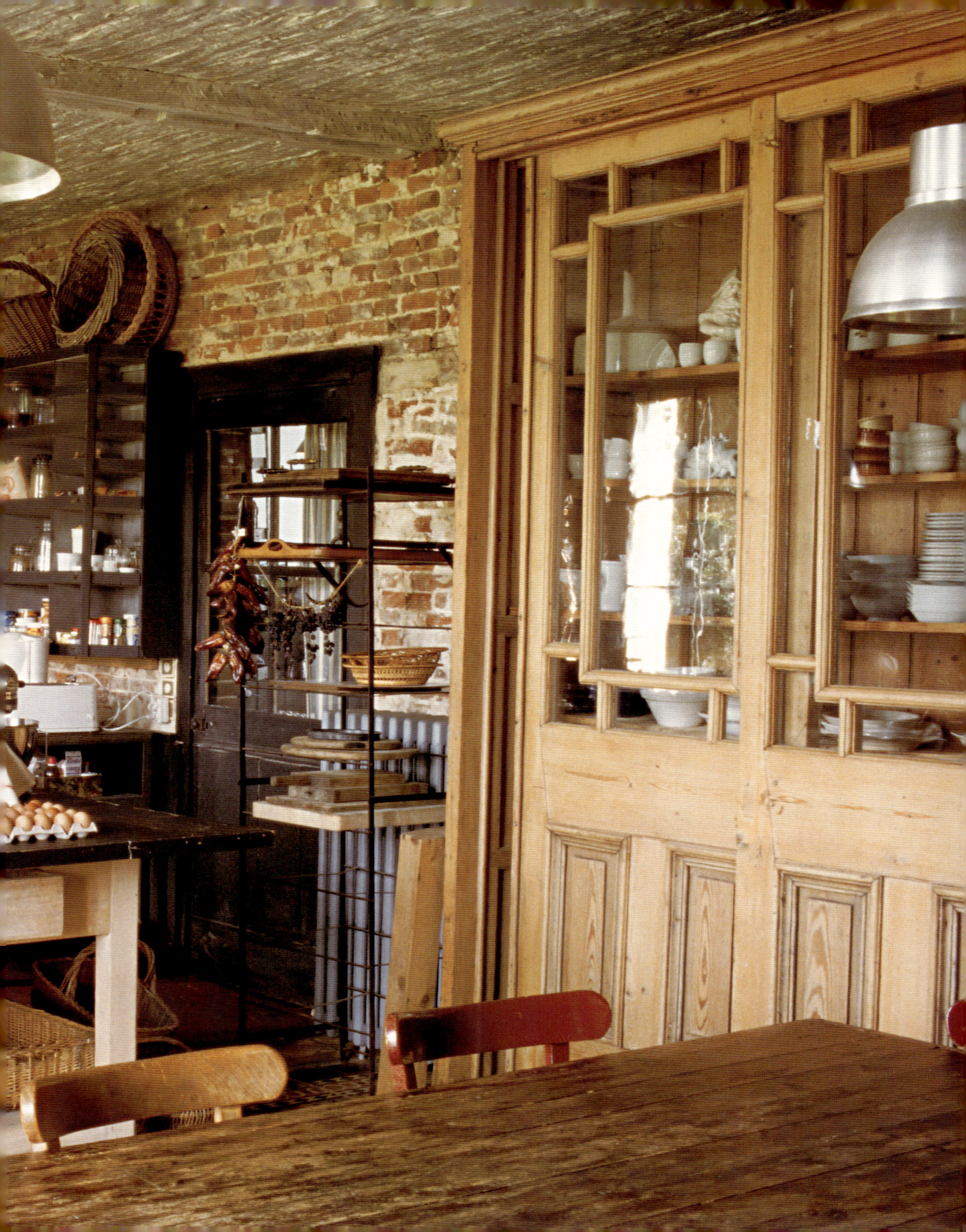

カントリー・キッチン

カントリー・キッチン

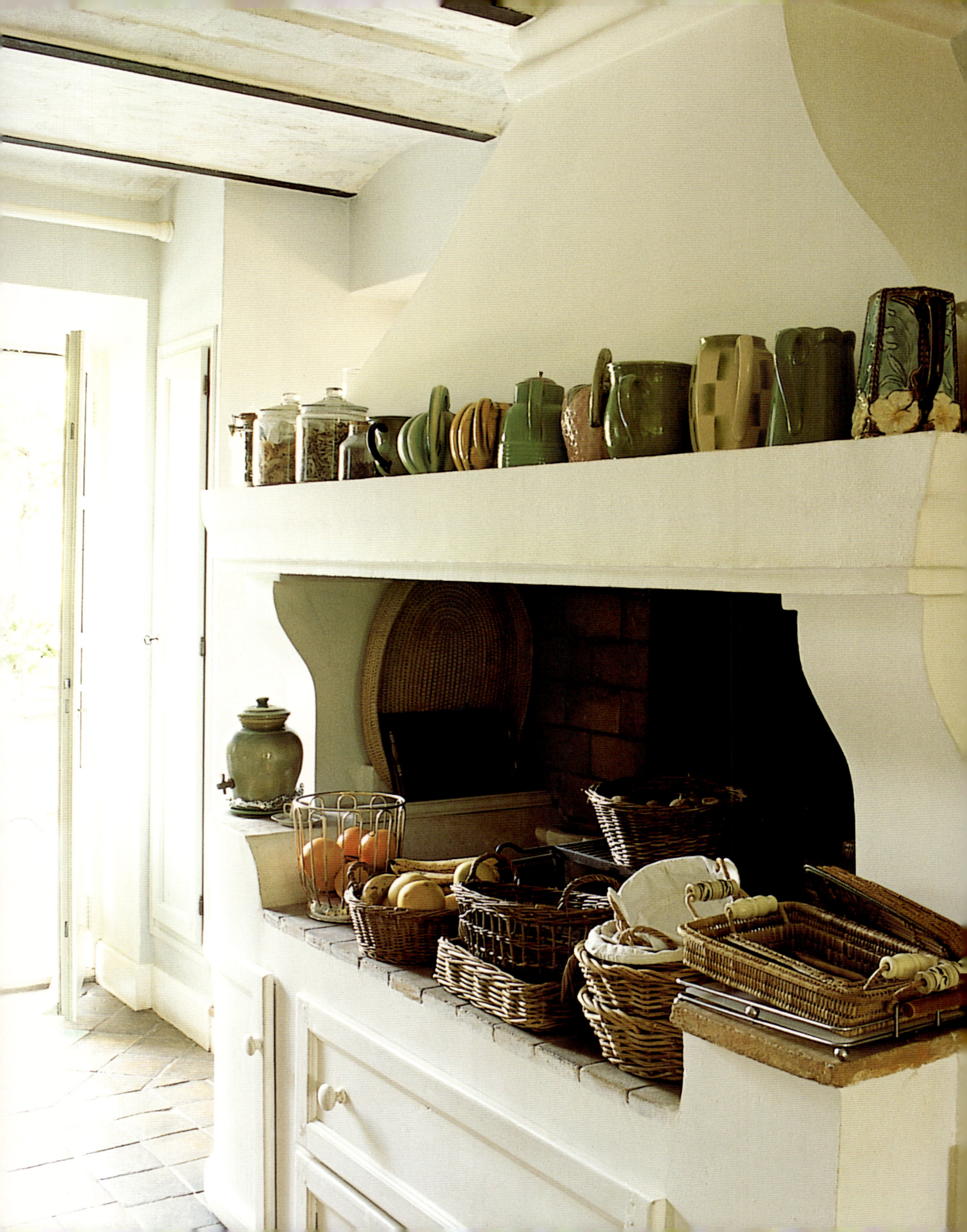

カントリー・キッチン

カントリー・キッチン

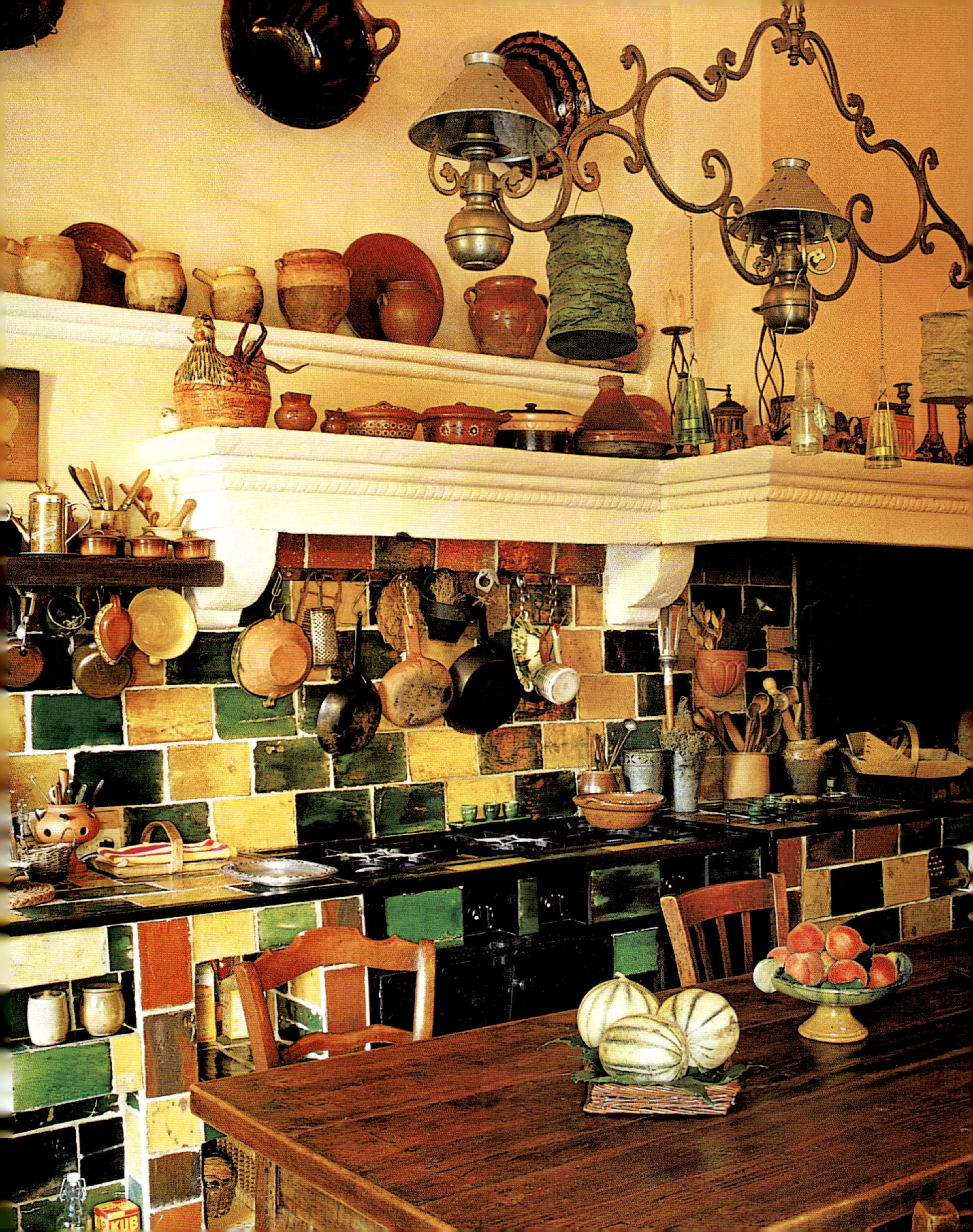

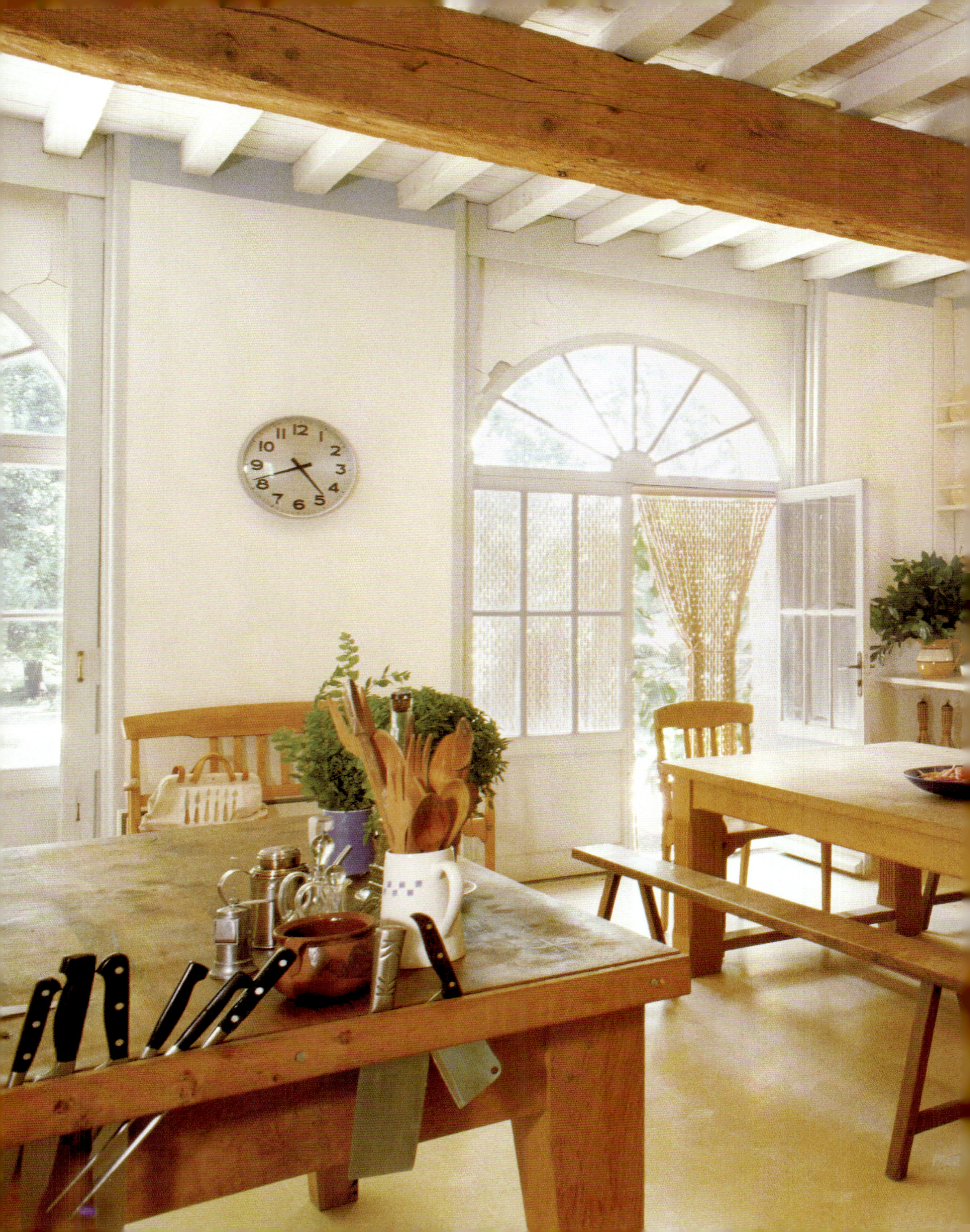

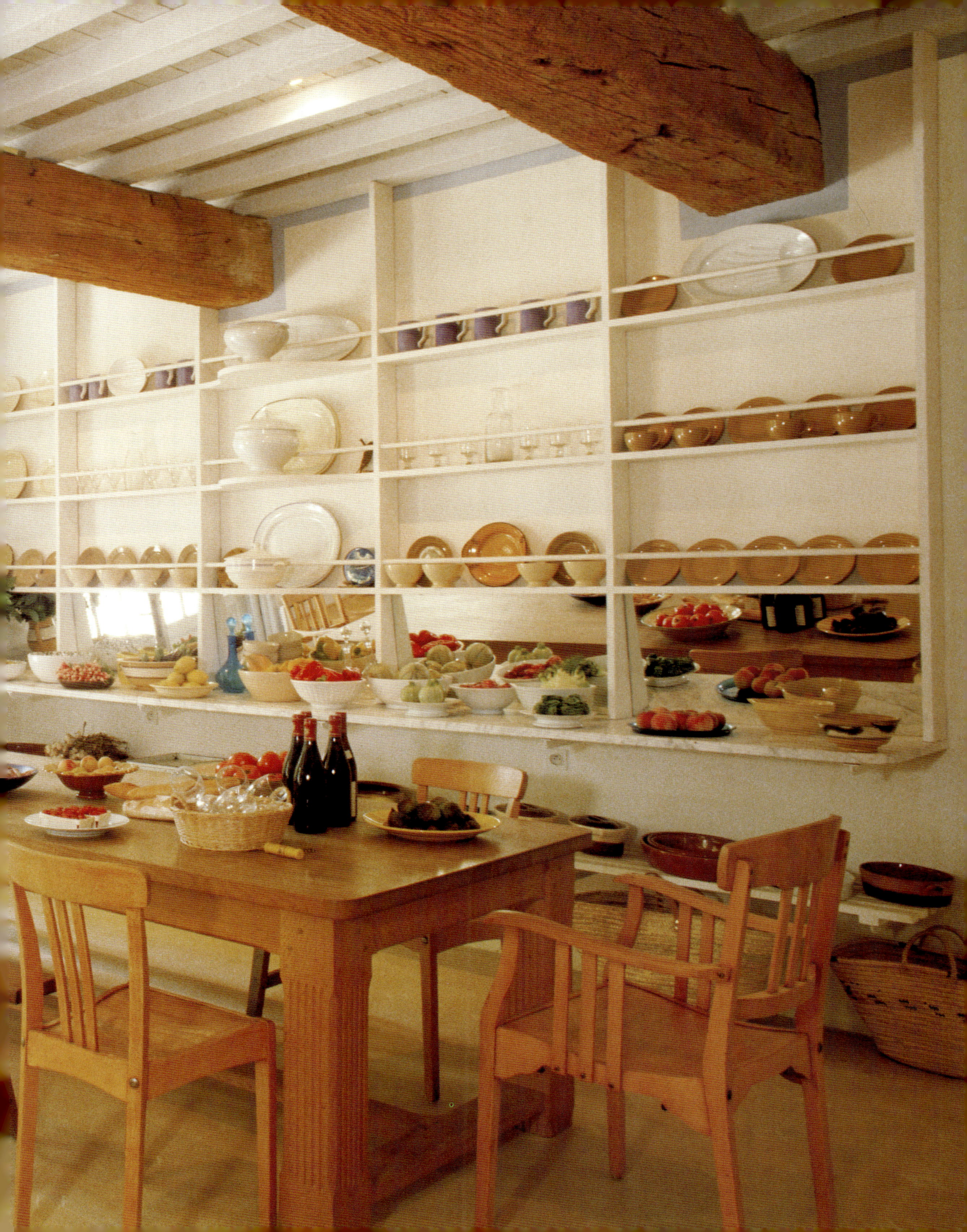

カントリー・キッチン

カントリー・キッチン

カントリー・キッチン

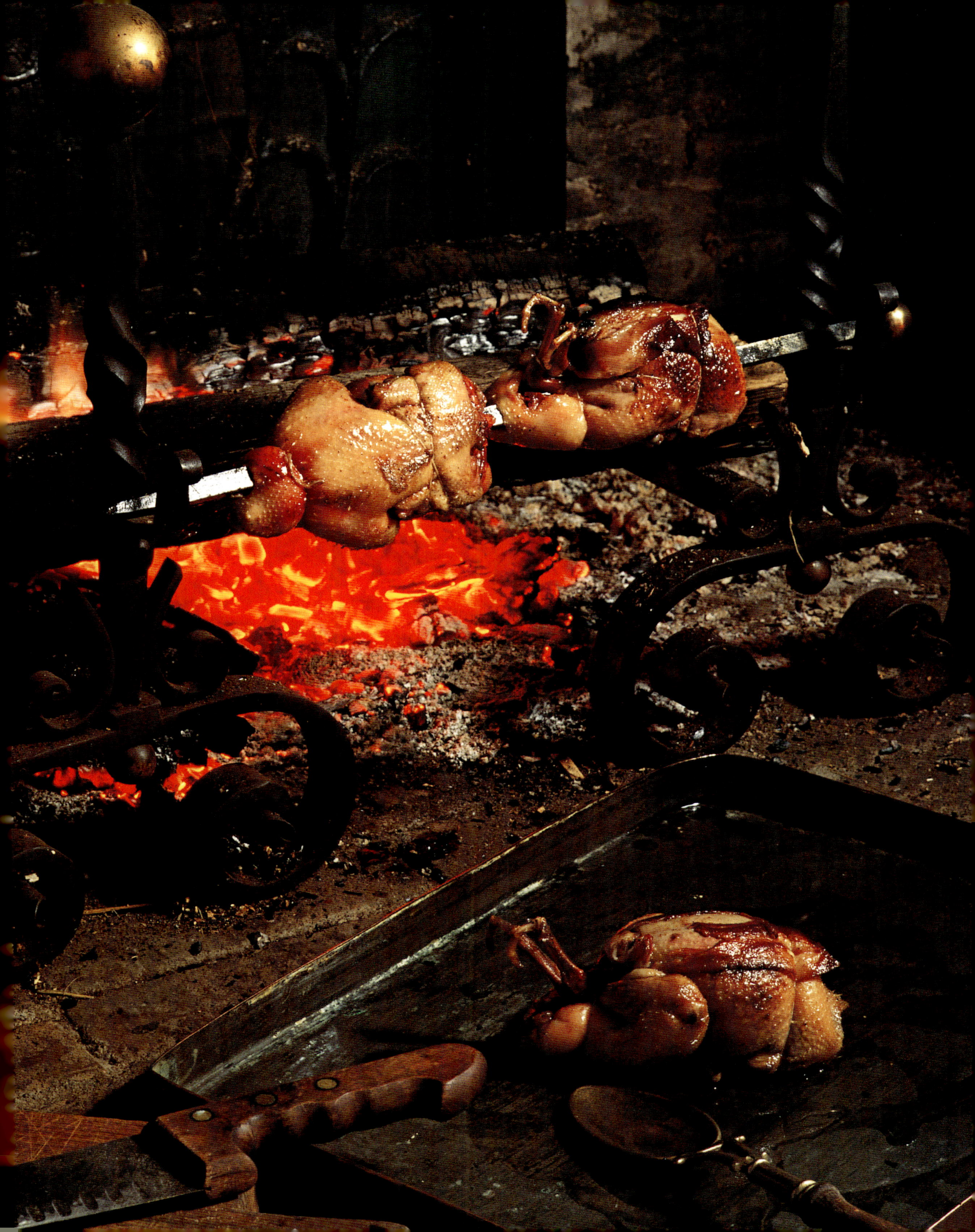

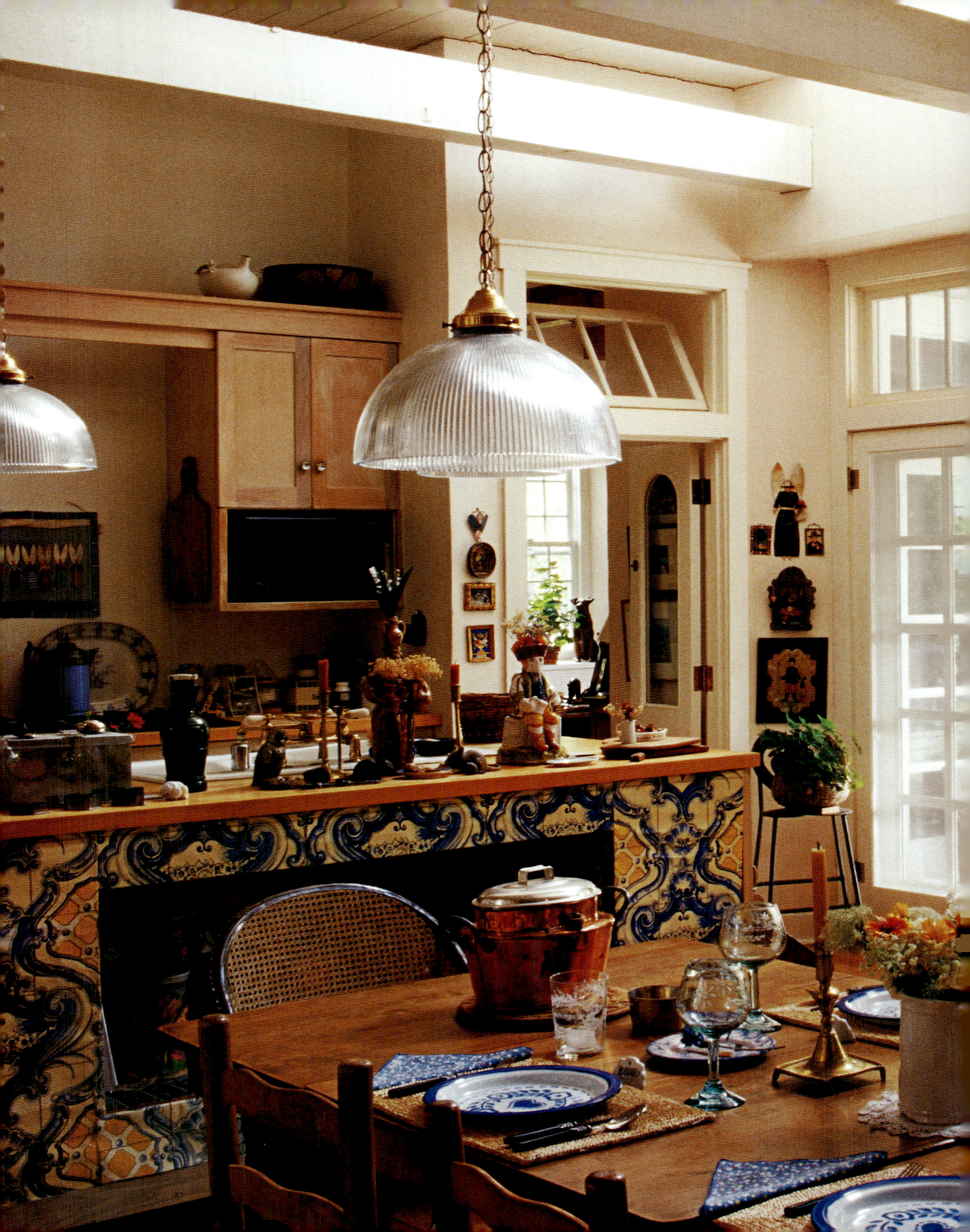

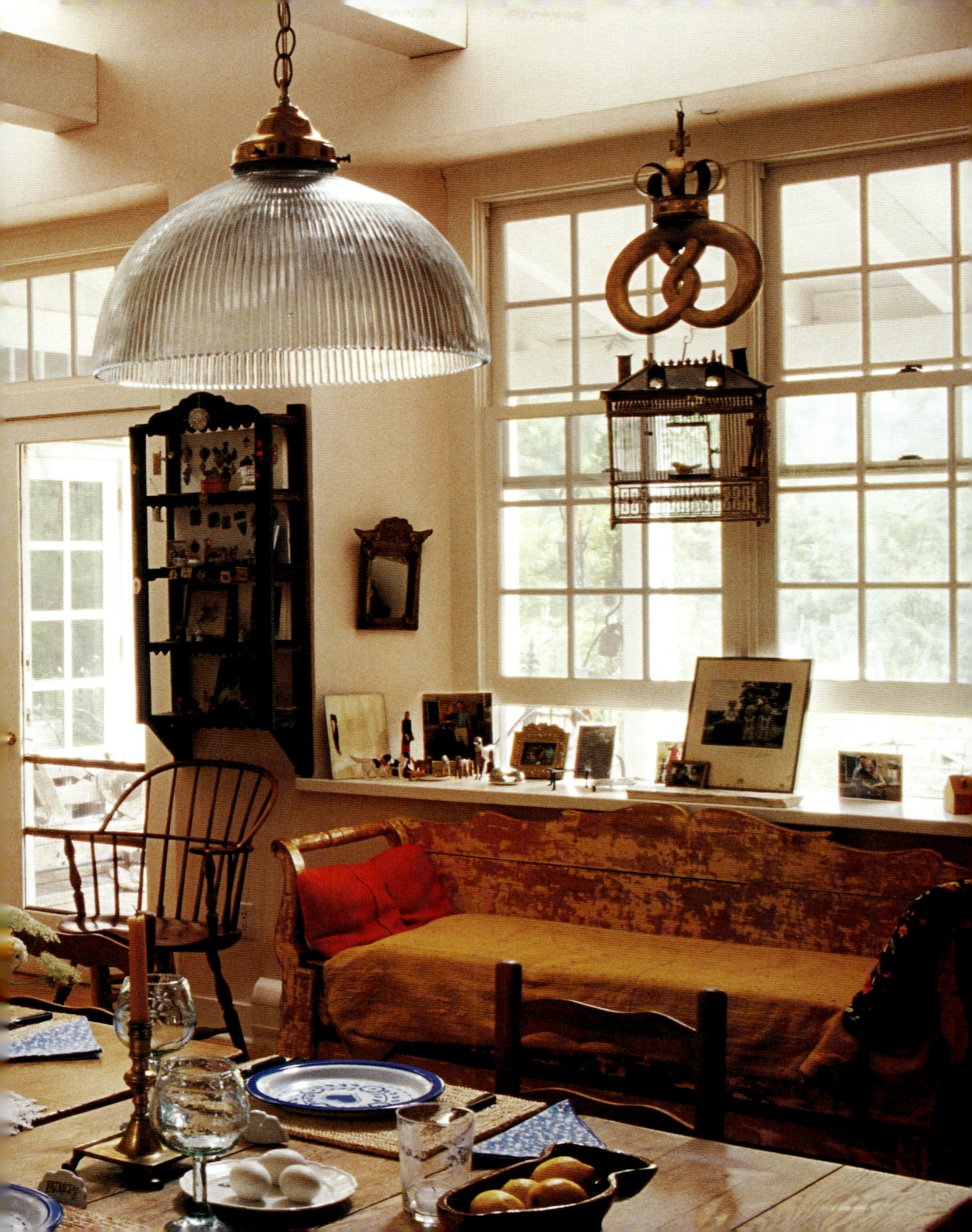

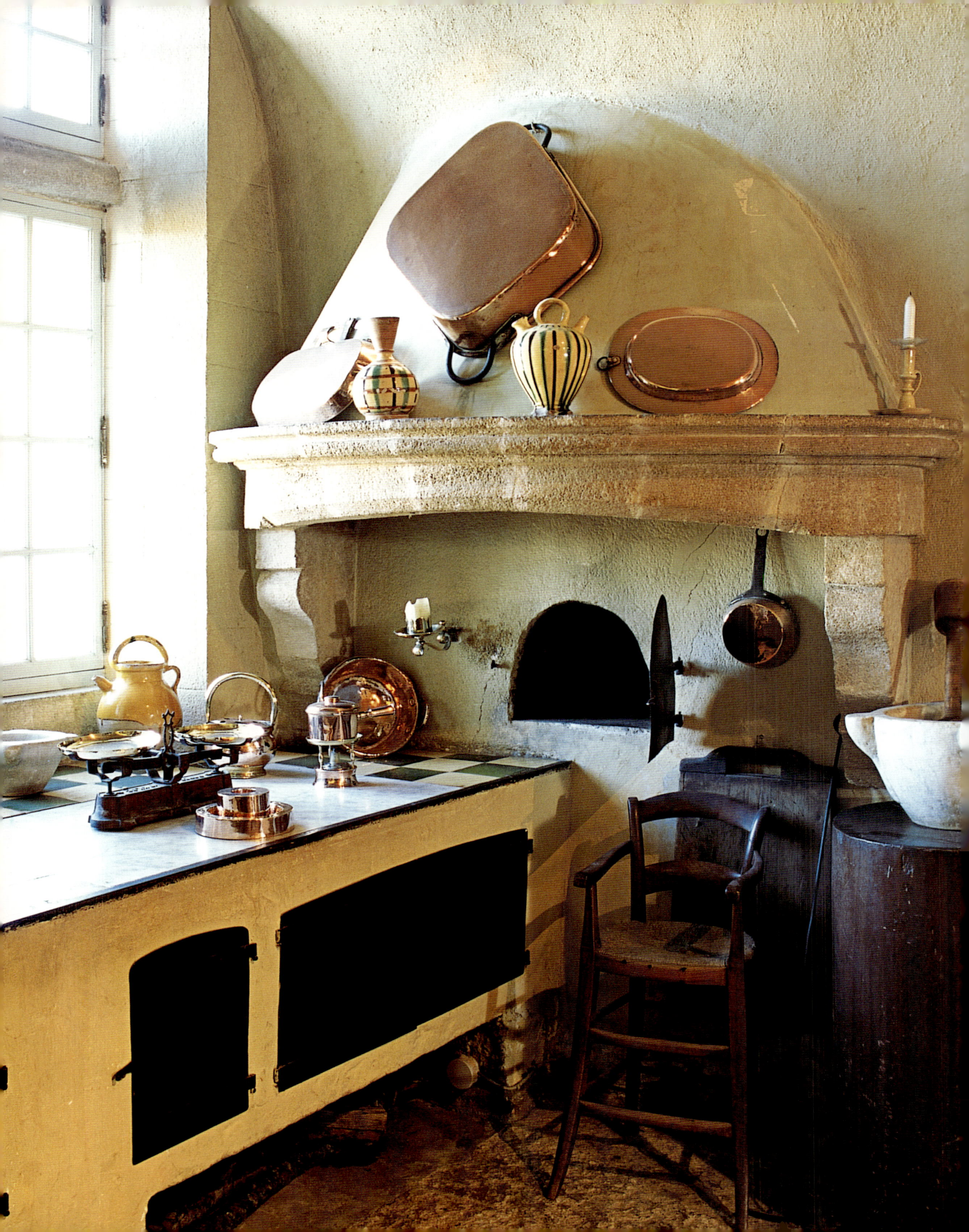

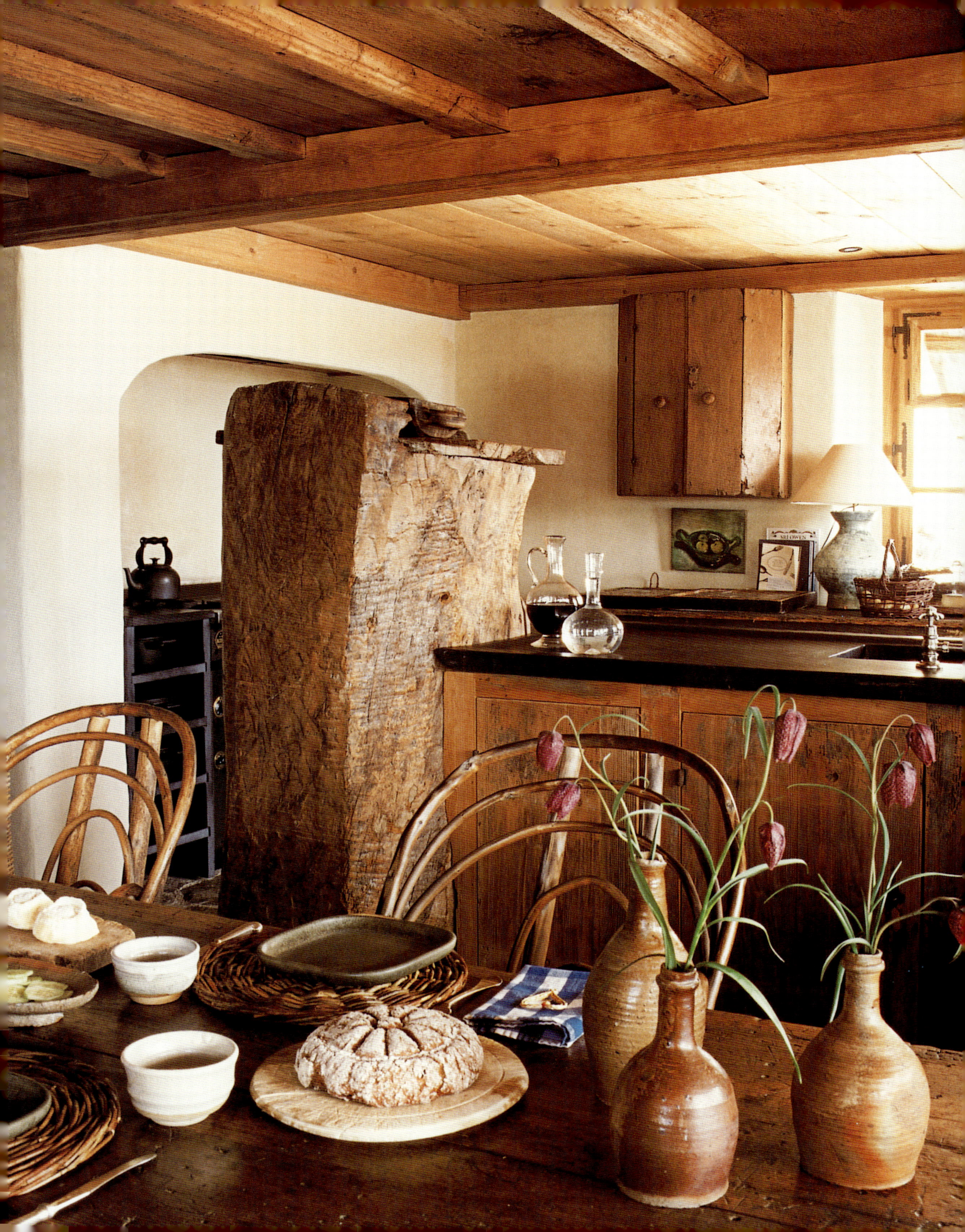

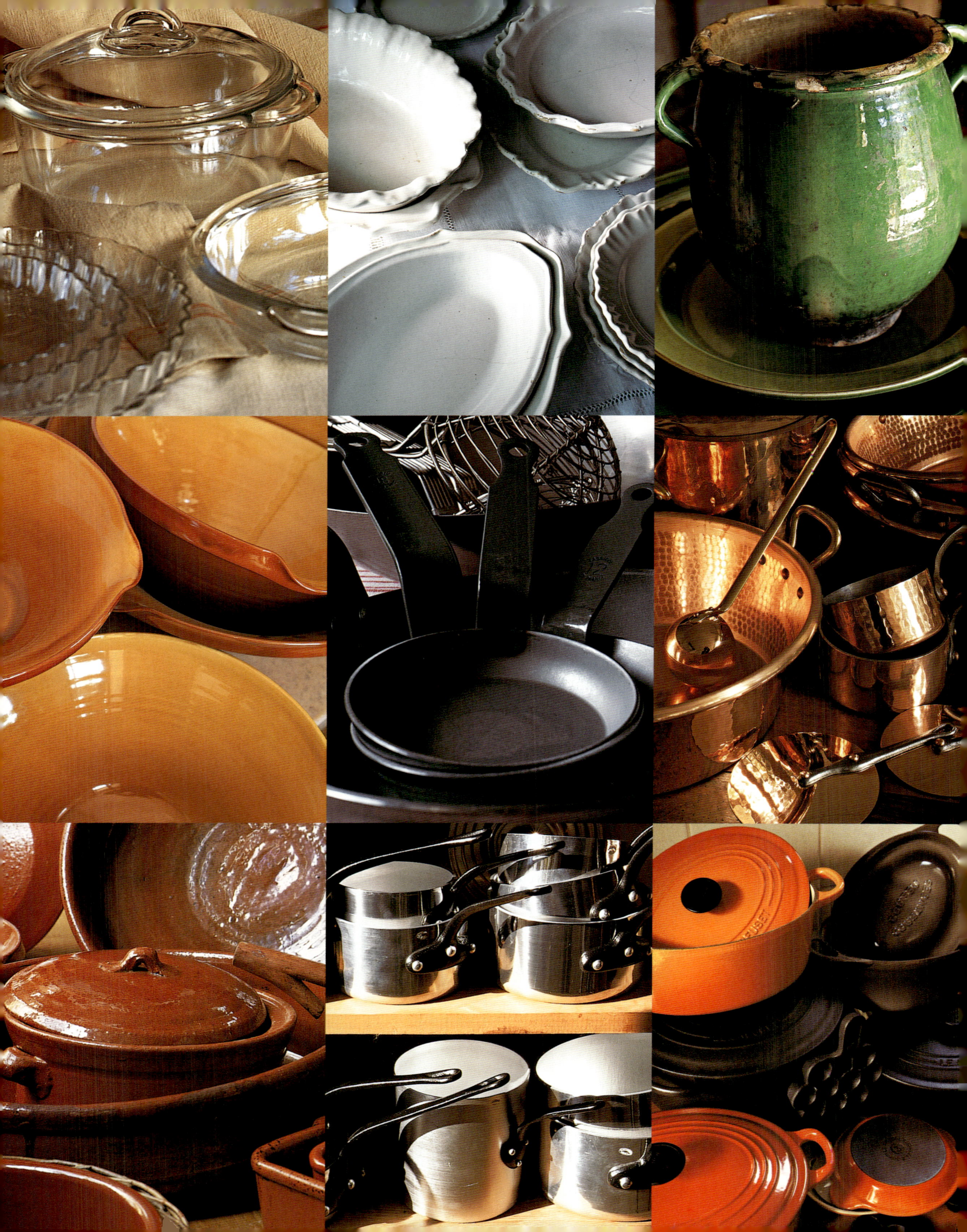

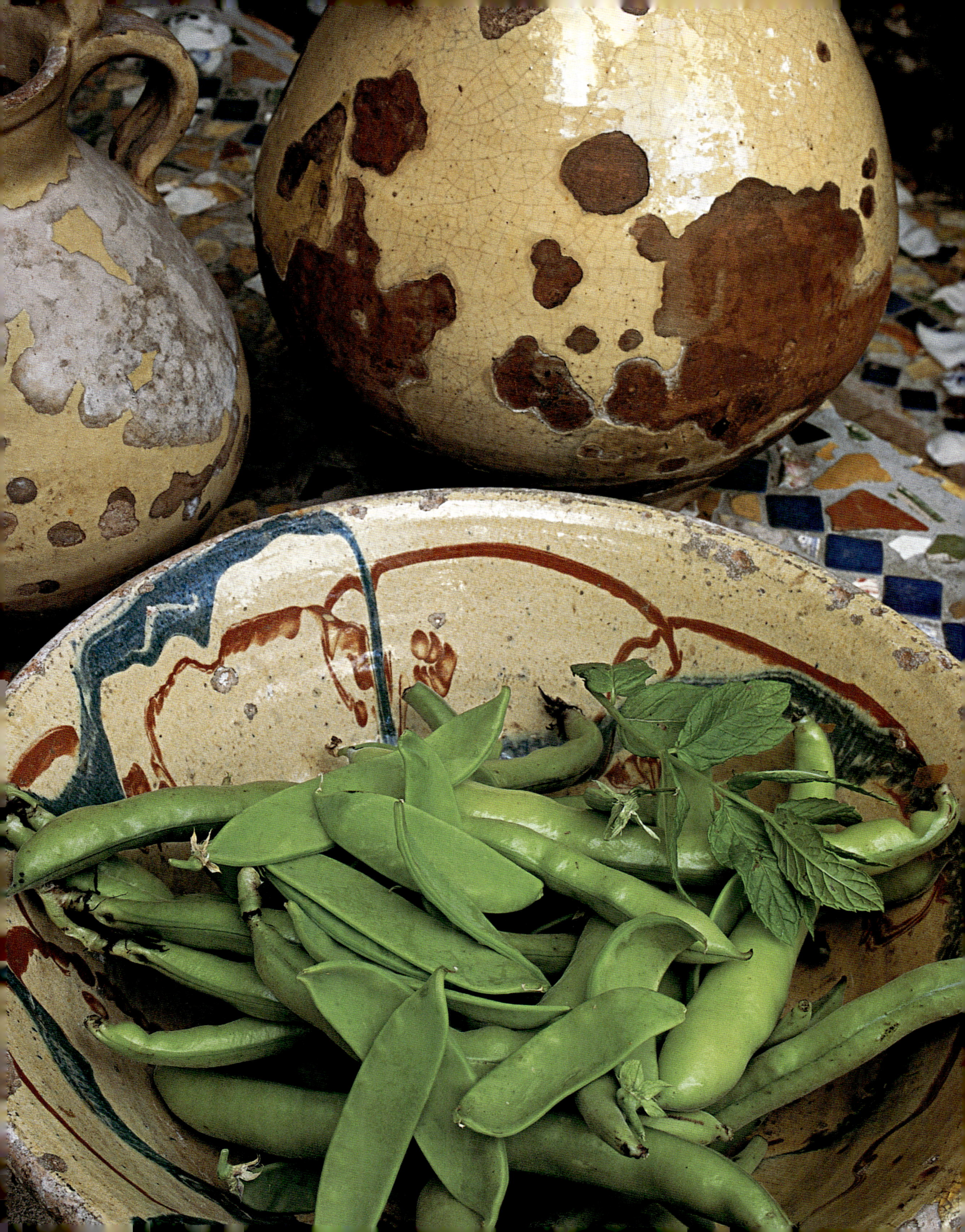

シティ・キッチン

The City Kitchen

「シティ・キッチン」という名称は、都市に住宅があるかどうか、ということより、キッチンのサイズや、スタイルで定義される傾向が強くなってきました。住まいの中には、広々としたスペースそのものが、強い印象と、洗練されたデザインの鍵になっている部屋もあります。しかし、キッチンは、こぢんまりとしたスペースに納めなければならないことが、多いものです。1950年代に人間工学の研究が進み、専業主婦は、キッチンでの家事のために、かなりの距離を歩いていることが分かりました。そこで、向きを変えるだけで、両側のカウンターに手が届く、「ギャレー・キッチン」が開発されました。「動線を三角形にする」という概念に基づき、冷蔵庫、シンク、コンロの理想的な配置が確立しました。その後、住まいの中で、キッチンに割くスペースは広くなっていき、「アイランド型キッチン」が開発されました。最初は、「朝食用カウンター」として完成しましたが、その後進化し、今では、シンクか、コンロが組み込まれています。「インテグレート（統合する）」という言葉が流行し、最新の設備が、すっぽりと、あつらえた収納棚の中に隠されるようになりました。シティ・キッチンにとって色選びは重要ですが、仕上げと素材——たとえば、大理石、ガラス、磨いた鋼や、ワークトップの人造大理石など——は、いっそう重要です。すべてが直線的で、形が角張っていた時代は終わりました。キャビネットがカーブしていたり、シンクが円形だったり、コンロにもまるみがついていたりします。モダンなシティ・キッチンは彫刻的で、その設備は——洗練されたレンジフードにしても、金属とガラス扉のツインドア冷蔵庫にしても——調和しない物たちの、単なる寄せ集めではなく、すべてが自然に溶け合うようにデザインされています。

City kitchens tend to be defined more by their size and style than by their location. Whereas some rooms depend on being large for their impact and stylishness, a kitchen often has to fit into a small, compact space. With the ergonomic studies of the 1950s, it was found that the distance housewives had to walk to perform a simple kitchen task could be enormous. So the galley kitchen, in which you could stand in the middle and reach either side just by turning around, was invented. The concept of the 'work triangle' established the ideal position for the cooker, the fridge and the sink unit. Since then the space given to the kitchen in the home has become more generous and we have seen the invention of the island unit – which at first came complete with a 'breakfast bar' and has now evolved to include either a sink or a hob. 'Integrated' has become the buzzword, with state-of-the-art equipment all seamlessly concealed within bespoke cabinetry. While colour is important in the city kitchen, finish and materials – such as marble, glass or polished steel, as well as surfaces such as corian – are more so. Gone are the days when everything had to be straight- or square-sided. Cabinetry can now curve or bow, sinks can be round and hobs semi-circular. The modern city kitchen is sculptural, its fittings – whether a stylish modern cooker hood or a twin-door metallic and glass-fronted fridge – are designed to blend into a totemic whole, rather than being simply a jumble of mismatched bits.

シティ・キッチン

シティ・キッチン

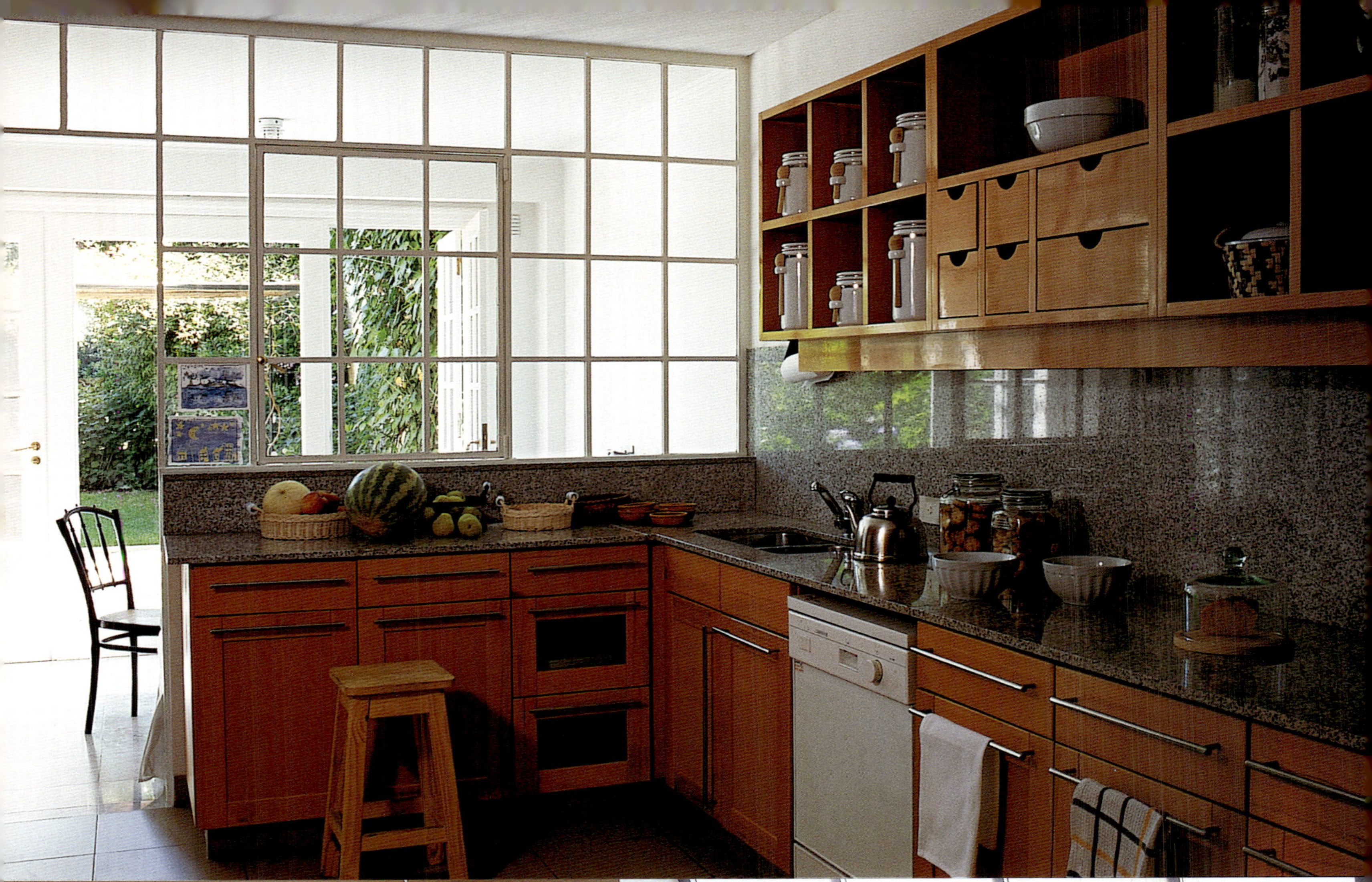

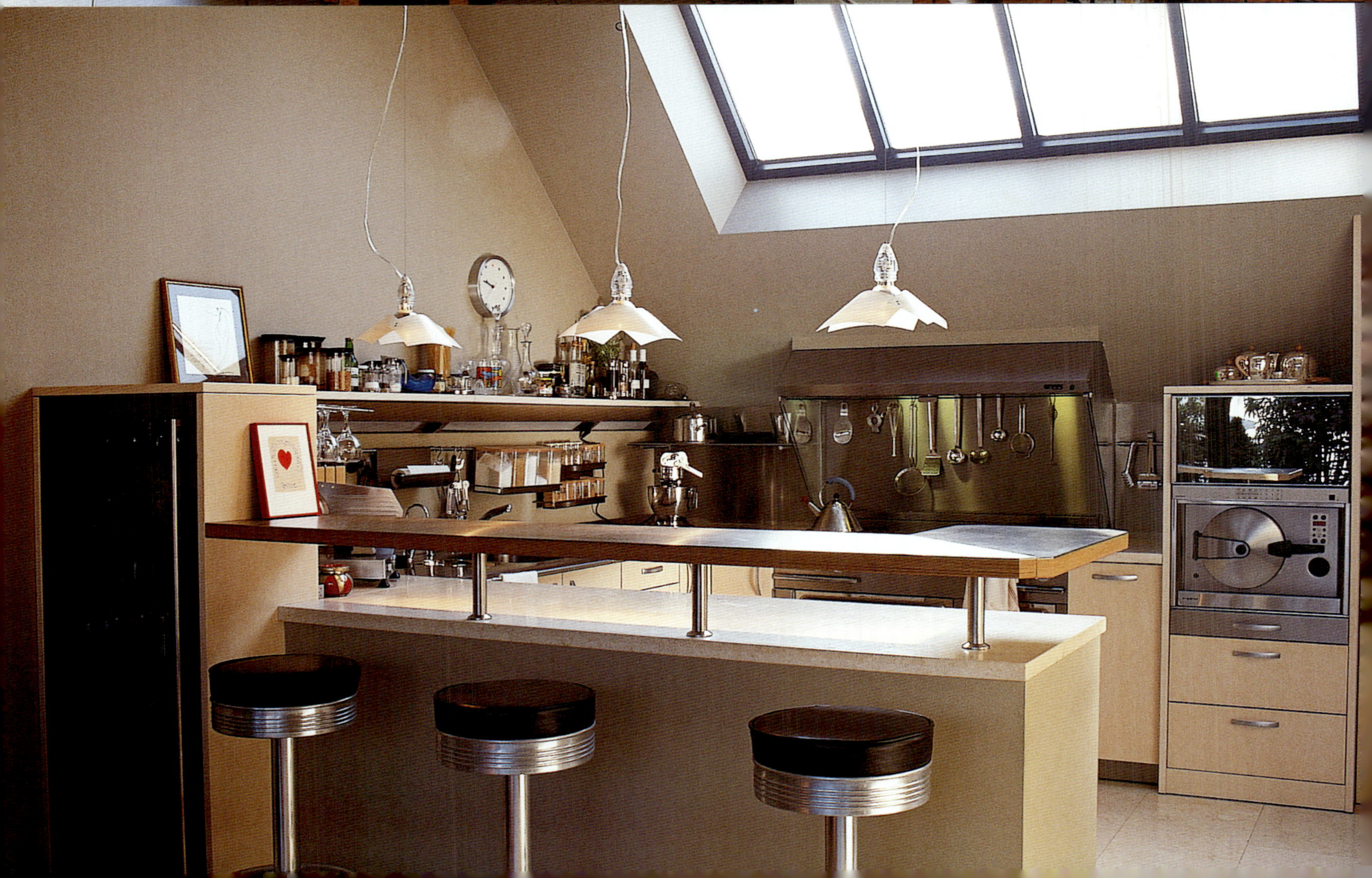

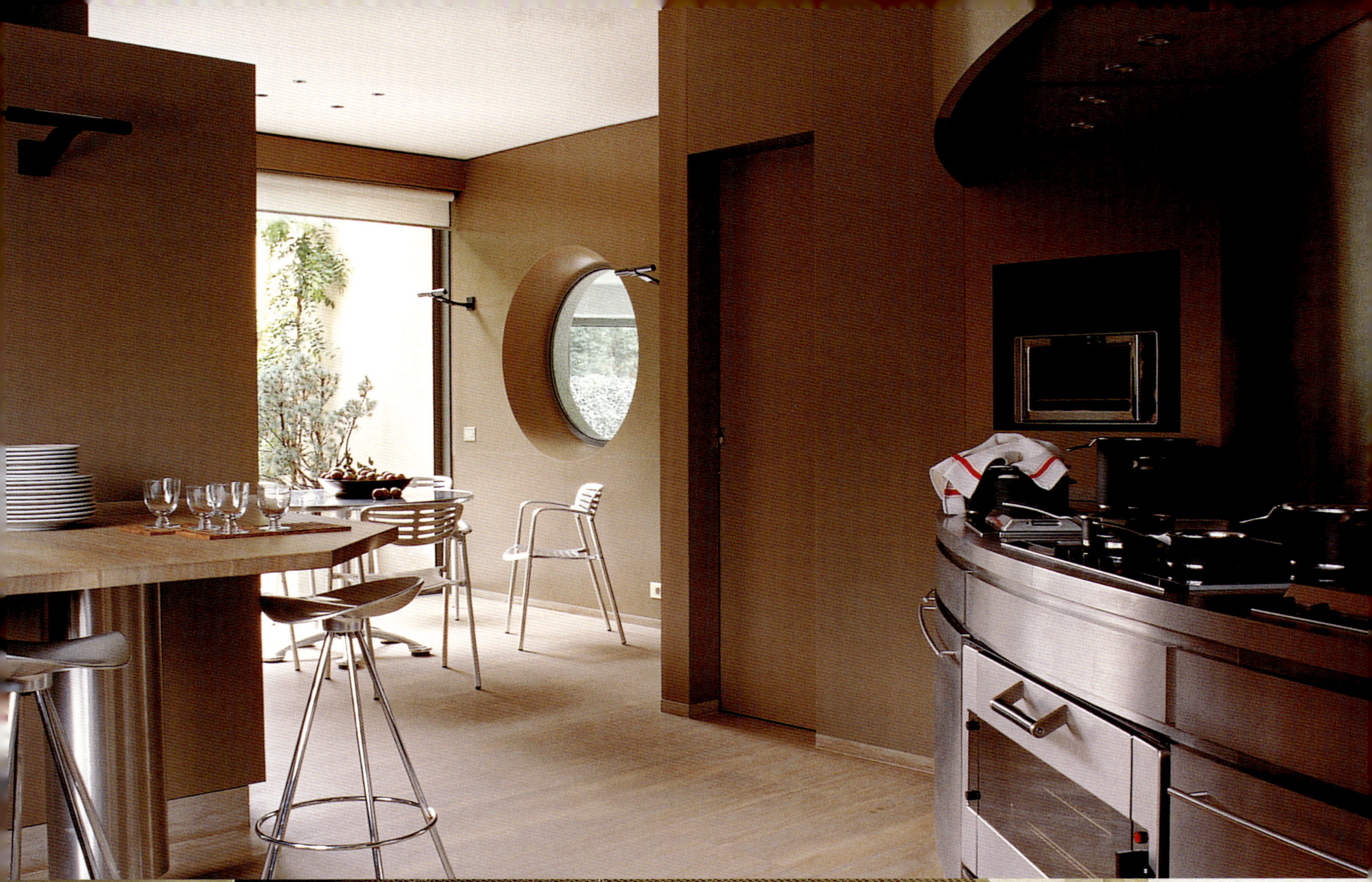
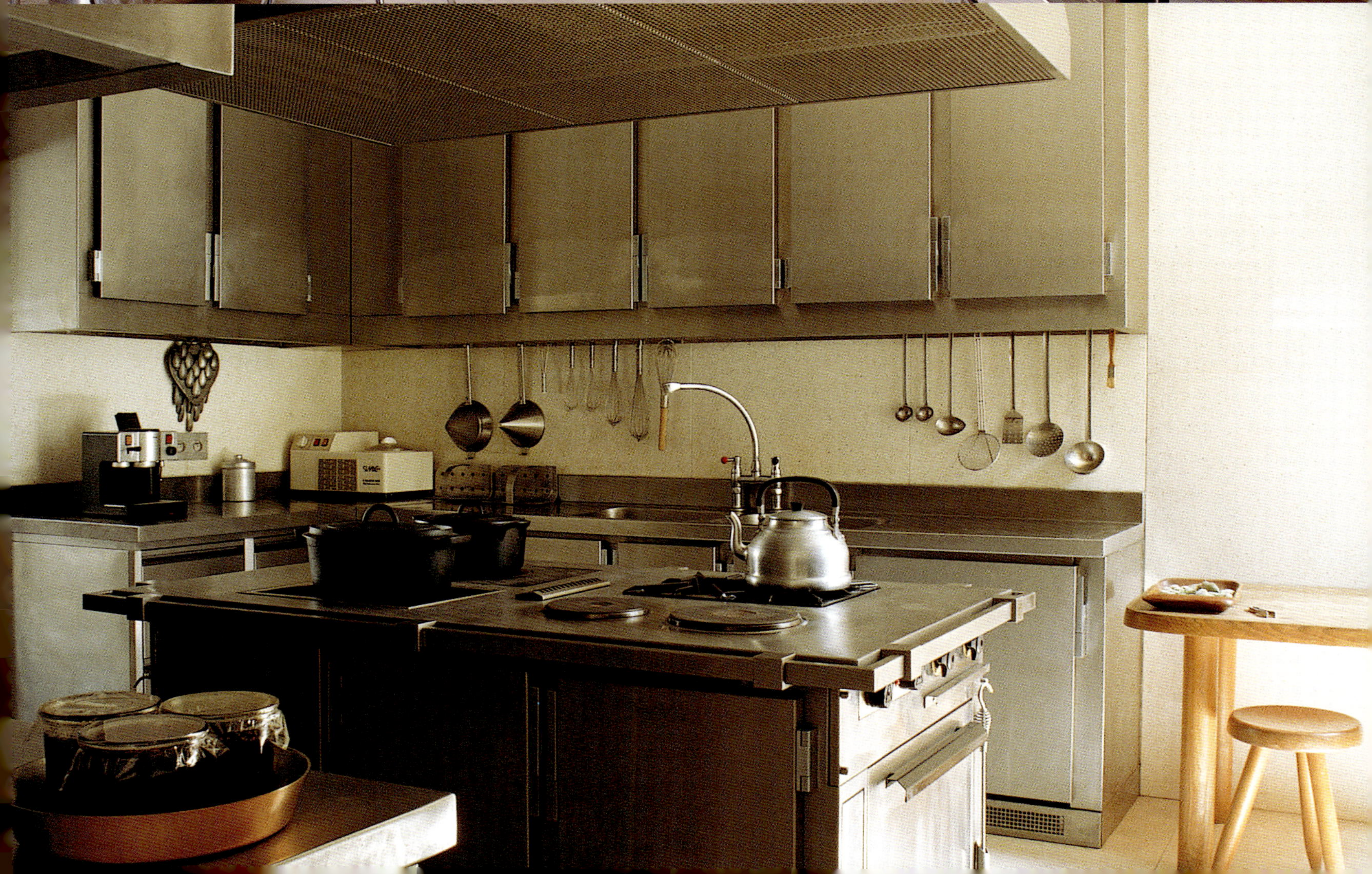

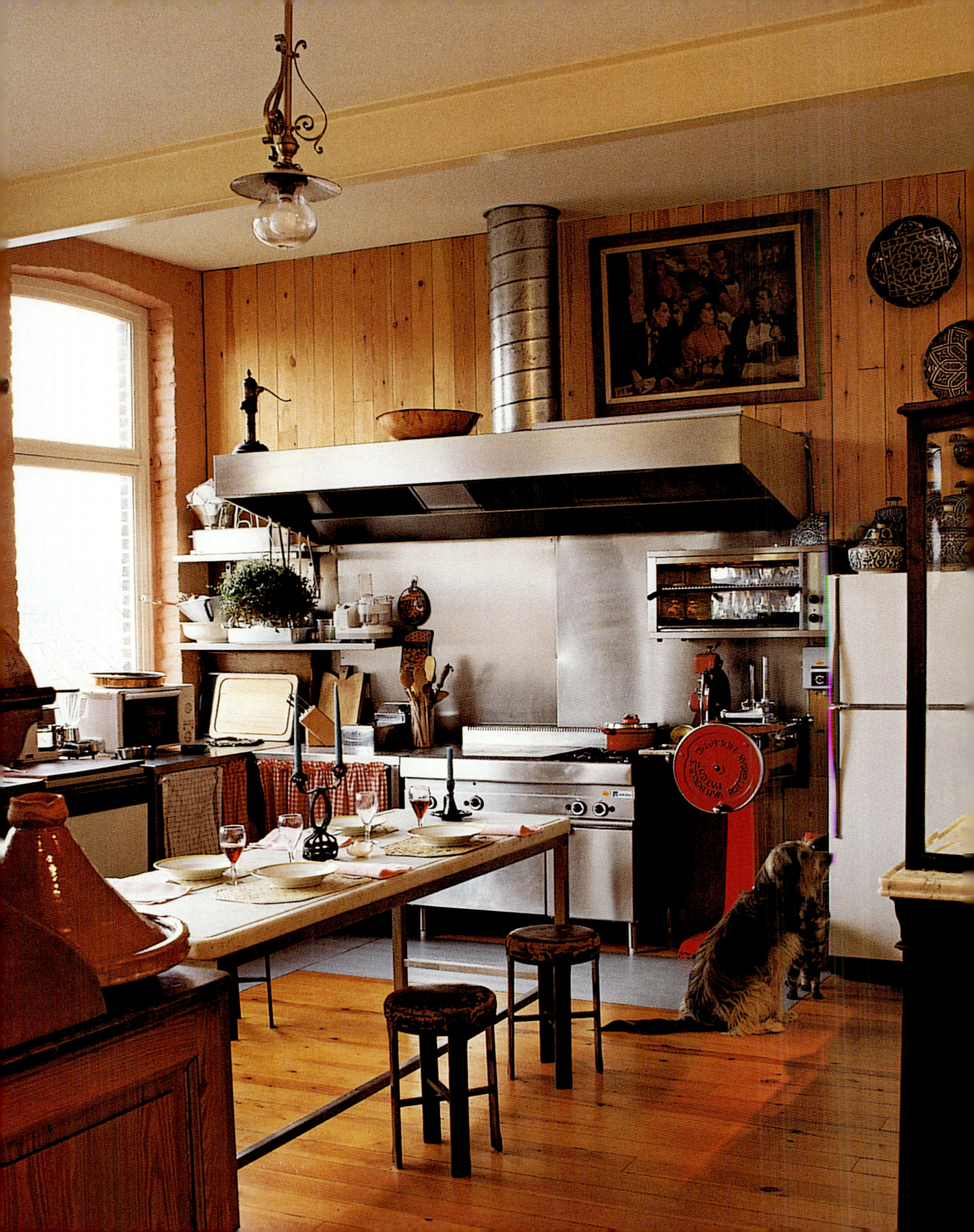

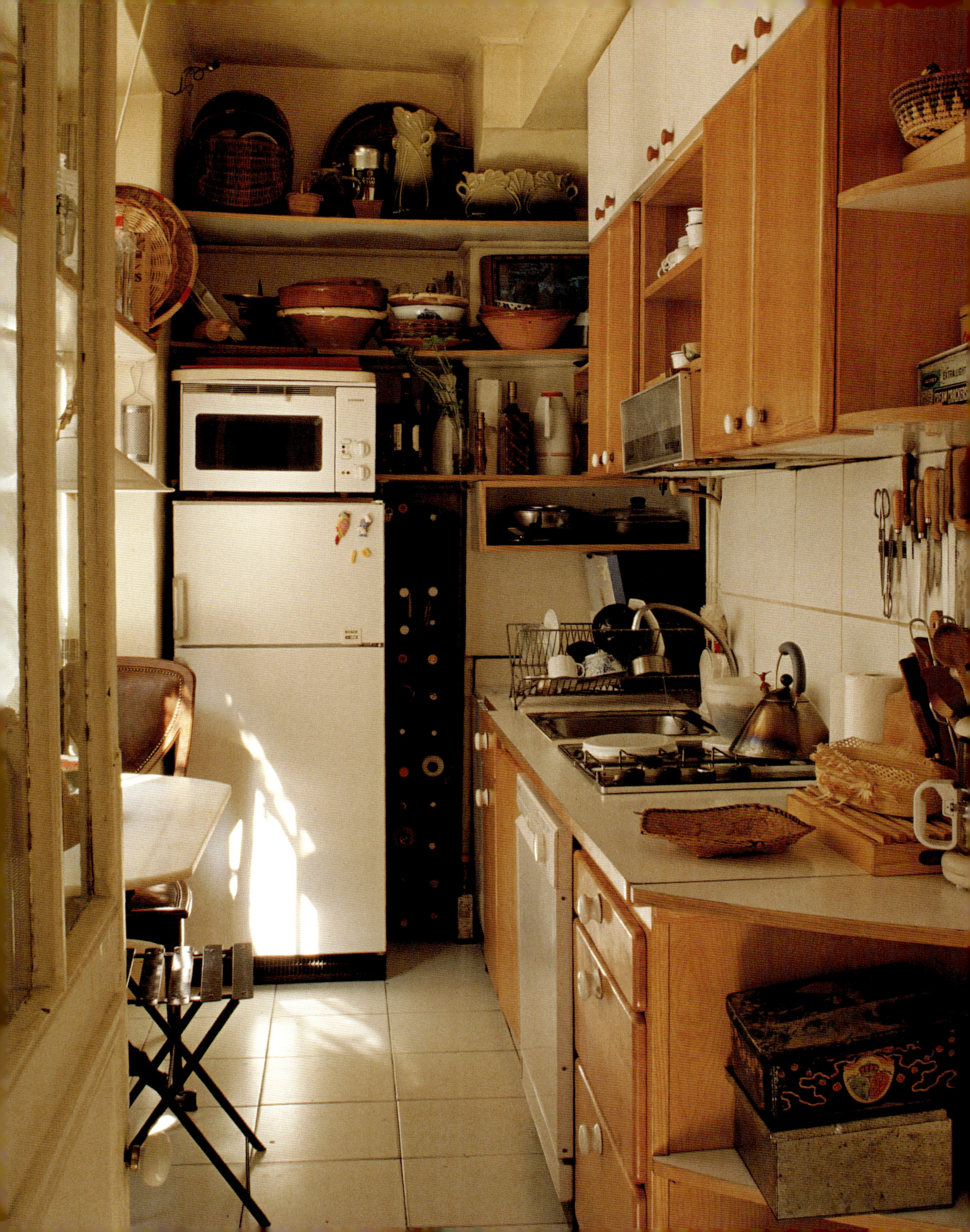

シティ・キッチン

シティ・キッチン

シティ・キッチン

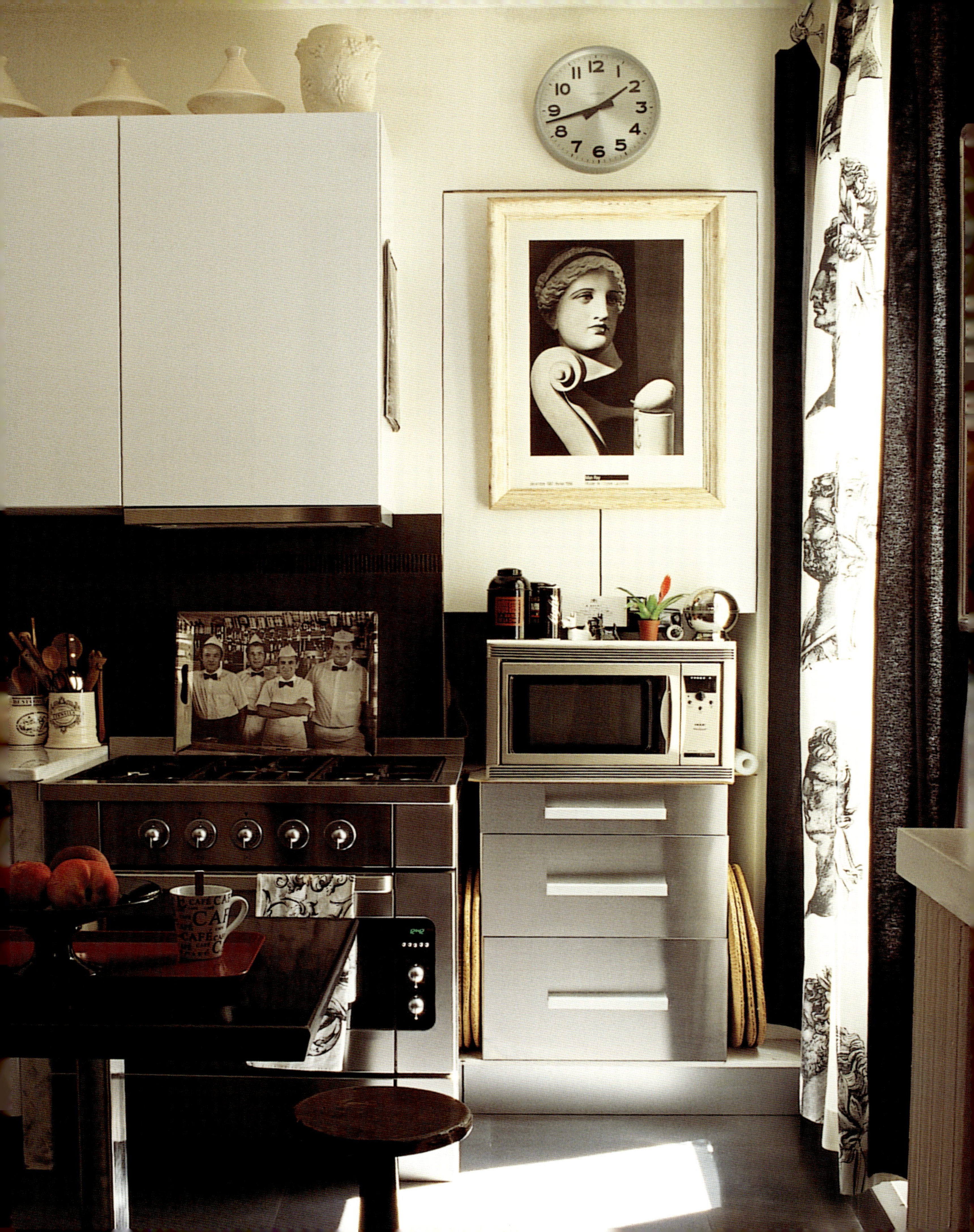

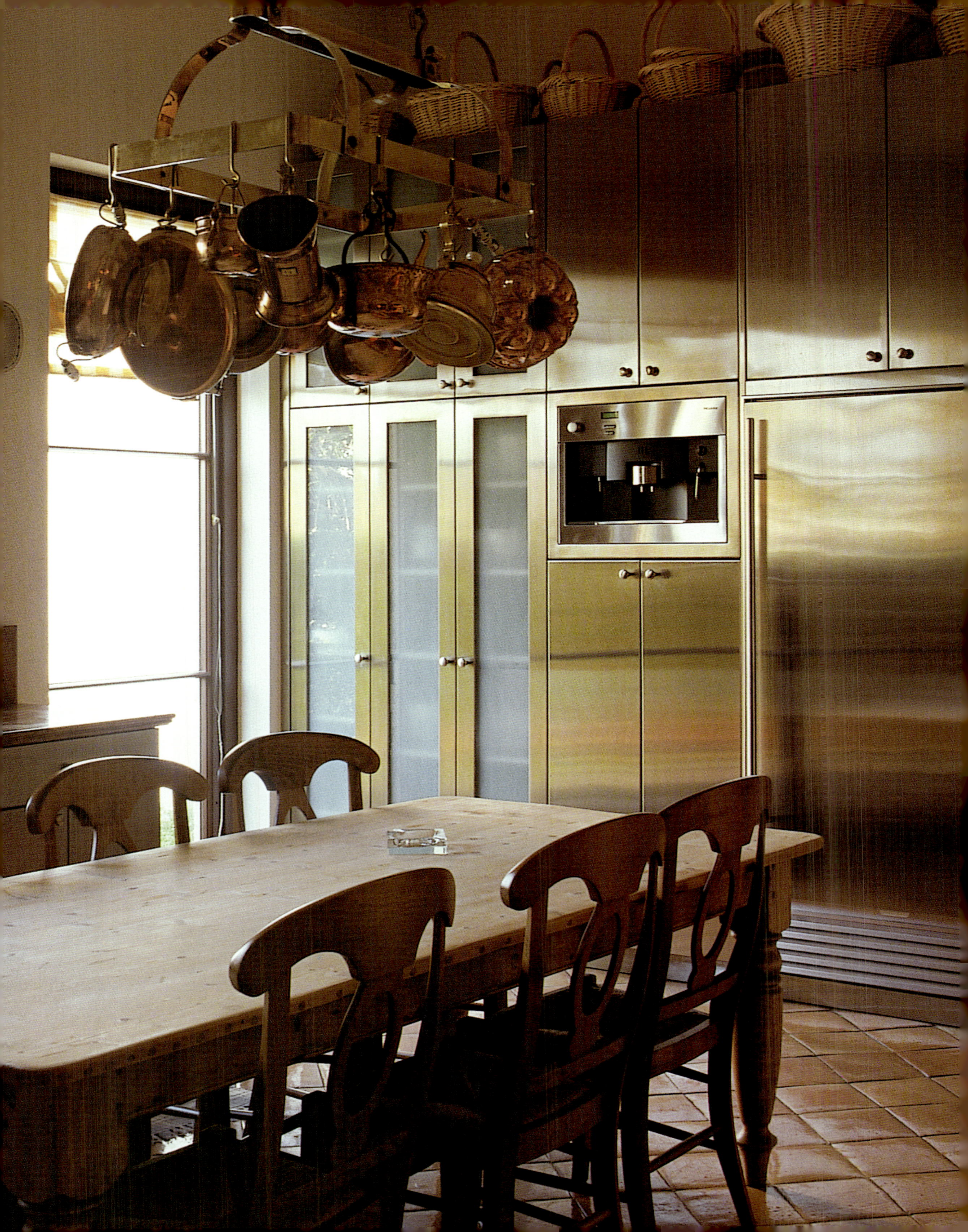

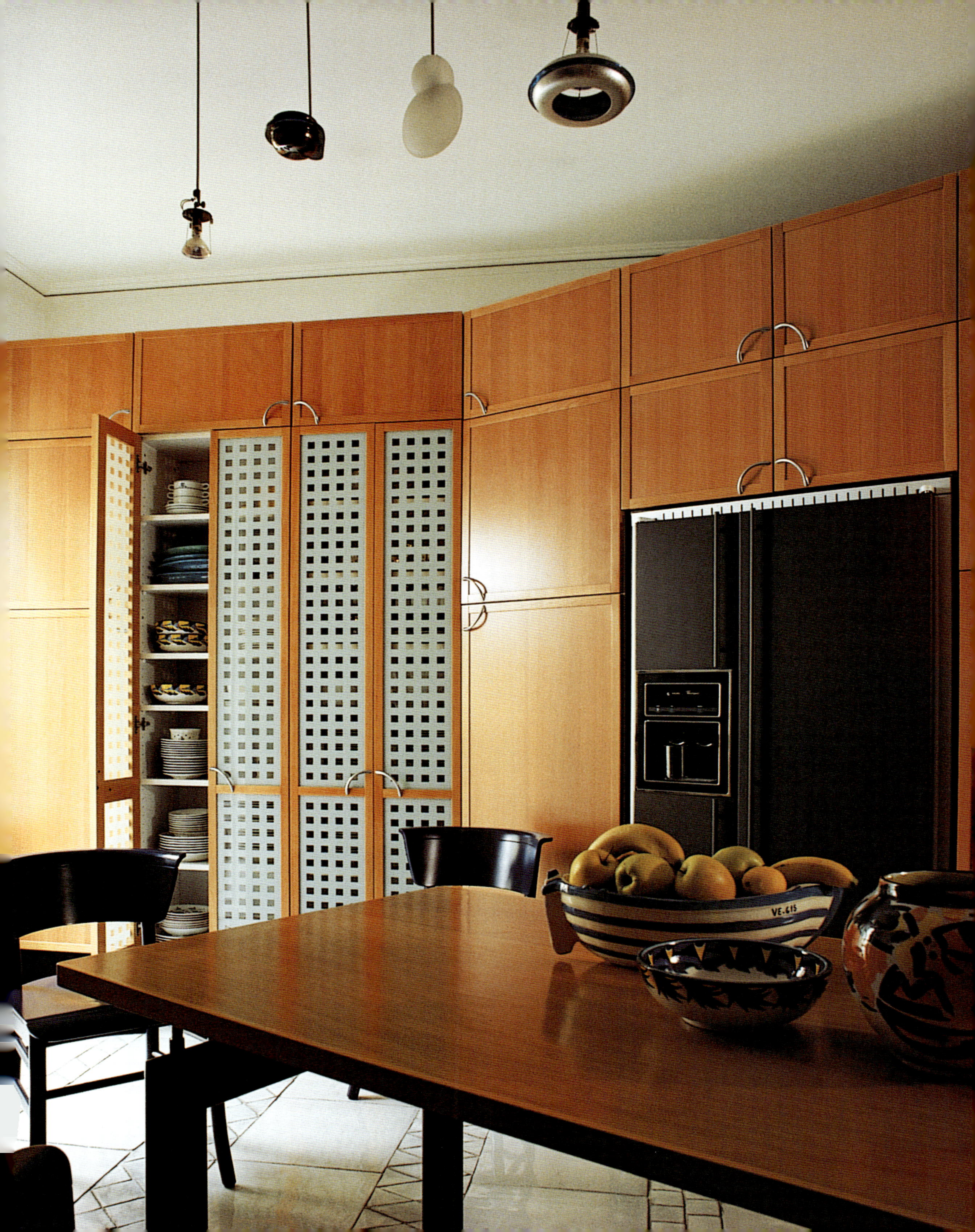

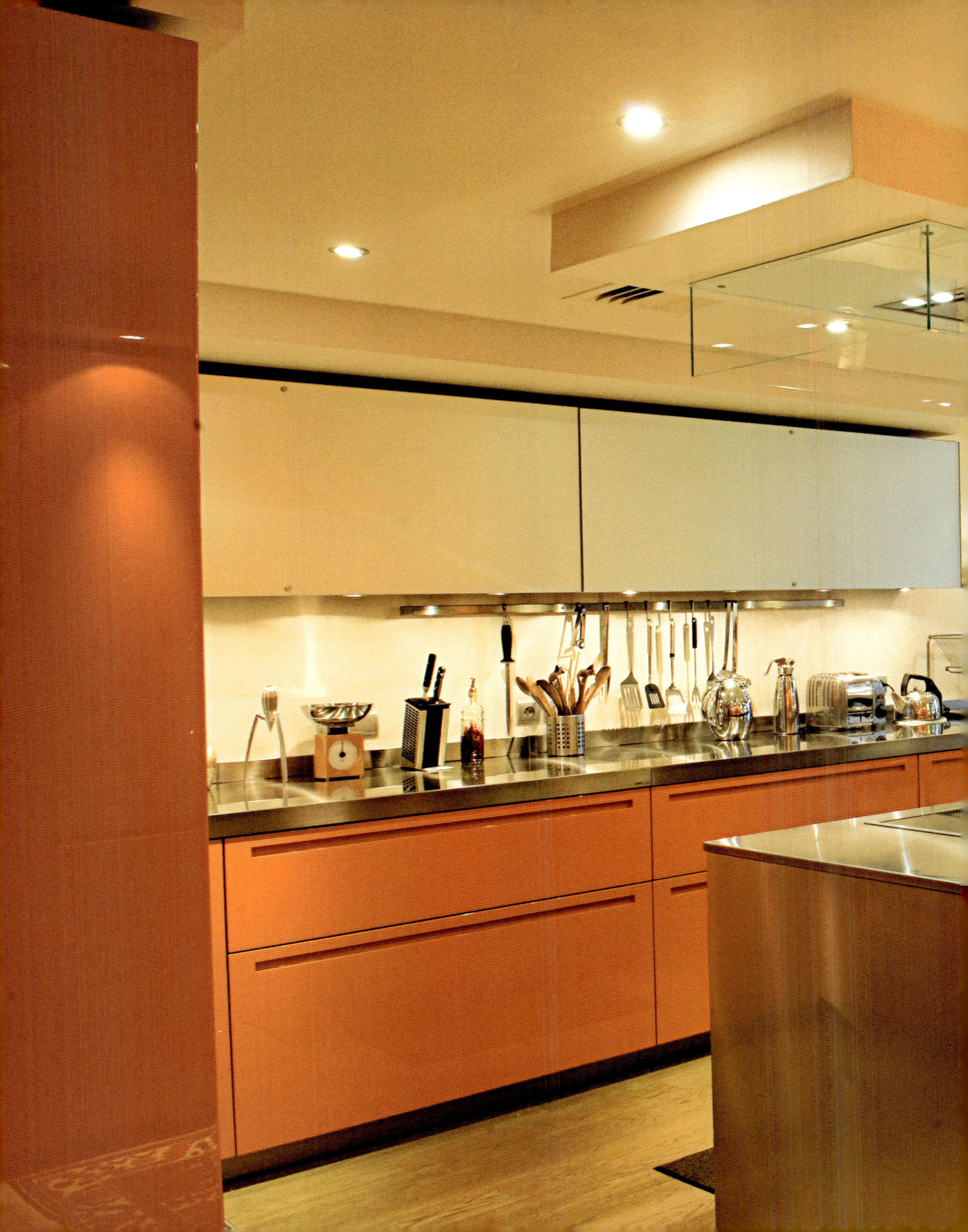

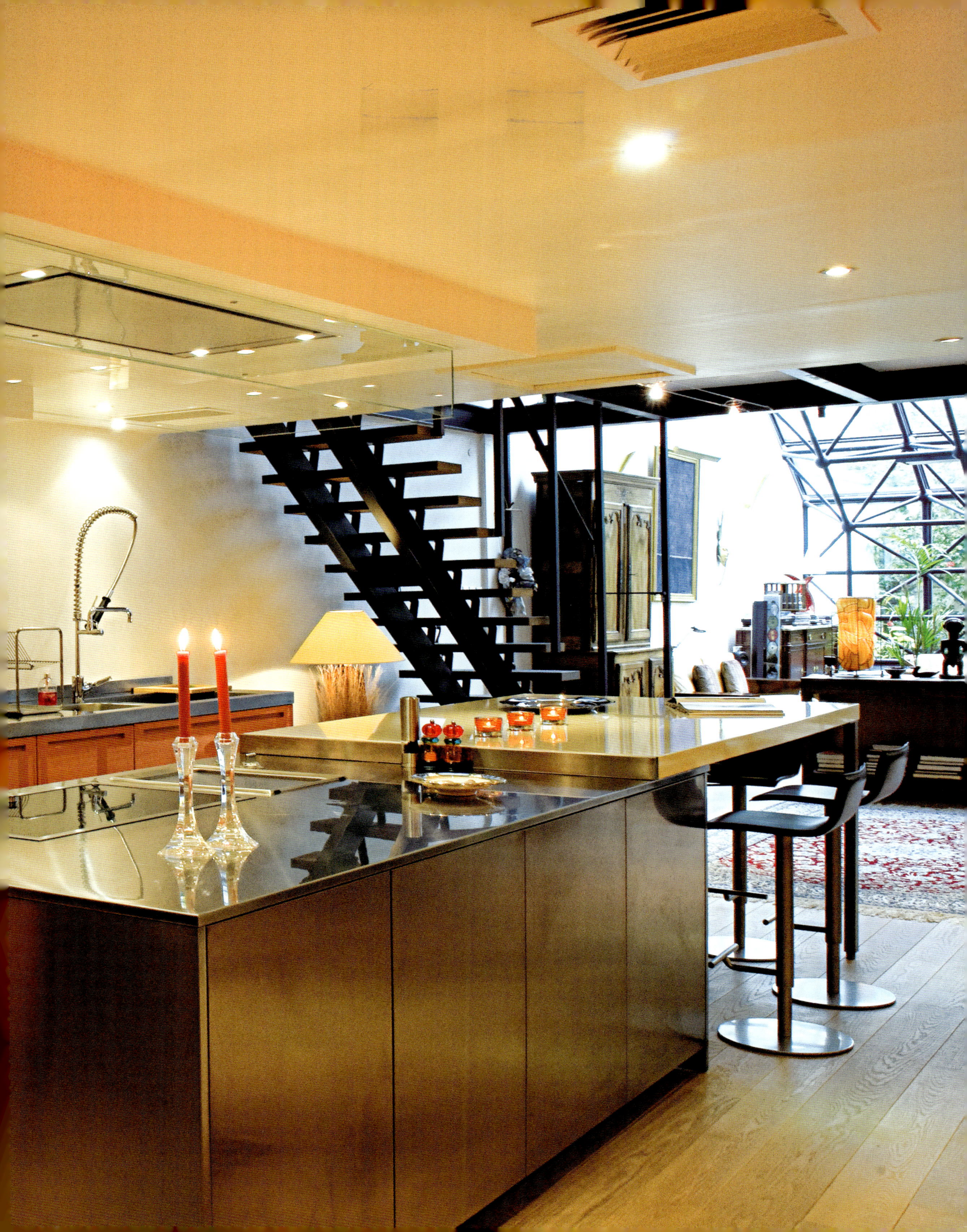

シティ・キッチン

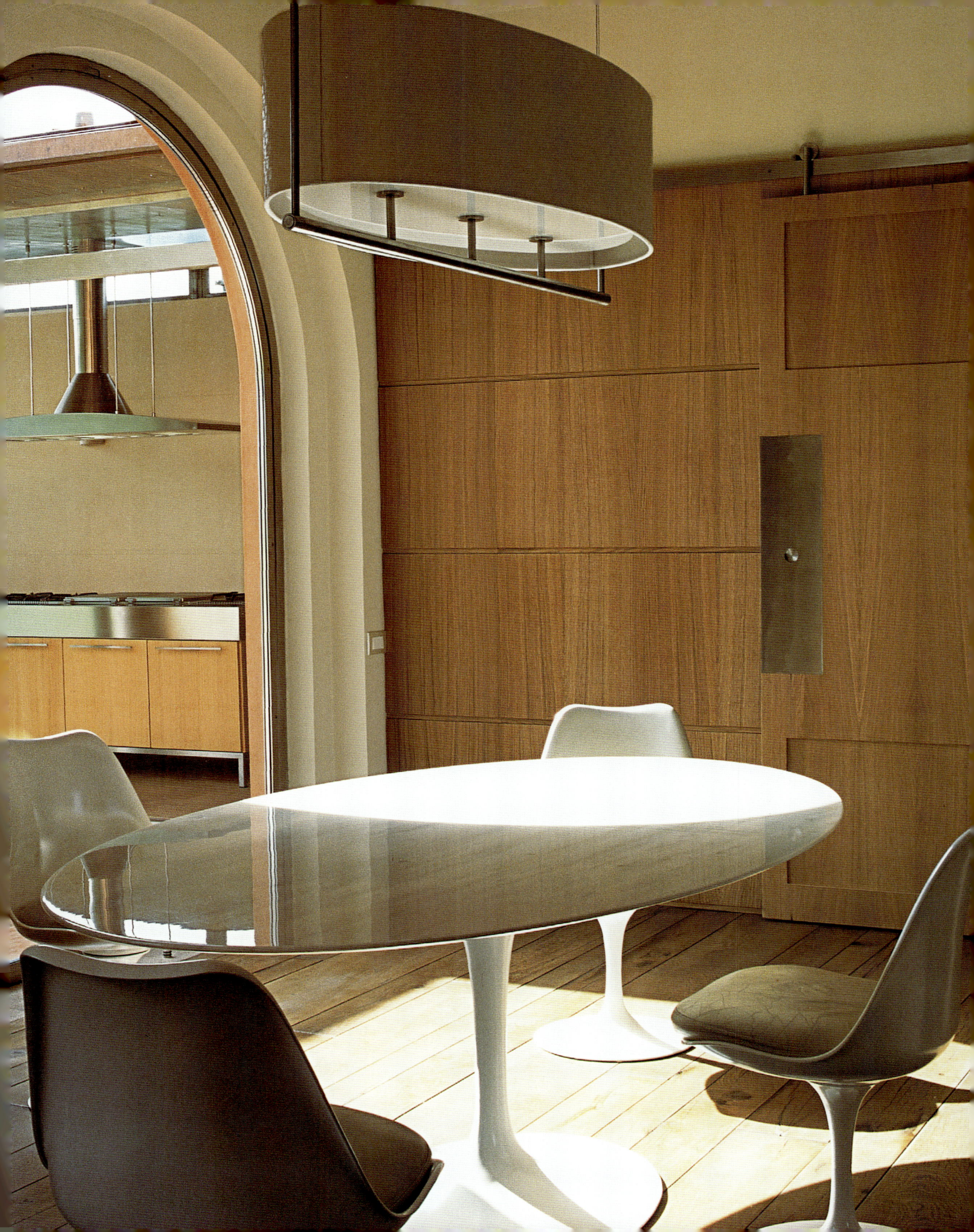

収納スペース

Storage Solutions

新しいキッチンにする時、考慮すべき事項で、もっとも重要なのは、どのくらいの収納スペースが必要か、または、作りたいかという点です。もし、自分にとってのぜいたくが、こまごました物をすべて視界から隠してしまうことだとしたら、今では、とてもいい解決策が用意されています。通常なら、手の届きにくい部屋の隅に、回転式の収納棚を取り付けるのです。それに、すべての調理器具と、カップ、ボウルなどを収納できる引き出しもあります。昔ながらのキッチンには、たいがい年代物のウェルシュ・ドレッサーか、ブレーク・フロント、チャイナ・キャビネットといった家具に食器がしまわれていると思います。また、16世紀から17世紀にかけて、ドイツ、フランス、スカンジナビア諸国では、こまごまとした物を収納する戸棚が使われていました。ドアに、美しい彫刻や手描きの模様があしらわれている、これらの家具は、今日でも、高く評価されています。あつらえた戸棚に、食器類をしまうという伝統の始まりは、日本のたんすが生まれた7世紀にさかのぼります。しかし、より現代的な収納のヒントになっているのが、19世紀の食料品店です。こういった店では、売れ筋の品物はすべて、飾り気のない壁いっぱいの木製棚に並べられているか、腰丈よりも低い引き出しか、戸棚にしまわれていました。このような古い家具の多くは、再利用され、思いがけず、現代のキッチンに顔を出しています。造り付けのキッチンが誕生したのは1950年代に入ってからのこと。家具メーカーが、最初に「モダン」キッチンを導入するようになったのは、1920年代でした。それは自立型の家具で、天板は、焼き菓子を作るために、ホーロー引きになっていました。また、スパイスと卵ラック、保存容器、タオルかけ、折りたたみ式のアイロン台、買い物用のメモボード、そして、気の利いた粉ふるいの器具が、セットされていました。

When planning a kitchen, perhaps one of the most important considerations is how much storage space is needed or wanted. If your idea of luxury is to have everything stored away out of sight, there are now some ingenious solutions available. You will find shelves that rotate out from normally inaccessible corners, as well as drawers for storing every piece of equipment or utensil, cup or bowl. Many traditional kitchens include a cupboard like an old Welsh dresser, a breakfront or a china cabinet, and in Germany, France and Scandinavia in the 16th and 17th centuries, housewares were kept in beautifully carved or hand-painted cupboards that are still highly prized today. The tradition of a bespoke cupboard to store kitchenware can be traced back as far as the 7th century Japanese Tansu. More recent storage inspiration also comes from 19th century grocery stores – where all of the most popular wares were stocked on simple wall-to-wall wooden shelves, or in below-waist-height drawers and cupboards. Many of these original fittings are recycled and turn up in kitchens today. Fitted kitchens did not arrive until the 1950's. When manufacturers introduced the first 'modern' kitchen cabinet in the 1920's, it was a stand-alone unit that came complete with an enamel-covered work surface (for pastry rolling), integrated spice and egg racks, storage jars, towel rail, fold-down ironing board and shopping list reminder, as well as a nifty component for sifting flour.

収納スペース

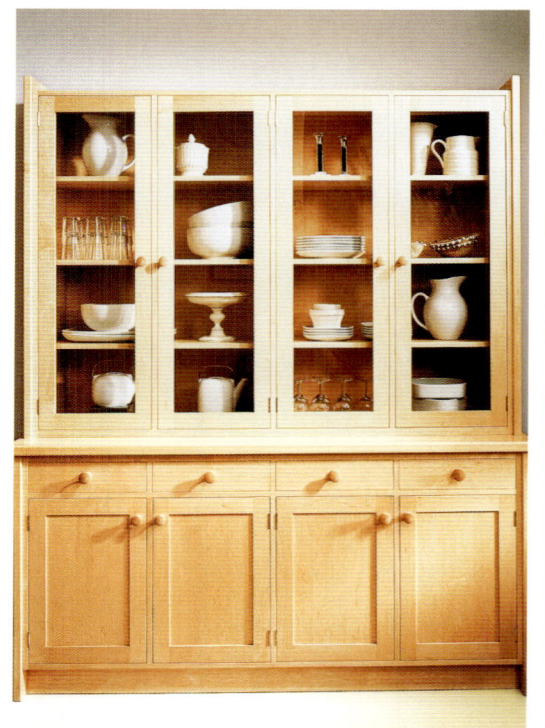

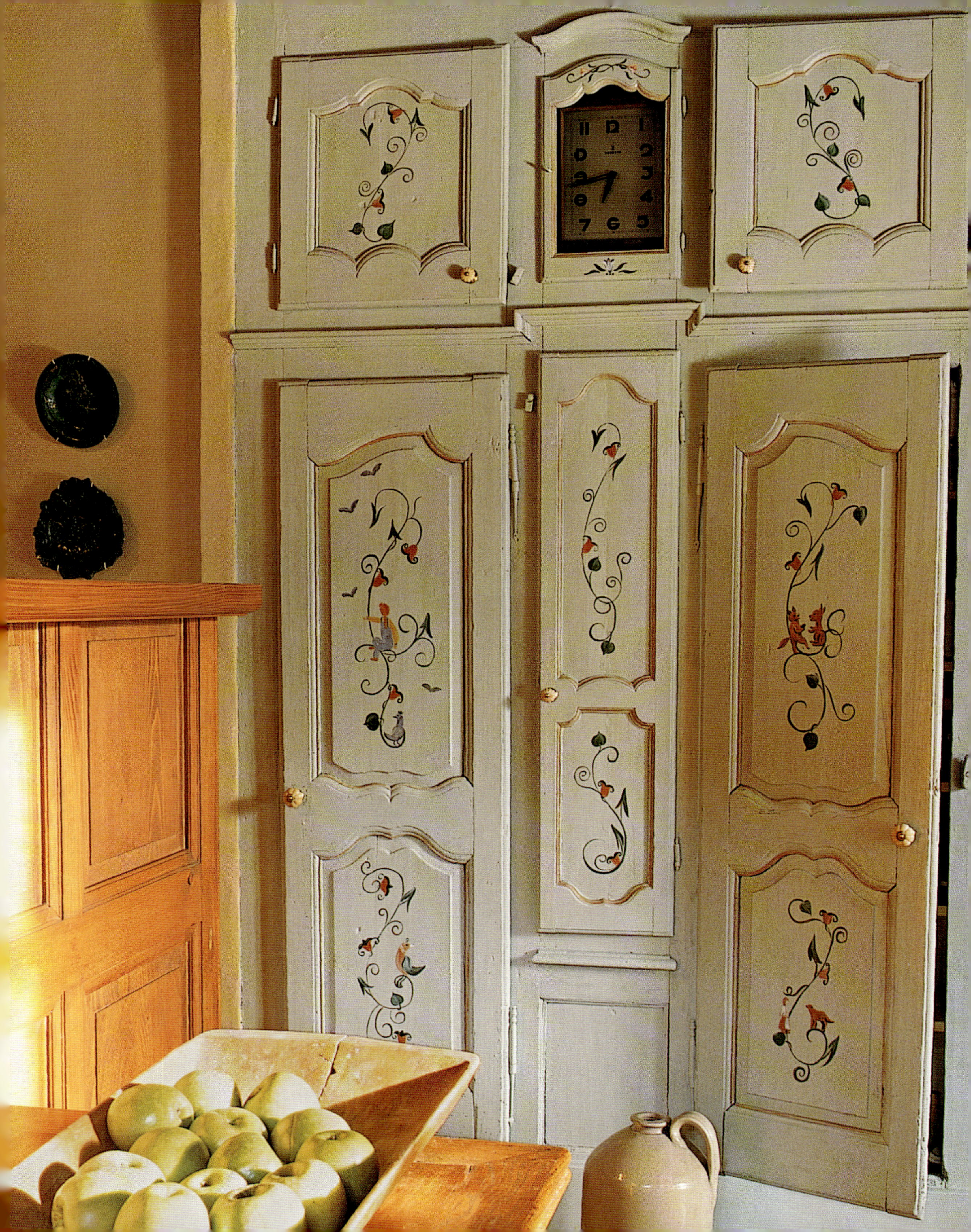

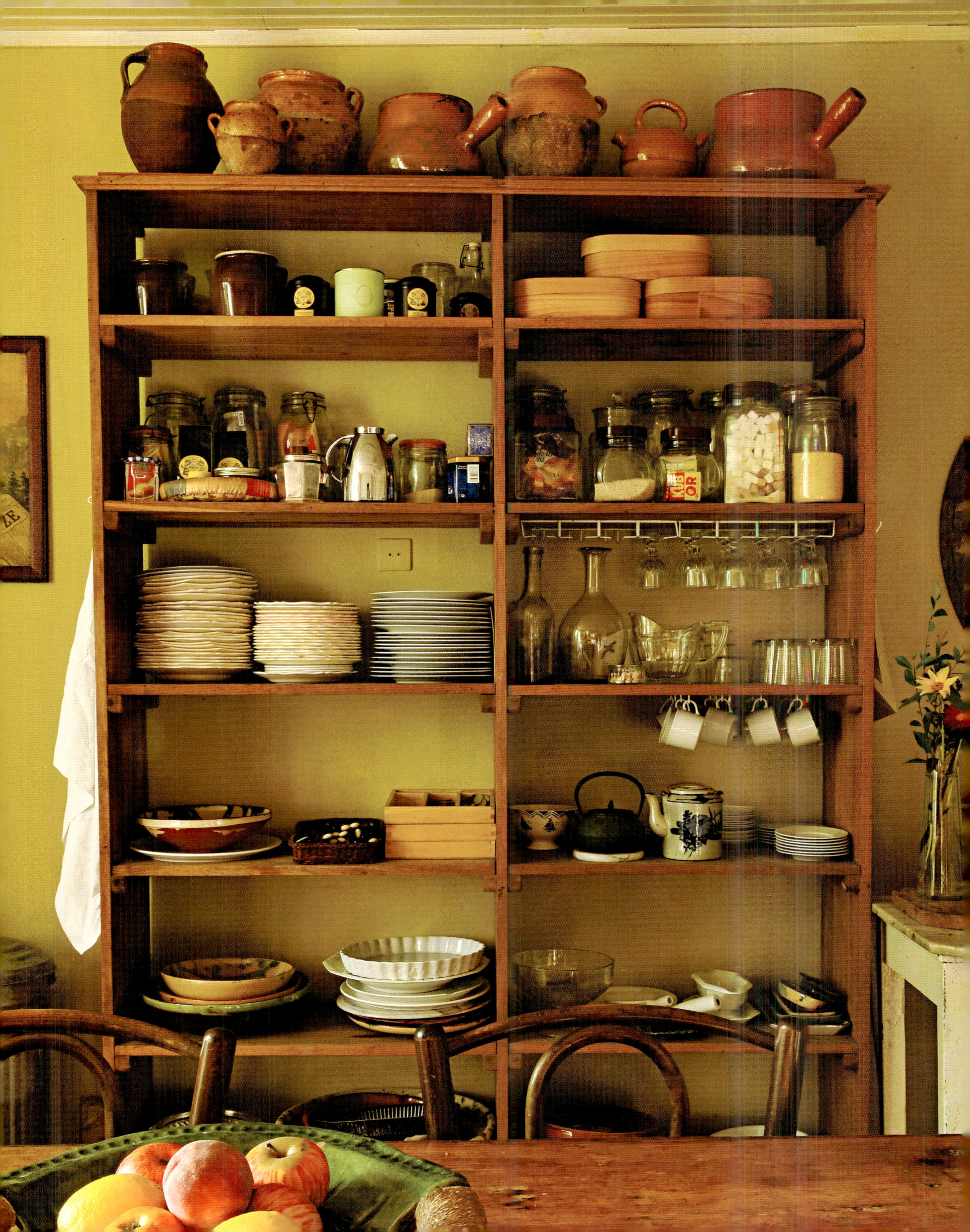

収納スペース

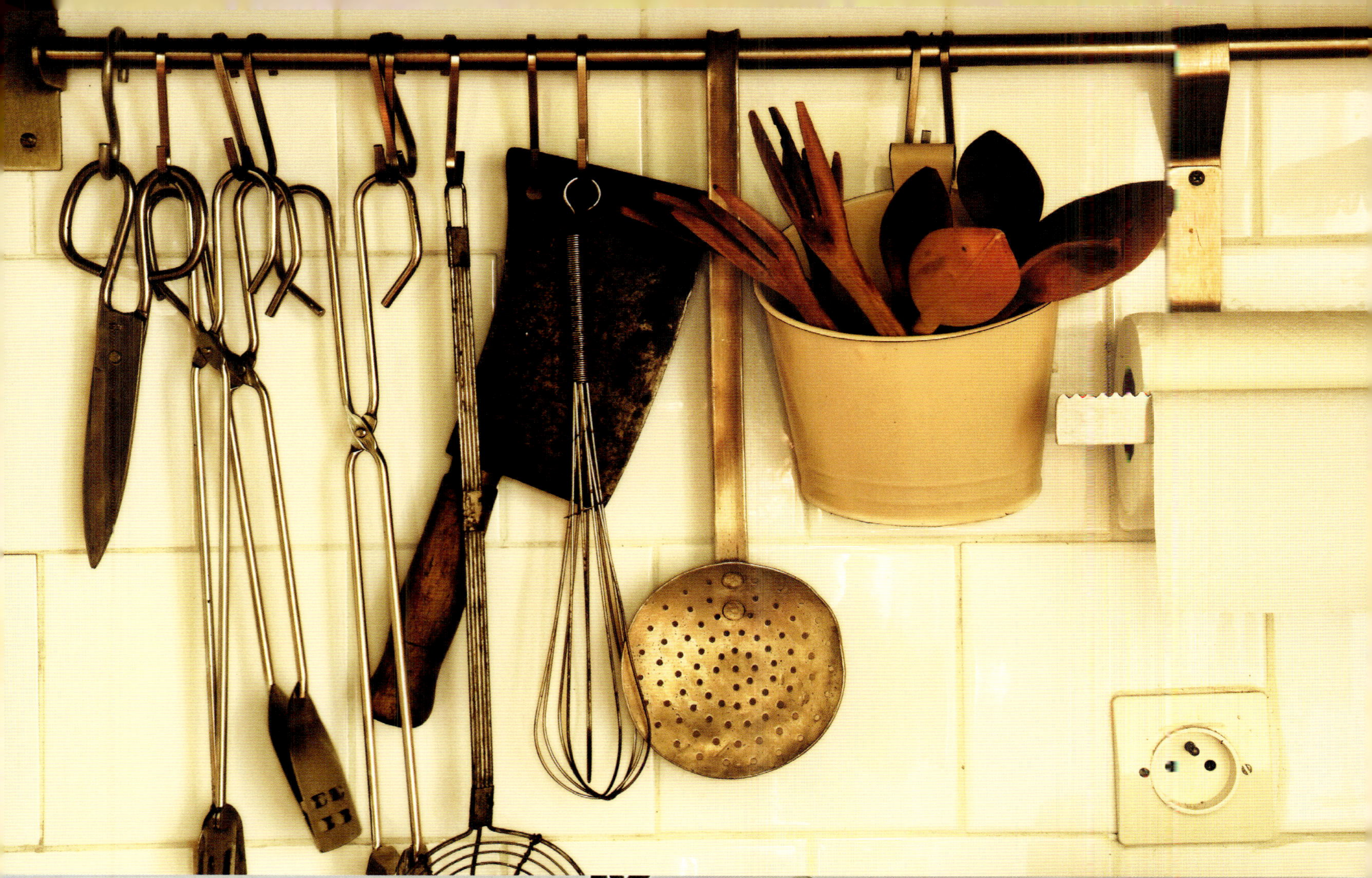

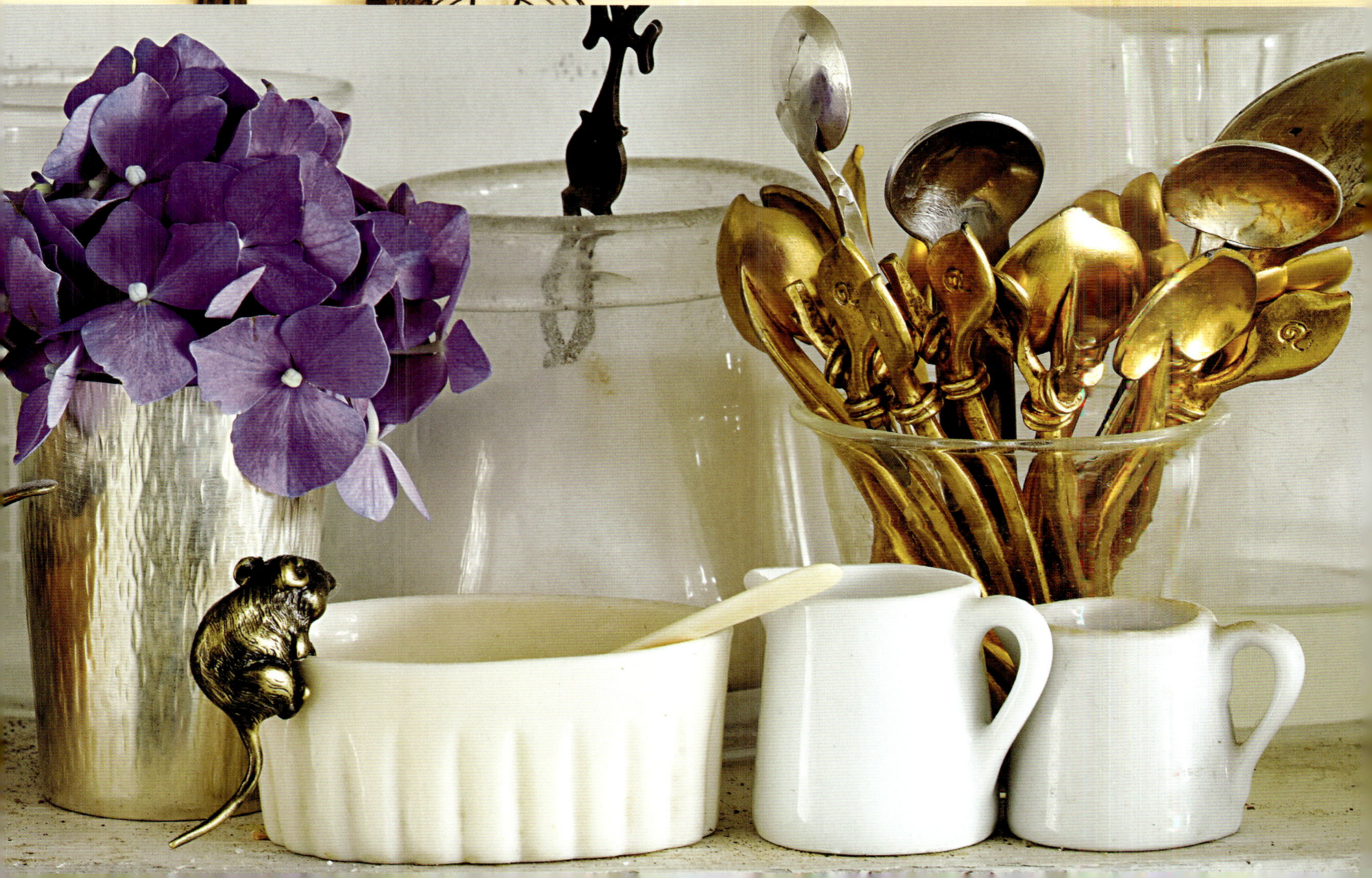

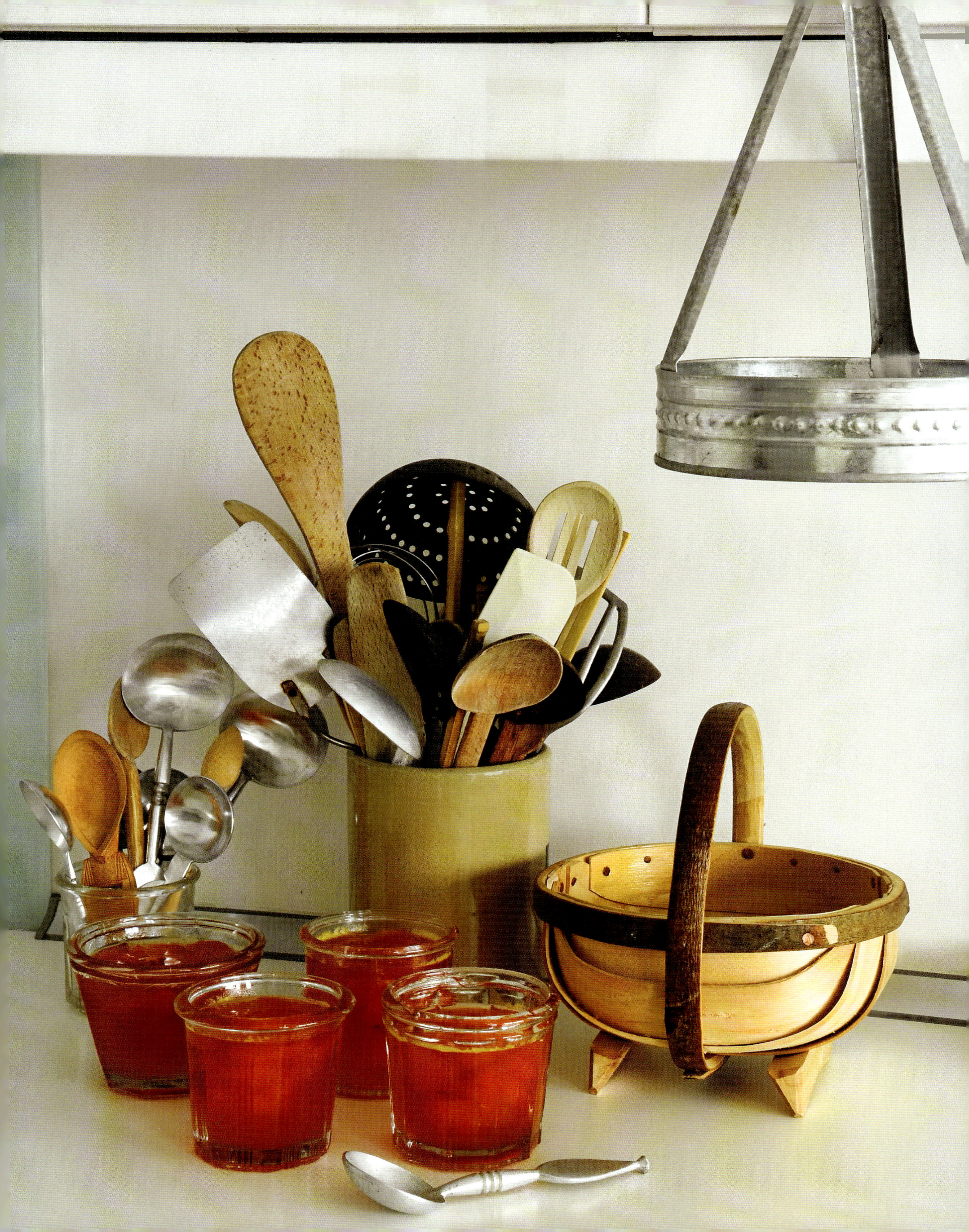

収納スペース

収納スペース

収納スペース

100

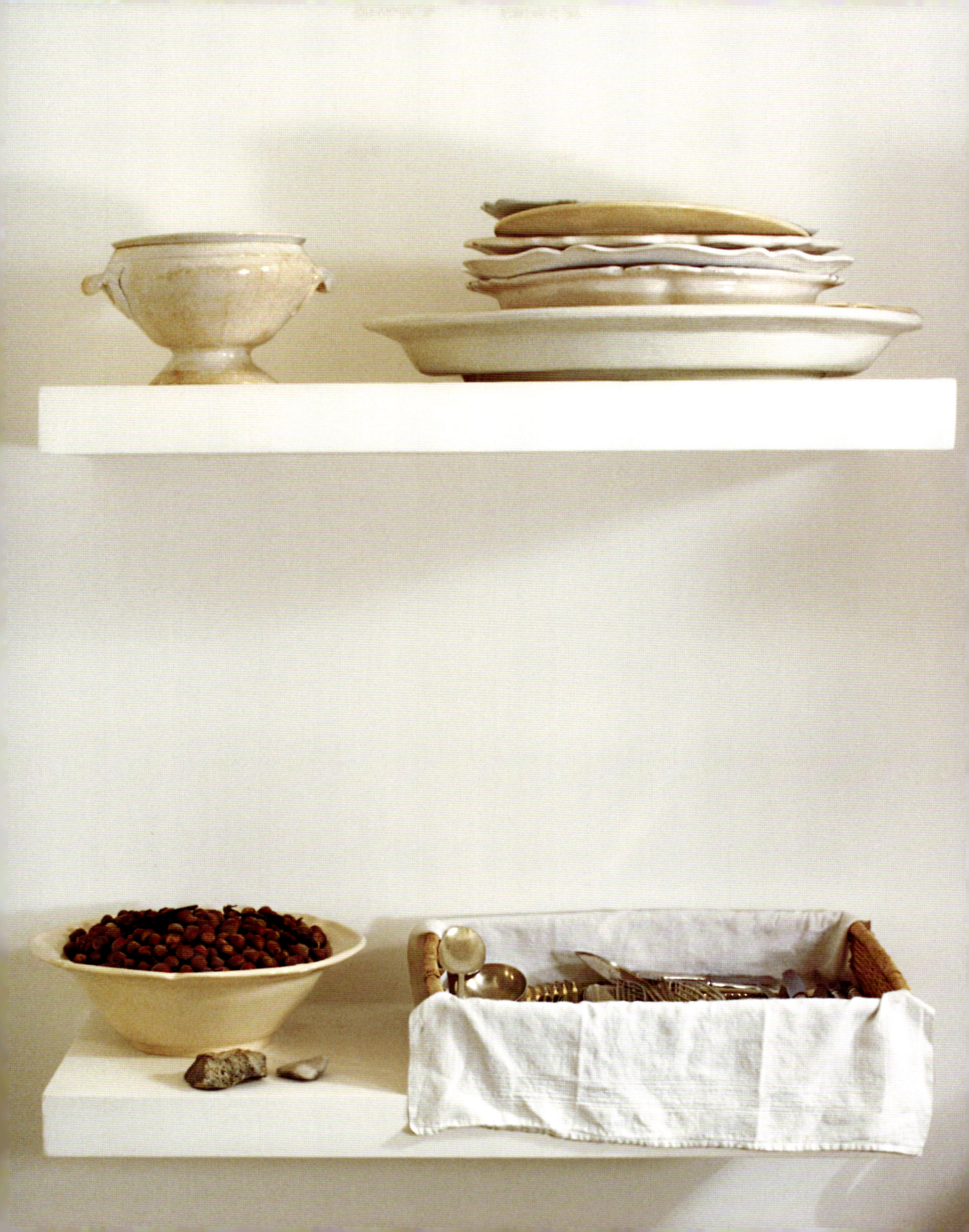

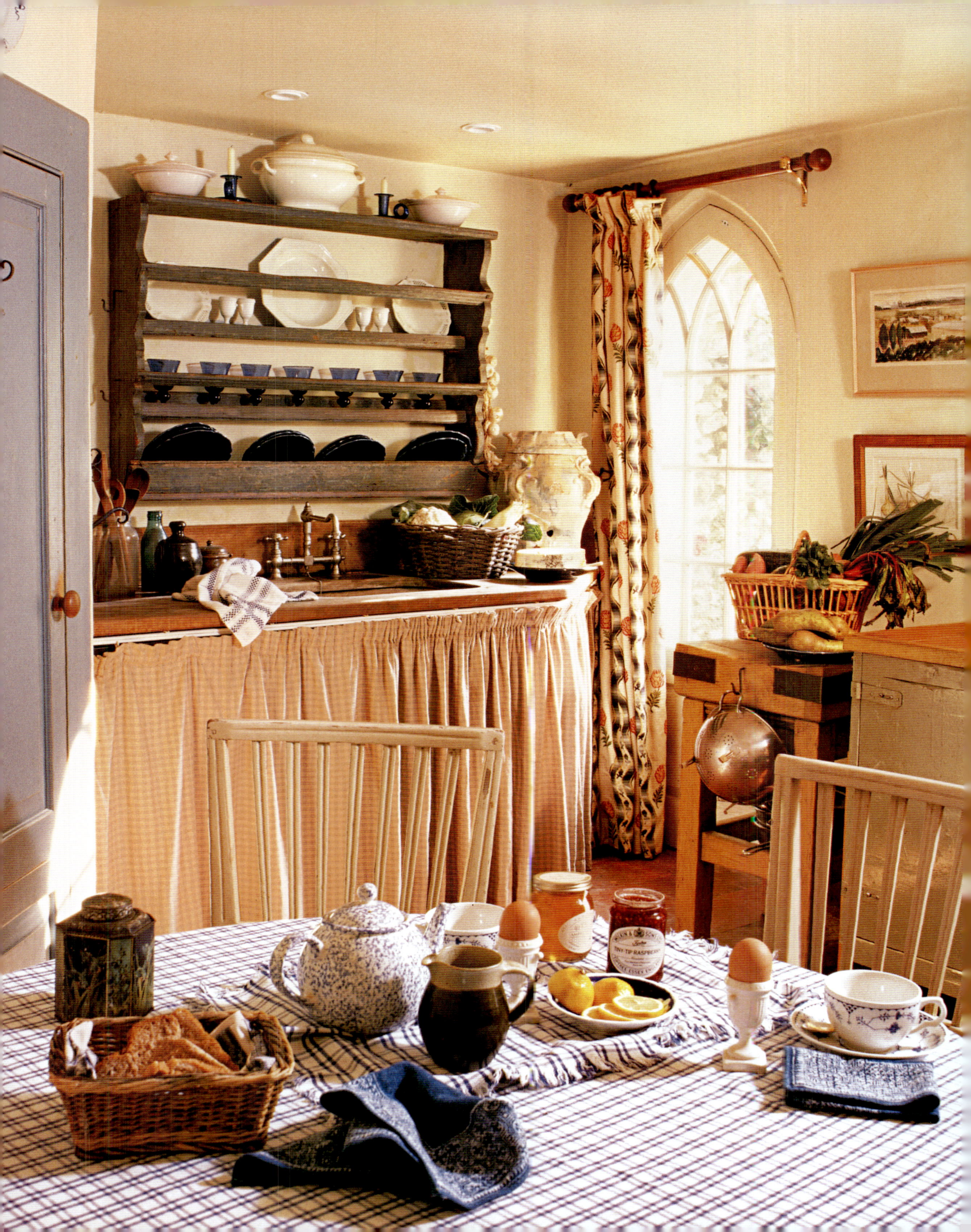
TINY TIP

収納スペース

収納スペース

収納スペース

収納スペース

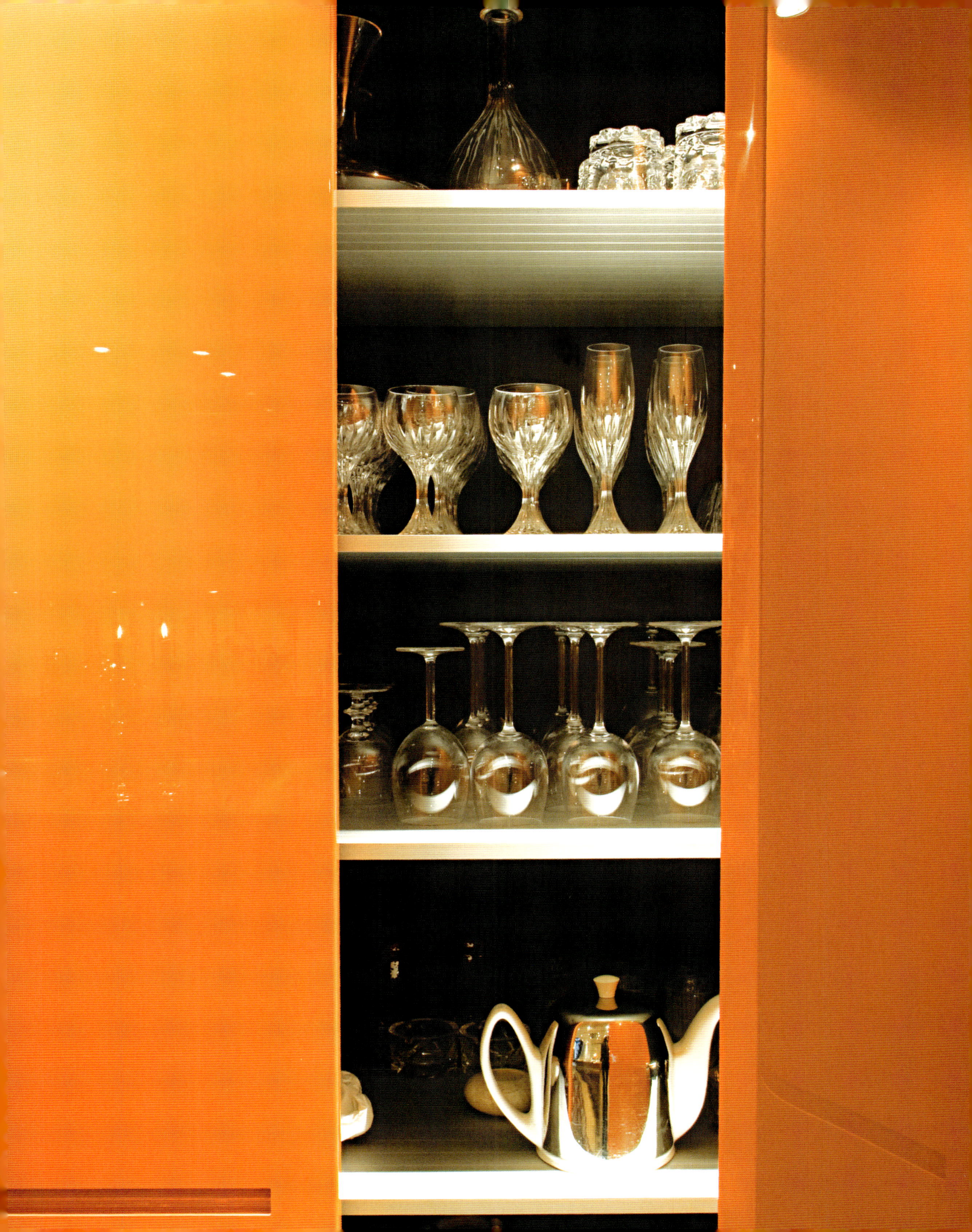

照明器具

Light and Shade

キッチンは、手術室並みに清潔であるべき、と言った人がいました。キッチンを清潔に保つためには、手術室の大きな特徴のひとつを、借用する必要があります。それは、効果的な照明です。部屋の照明は、夜はもちろん、昼も大切であり、それは芸術の一形式といっても過言でありません。照明には2種類あります。タスク照明とムード照明です。照明の基本は、自分の前に明かりを付けて、作業場所を照らすということです。そのための器具は、サイズも種類もたいへん豊富です。小さなハロゲン・ランプ、タングステン球、LEDを使った照明器具のほとんどは、壁面や天井に埋め込んだり、棚や作業台の上や下に取りつけたりできますから、部屋の中に薄暗い場所などできようもありません。けれども、こうこうとした明かりで、キッチンのムードを損ないたくないのも確かです。テレビ局のスタジオで、料理をしているわけではないのですから。光と影を上手に取り入れましょう。落ち着いた場所、輝きのある場所、もっとも明るい場所を、それぞれ室内に作るのです。照明には、変化のつけやすさも大切です。空がどんよりとしている朝は、元気に朝食が取れそうな明るい光を、また友人と「キッチンでの夕食」を楽しむなら、ムードを演出してくれる光が欲しいものです。そして照明には、キッチンに高級感を出し、目を引きつけるという効果もあります。シャンデリアは、驚くほどキッチン用としても人気があります。特に、ダイニングテーブルか、アイランドキッチンの上に吊ることが多いようです。シャンデリアのデザインには、クラシカルな真鍮製や、クリスタルを使った手の込んだ物から、異国情緒のある花や、クラゲを模したモダンなデザインまで、様々な物が揃っています。中でも、もっとも革新的なデザインは、割れた陶器や、小さなペットボトルを再利用して作ったシャンデリアです。

Somebody once said that a kitchen should be as spotless as an operating theatre. In order to achieve this, your kitchen will have to borrow one of the theatre's most important features – its very efficient lighting. Lighting a room can be a real art form, as important in daytime as at night, and should be divided into two types; task lighting and mood lighting. At its most basic you should have light in front of you, focused on the areas where you will be working. After that, there are hundreds of sizes and types of light fitting available – tiny halogen, tungsten and LED fittings, most of which can be set into, onto or under every surface. There is no excuse for a dark corner. And yet, at the same time, you don't want to blast your kitchen with light – you're not cooking in a television studio after all. You will want a bit of variety of light and shade; some pools and sparkles and highlights in places. You will need some flexibility too: bright cheerful light for breakfast on a grey morning, moody atmospheric effects for a 'kitchen supper' with friends. Then there is the showy fashionable aspect to lighting – chandeliers are now surprisingly popular in kitchens, particularly hanging over a dining table or an island unit. These range from old-fashioned brass fittings and elaborate crystal creations to modern designs resembling exotic blooms or jelly fish; the most innovative of which are composed of fragments of broken china, or clusters of tiny recycled plastic bottles.

照 明 器 具

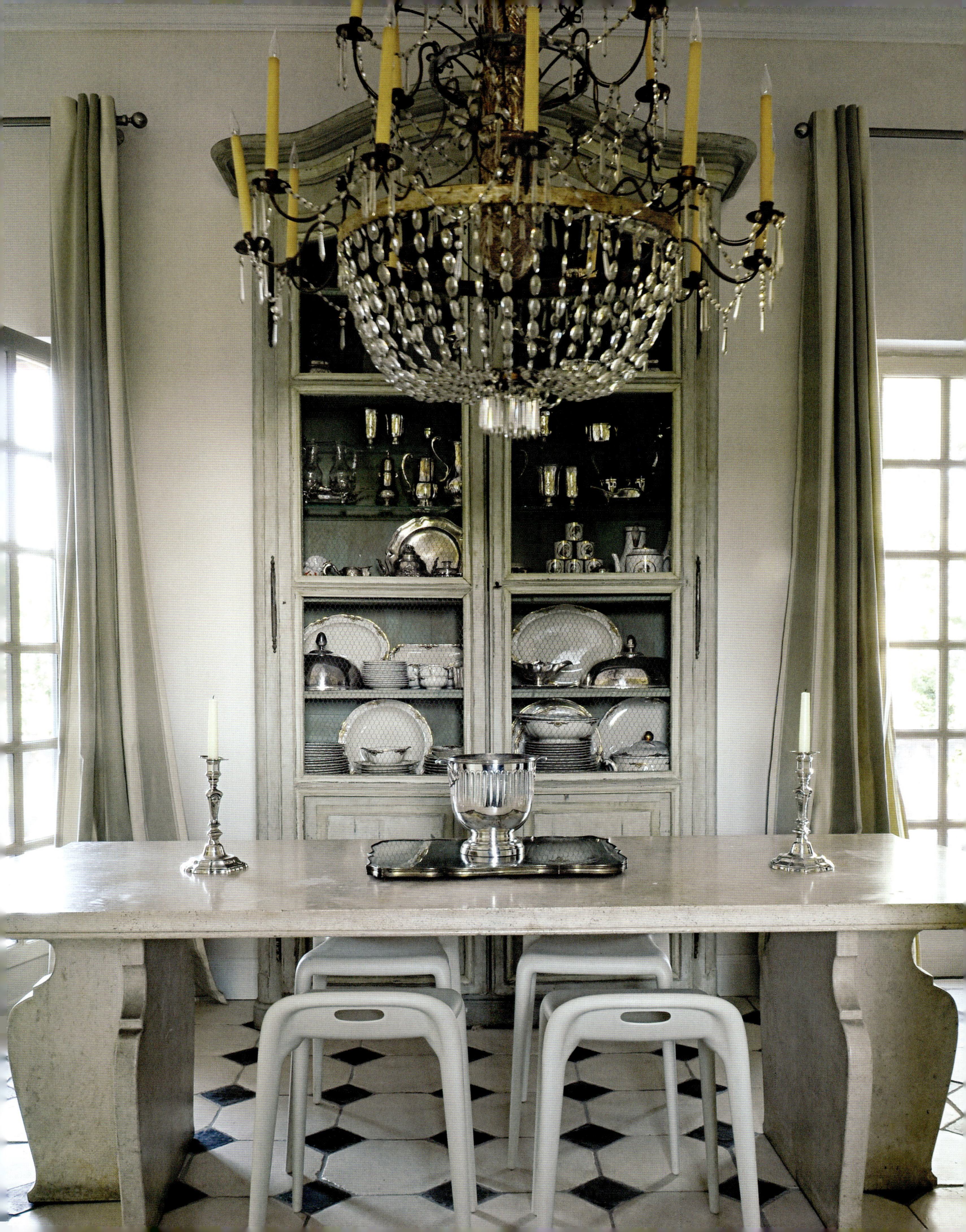

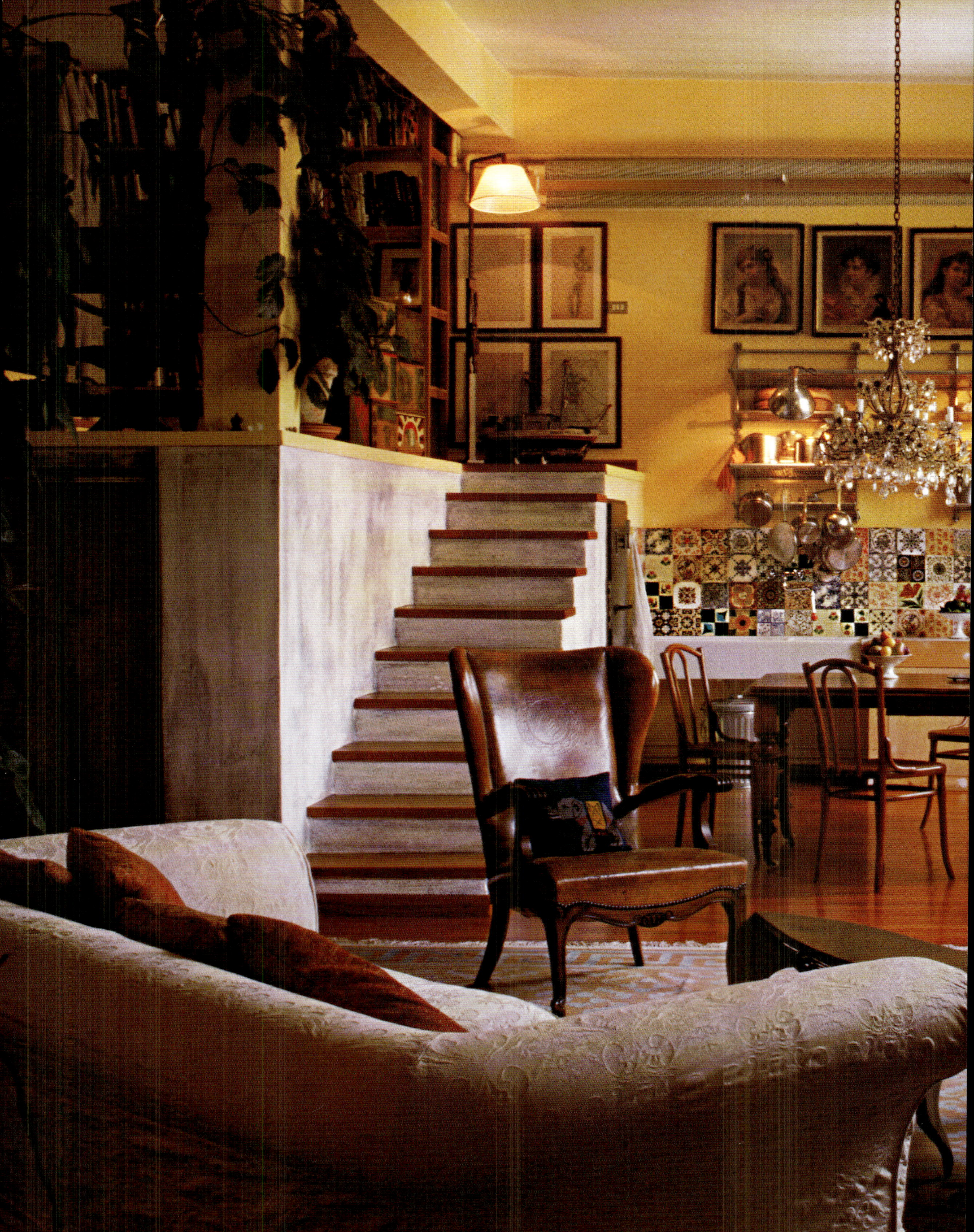

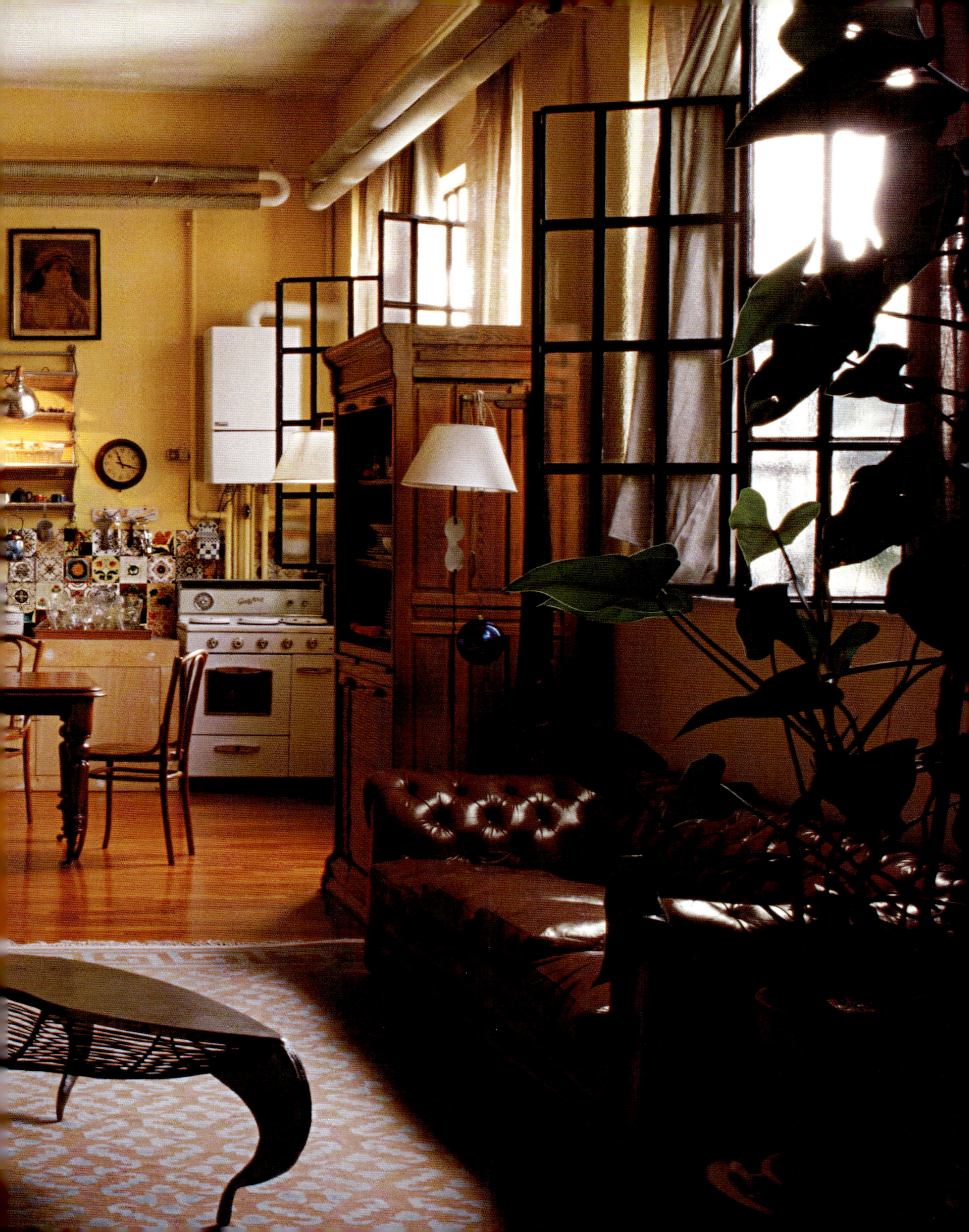

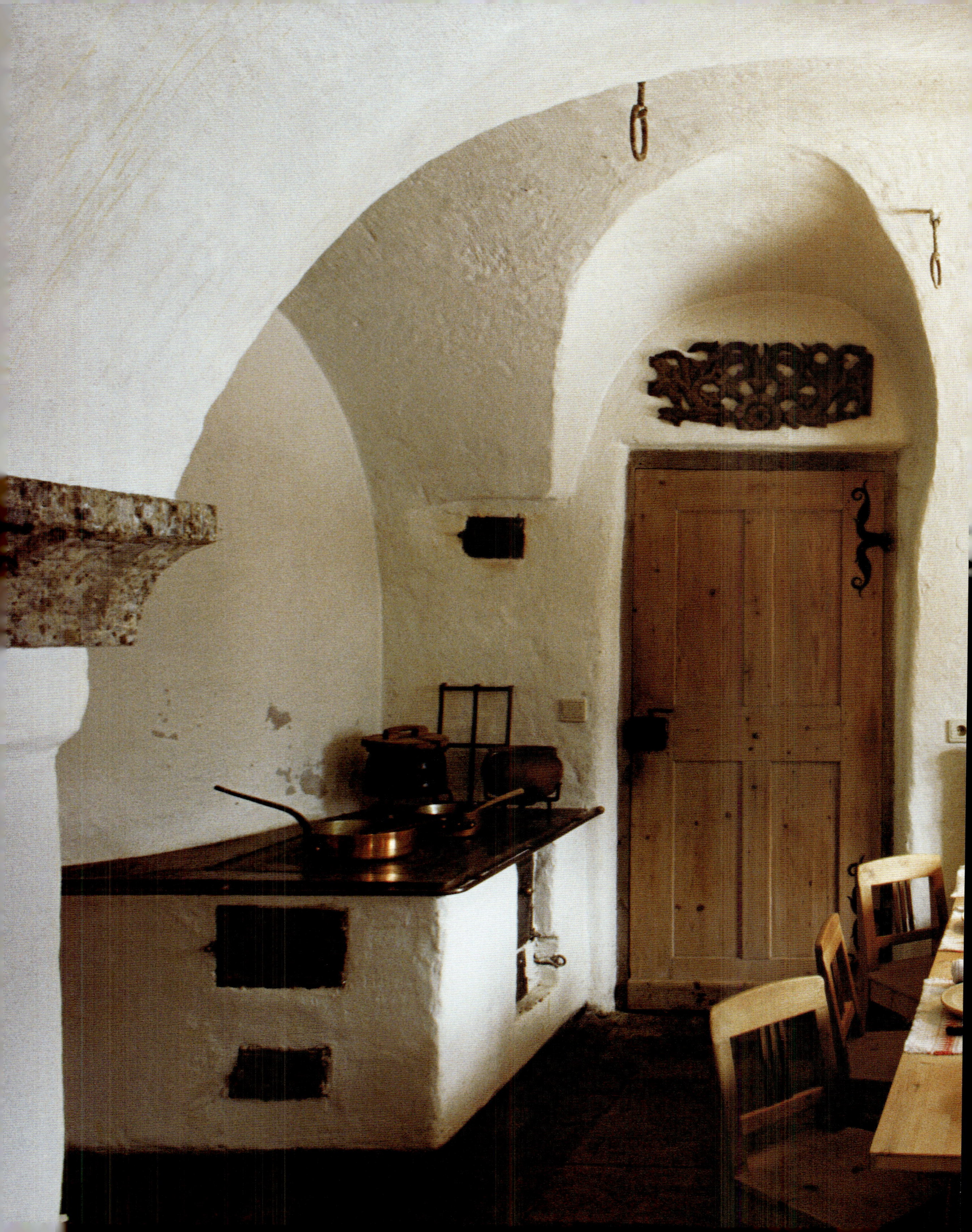

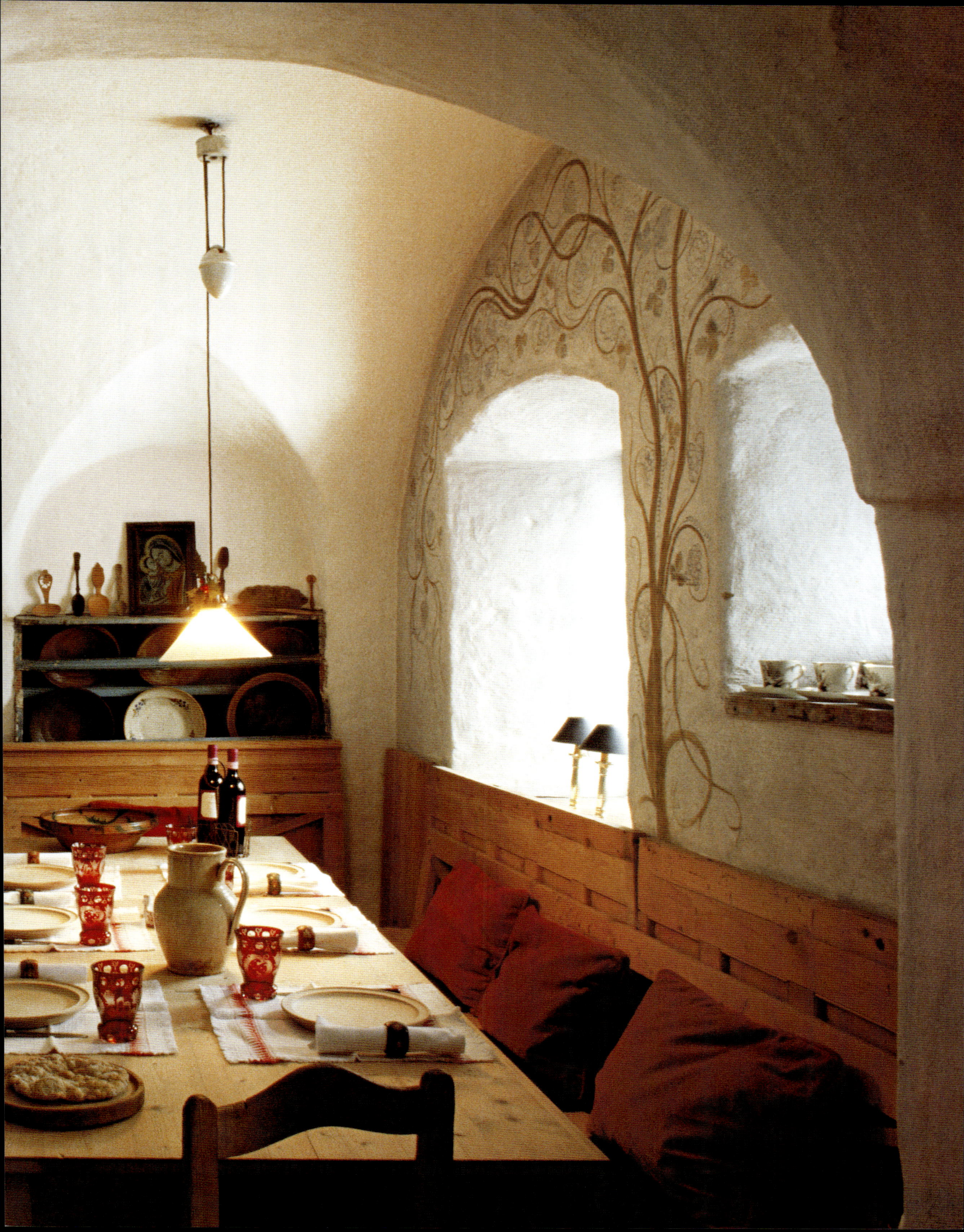

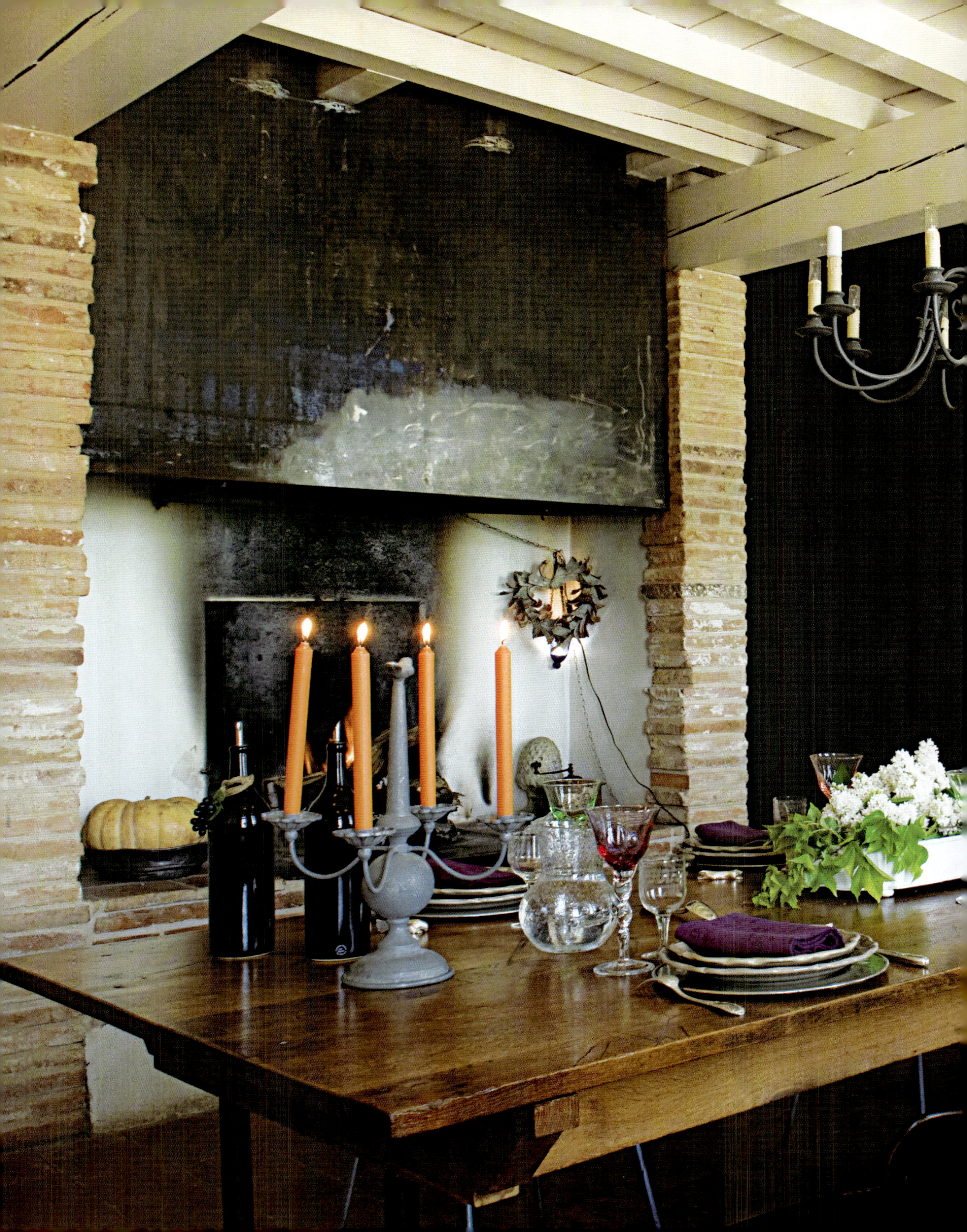

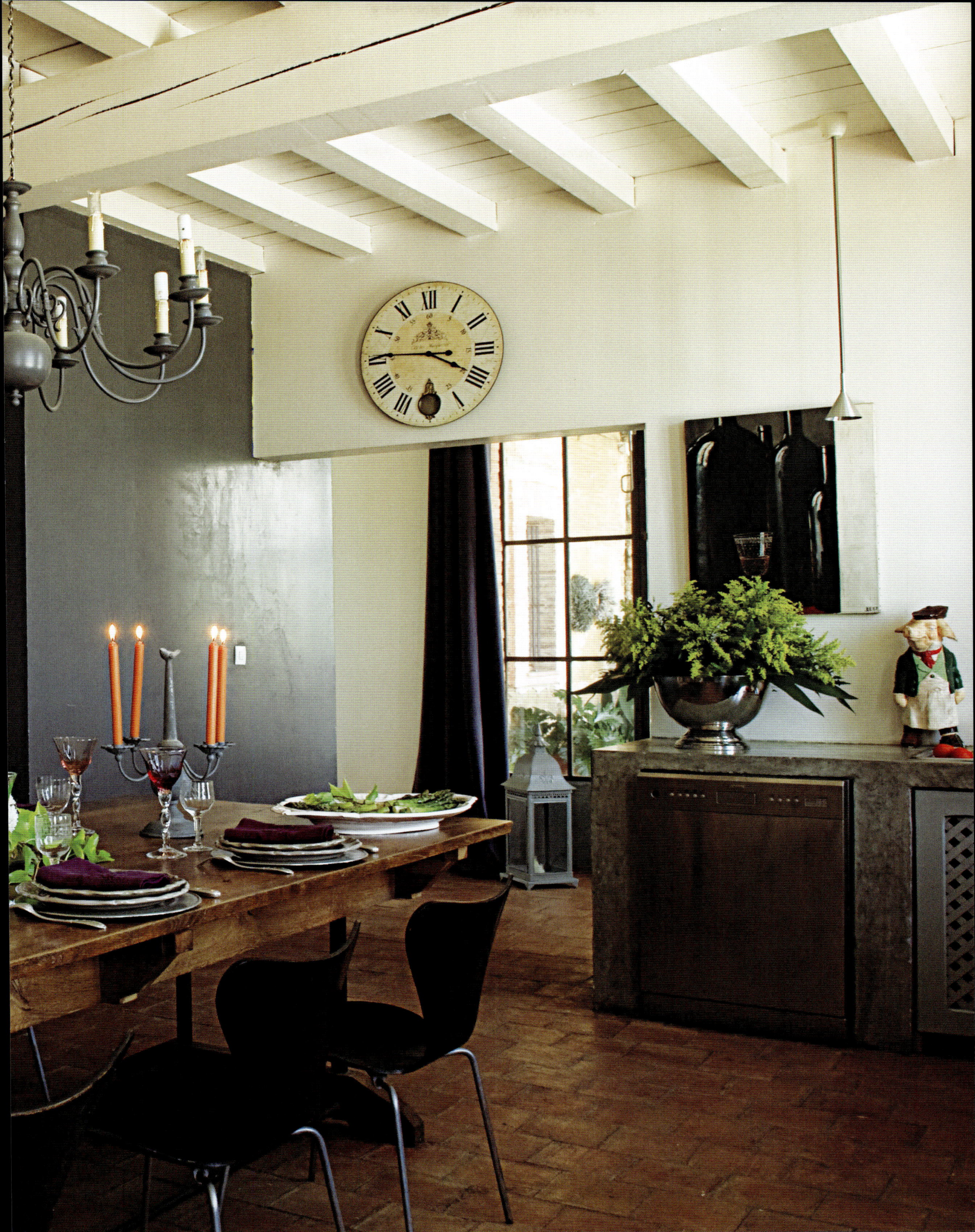

照明器具

照明器具

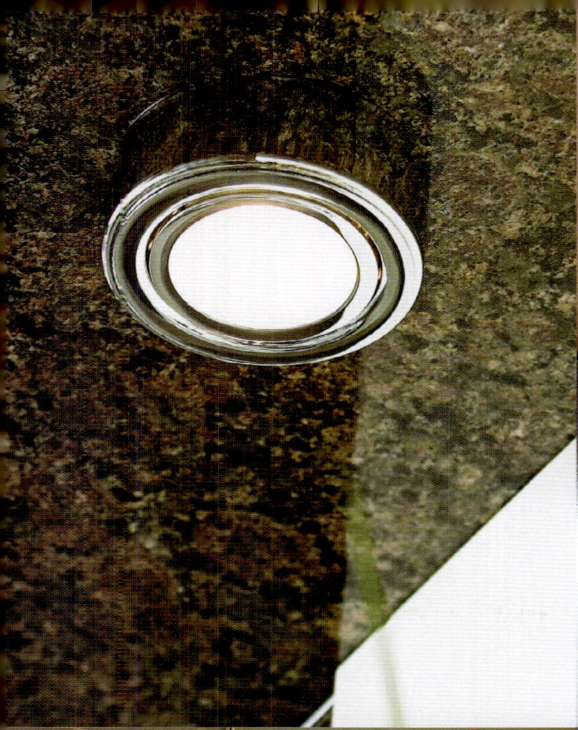
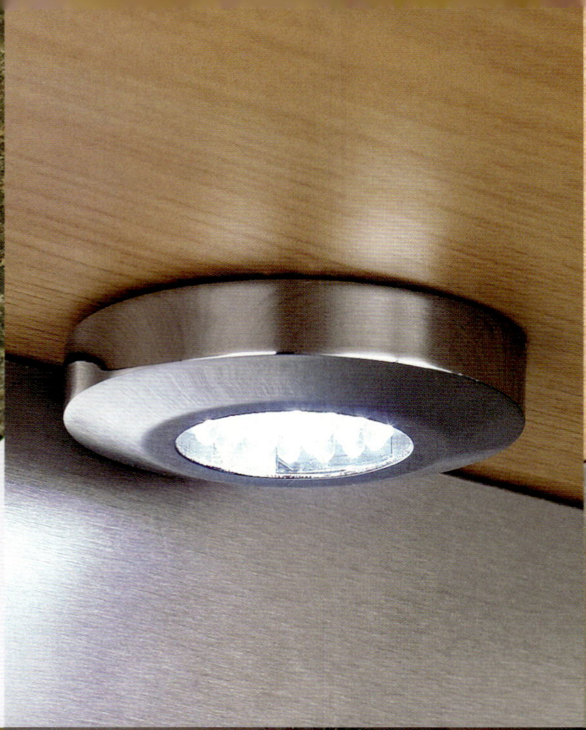
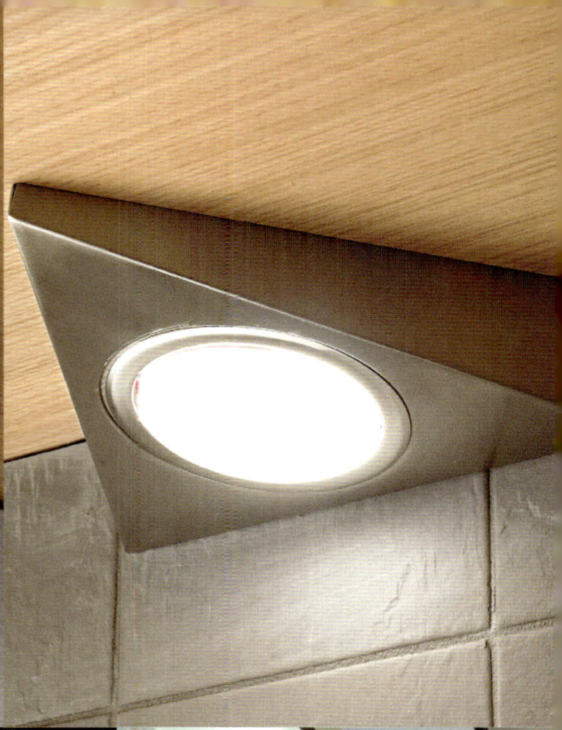
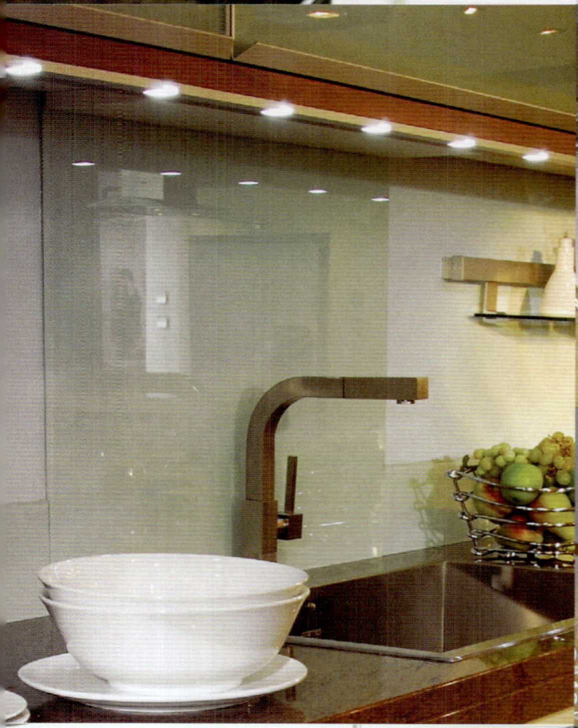
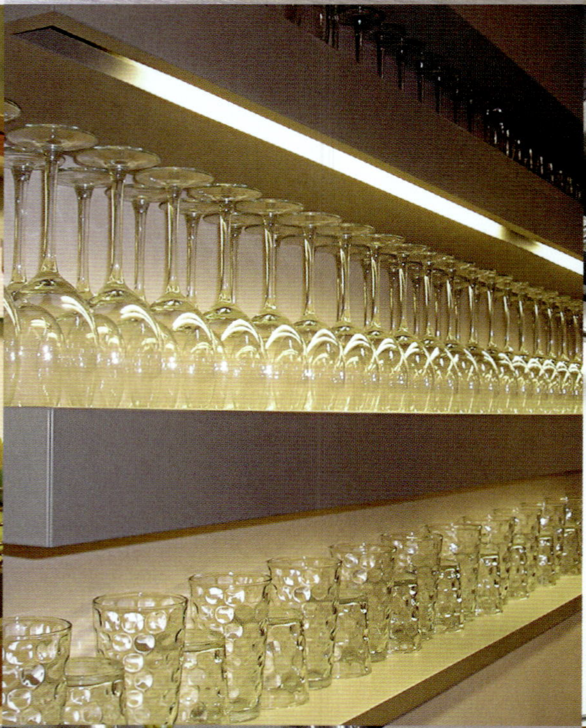
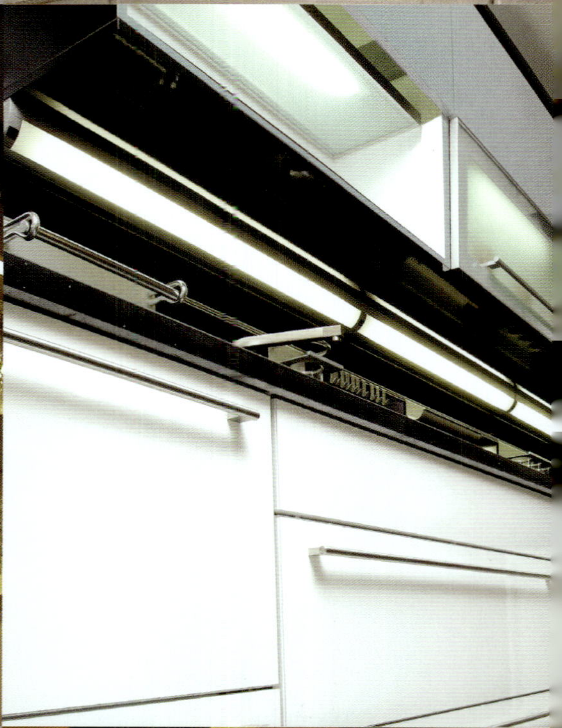
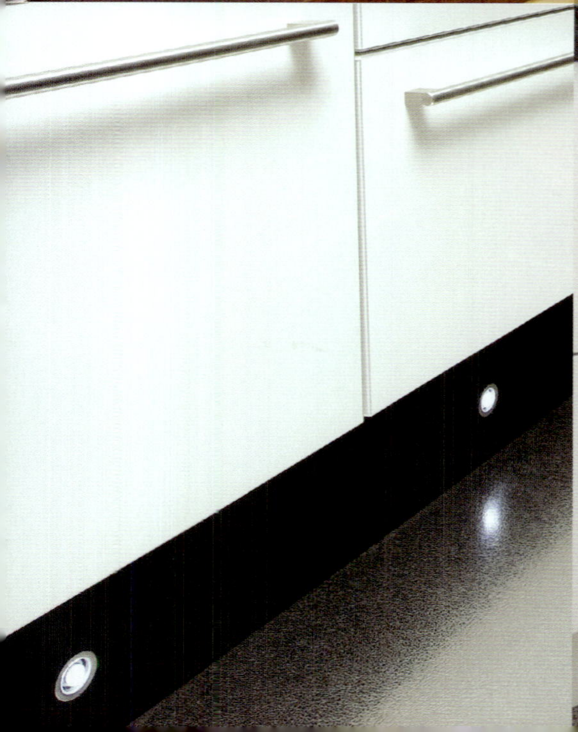
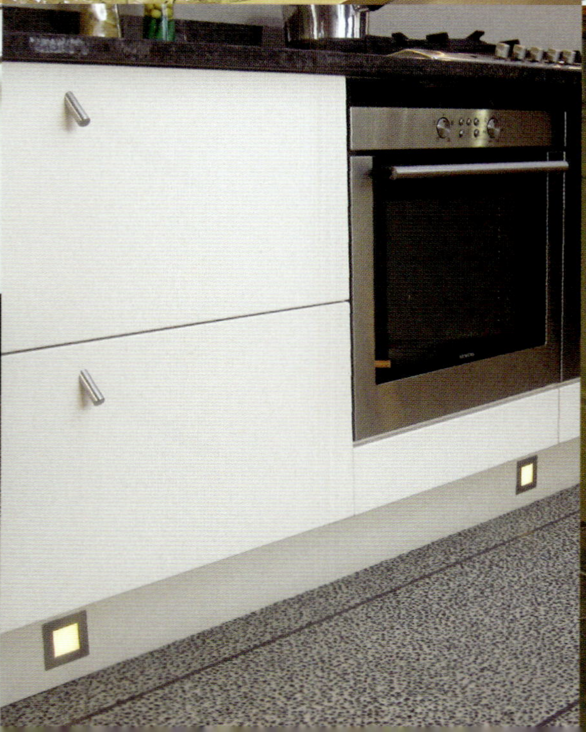
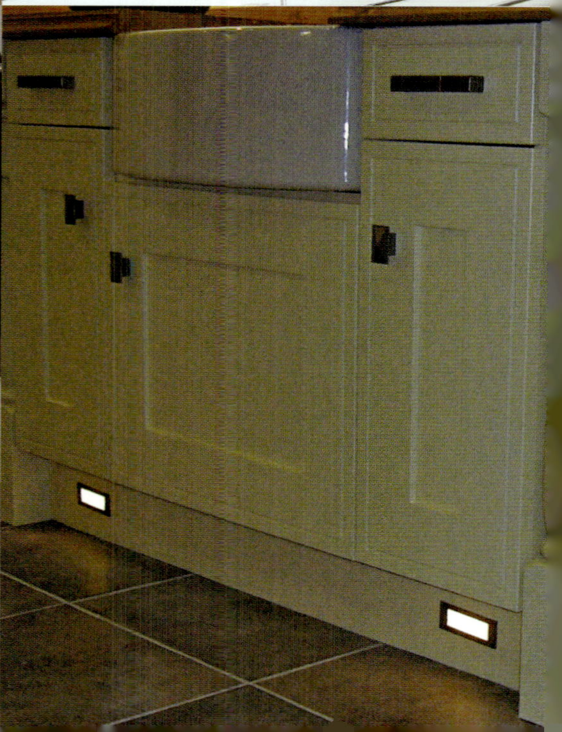

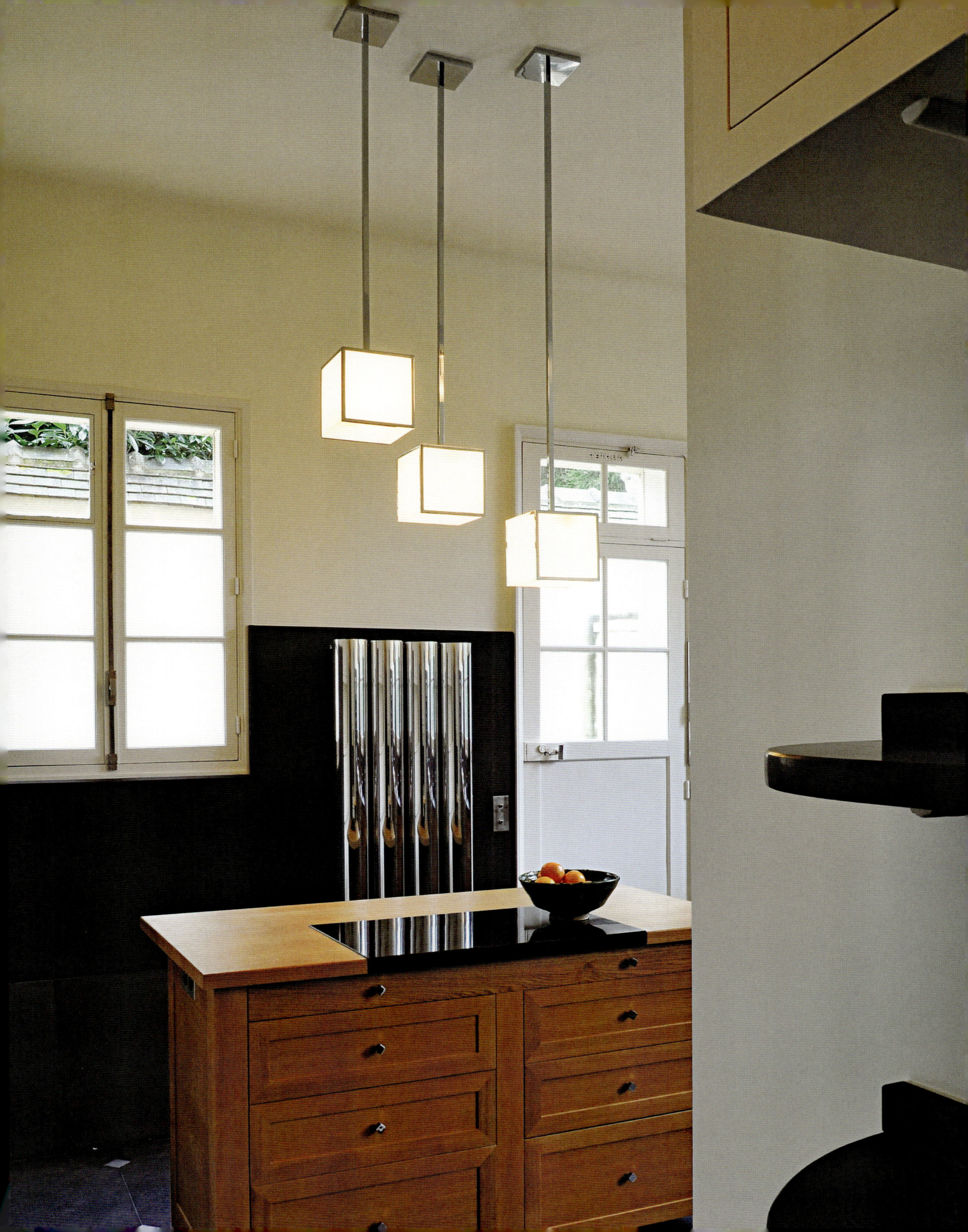

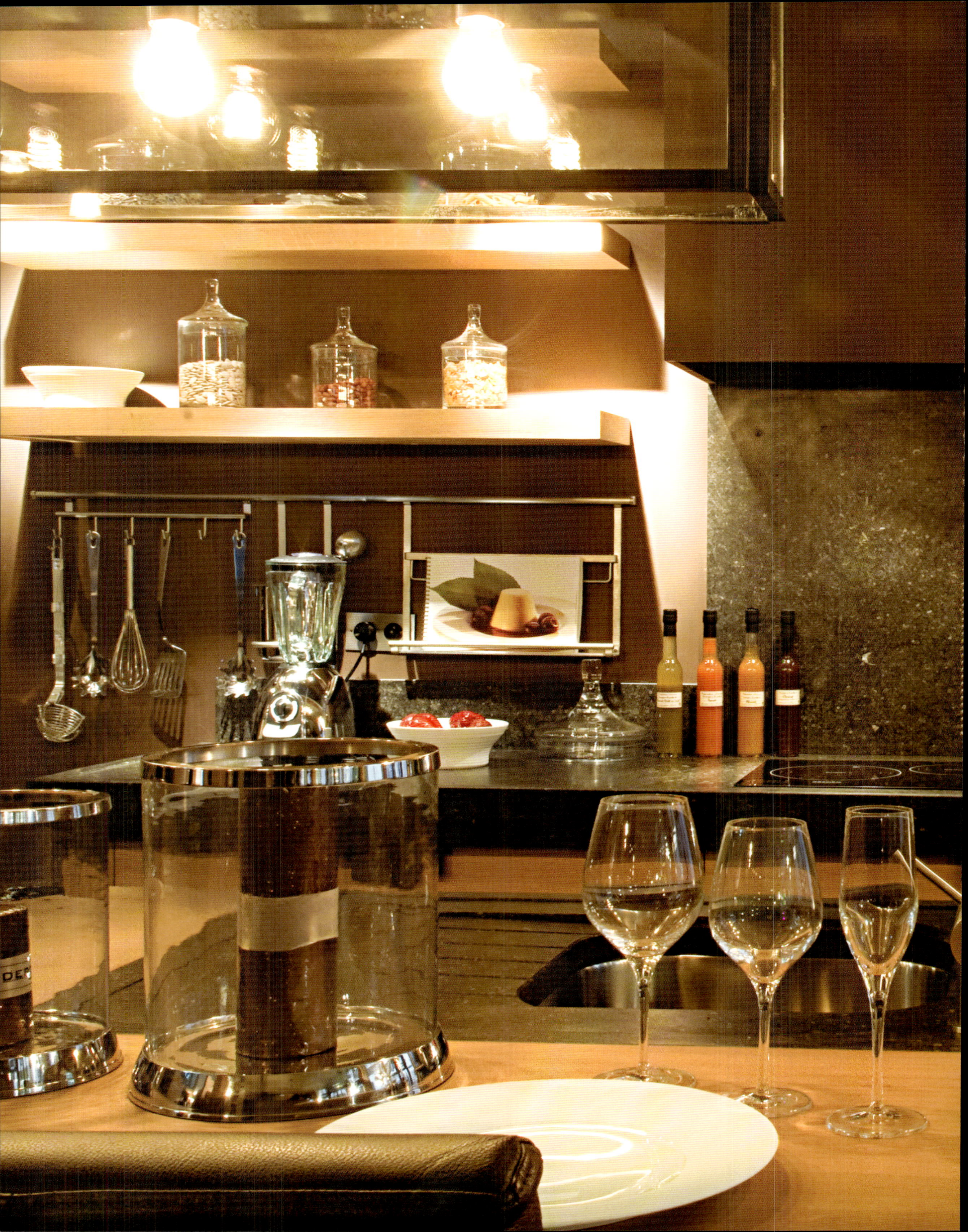

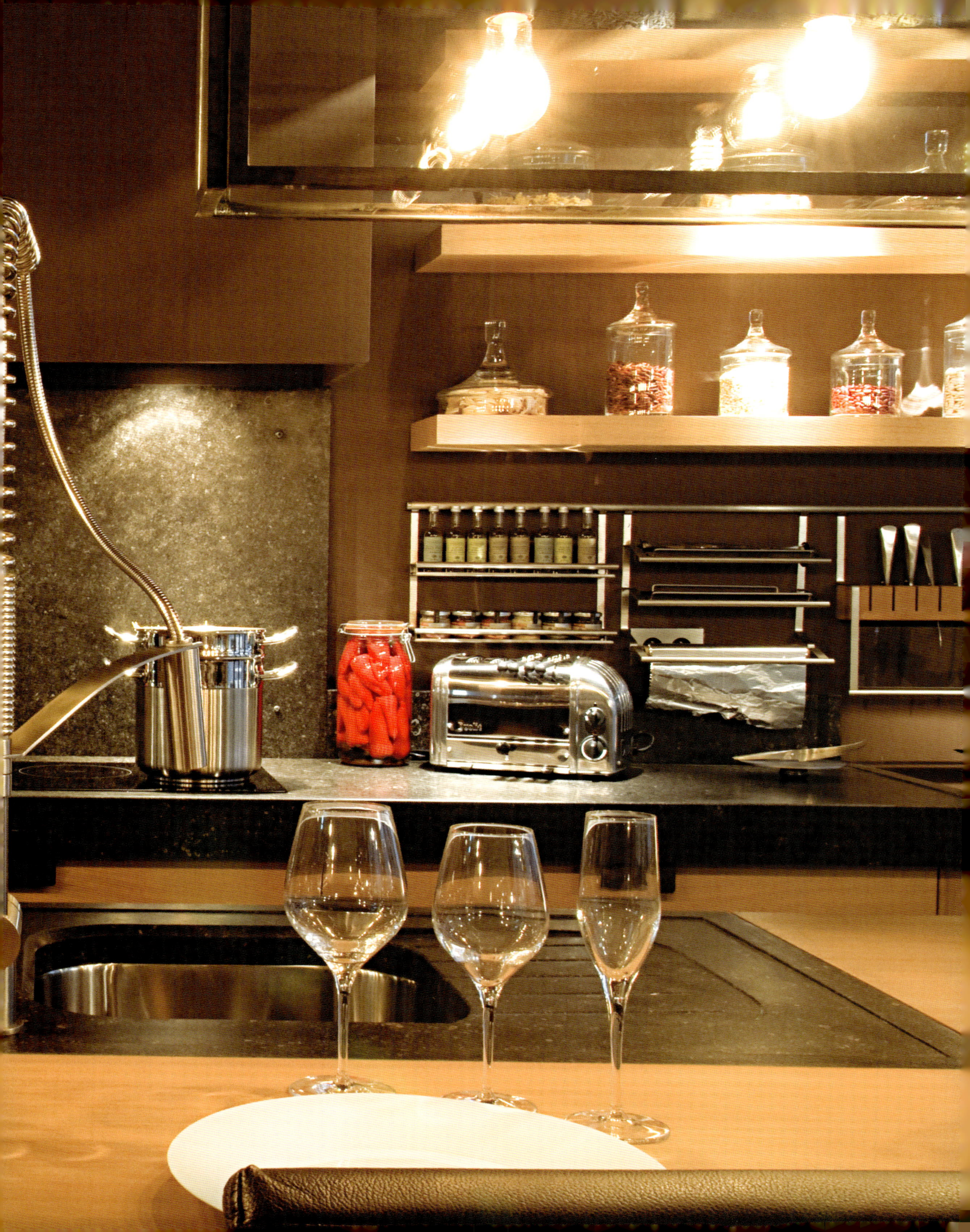

見せる収納

Display Options

スタイルで大別すると、キッチンは2種類に分けられます。雑然としているか、物が少ないかです。雑然としていると言っても、「汚い」とか「だらしない」という意味ではありません（確かにキッチンは、こういう状態を避けて通れない場所ですが）。反対に、物が少ないと言っても、「空虚」とか「面白みがない」という意味ではありません。物の少ないキッチンは、概して、モダンで都会的なスタイルです。特注の美しいキャビネットに取りつけてある、水圧式ドアの向こうや、引き出しの中に、すべてのキッチン用品が隠されています。一方、雑然としたキッチンでは、物を飾って収納します。この後の数ページで、その実例がたくさん出てきます。飾る収納には、調理器具や食器を並べる、扉のない棚が欠かせません。実用的でありながら、美しい。それは調理器具ならではの、特長です。その品物が古くても、新しくても、美しく飾ることができます。鍋類、こまごまとした調理用具、ナイフやフォーク、ガラス器、古いカゴをまとめて飾ると、どれも、たいへん見映えがします。こういったキッチン用品は、「キチネリア」と呼ばれ、もし、家に伝わる古い品物がなくても、目の越えた人なら、世界中のアンティークの定期市や、フリーマーケット、ガレージセールで手に入れることができます。品物の種類ごとに――紅茶の缶から、トースター、やかん、コーヒーポットまで――収集し、交換し、語り、愛する人たちもいます。しかし、実際に使えるかどうかは、種類によって異なります。平皿、スープ用の蓋付きの深皿、グラス、ブリキ製品は、見かけもよく、実際に使えます。しかし、まな板や、木製のサラダボウル、古い刷毛は、目を楽しませるためだけに飾るのがいいでしょう。飾る収納では、使っていない間に、食器がほこりをかぶるかもしれませんが、心配無用です。その、ほこりにも名前が付いています。それは「趣」です。

Stylistically kitchens seem to fall into two categories, cluttered or minimal. I don't mean cluttered as in 'messy' or 'untidy' (though kitchens can certainly pass through that phase) and I don't mean minimal as in empty or uninteresting. Minimal kitchens are generally modern and city-based, with everything hidden behind beautiful tailor-made hydraulically opening and closing doors and drawers. Cluttered kitchens are where we see display, and over the next few pages, you'll find plenty of it. Essentially the concept depends on open-fronted shelves, on which cooking and eating wares are stored. Things as beautiful as they are useful; that is one of the unique elements of cookware – both old and new – it can look great. Groups of cooking pans, utensils, cutlery, glassware and old baskets all look wonderful. This stuff is called 'kitchenalia' and can, if it's not inherited, be found by the discerning collector in antique fairs, flea markets and yard sales around the world. For every type of object – from tea caddies to toasters, kettles to coffee pots – there is a group of people who collect it, swap it, talk about it, and adore it. But certain things wear better than others. Plates, tureens, glasses and tinware look fine and can all be put to good use, but wooden chopping boards, salad bowls and old brushes are best kept just for admiring. If any of these things on display gathers a bit of dust between uses, don't worry. That too has a name. It's called patina!

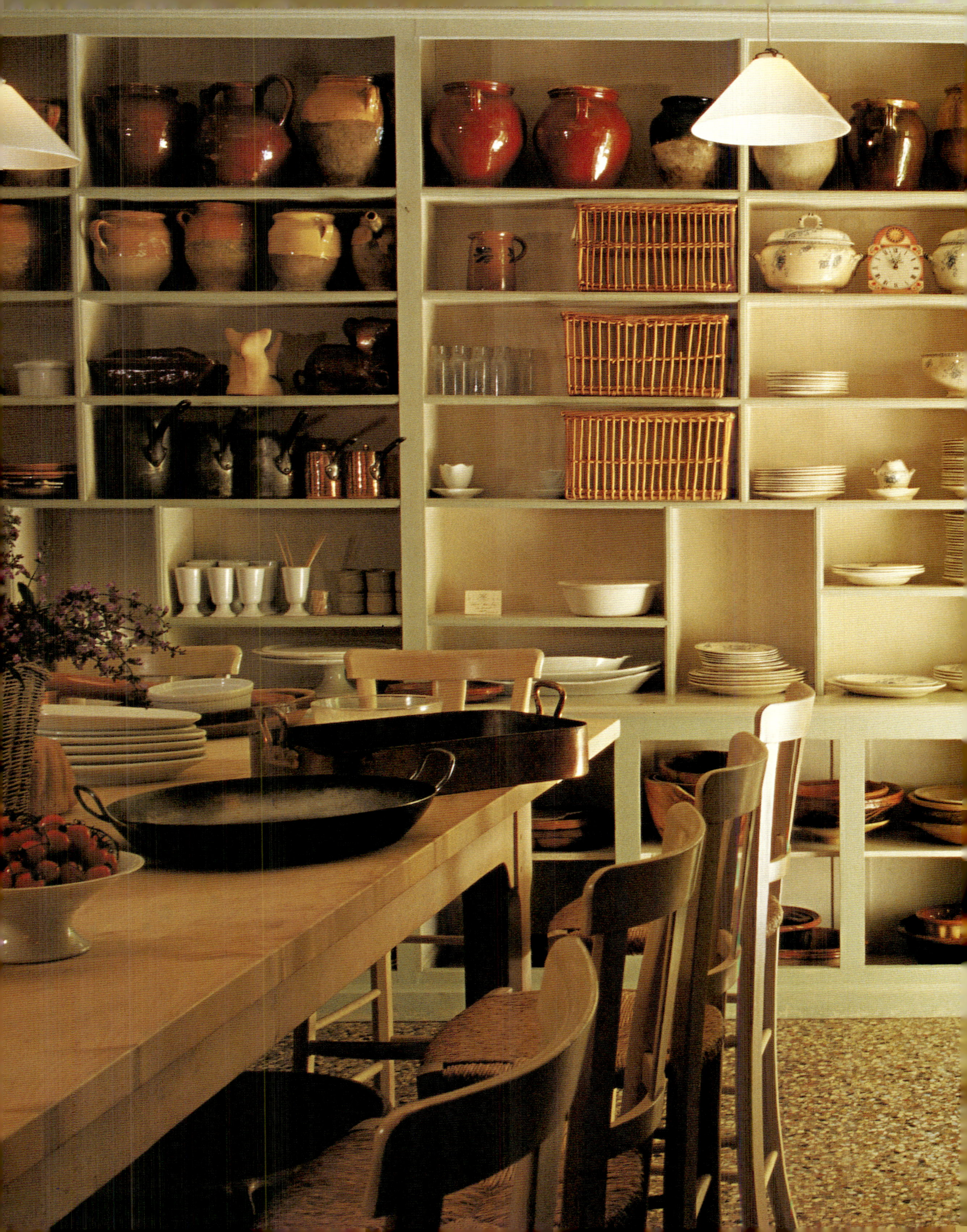

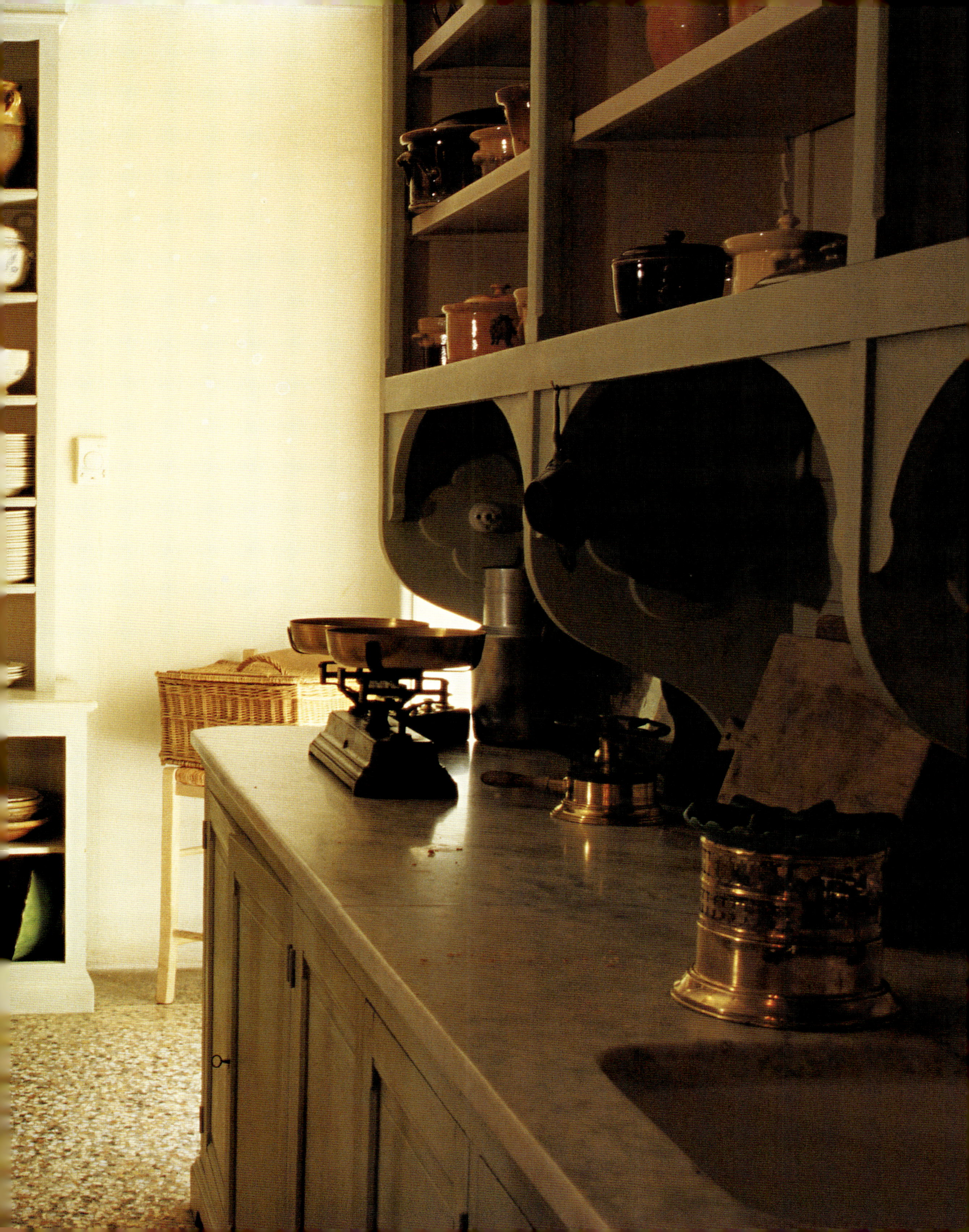

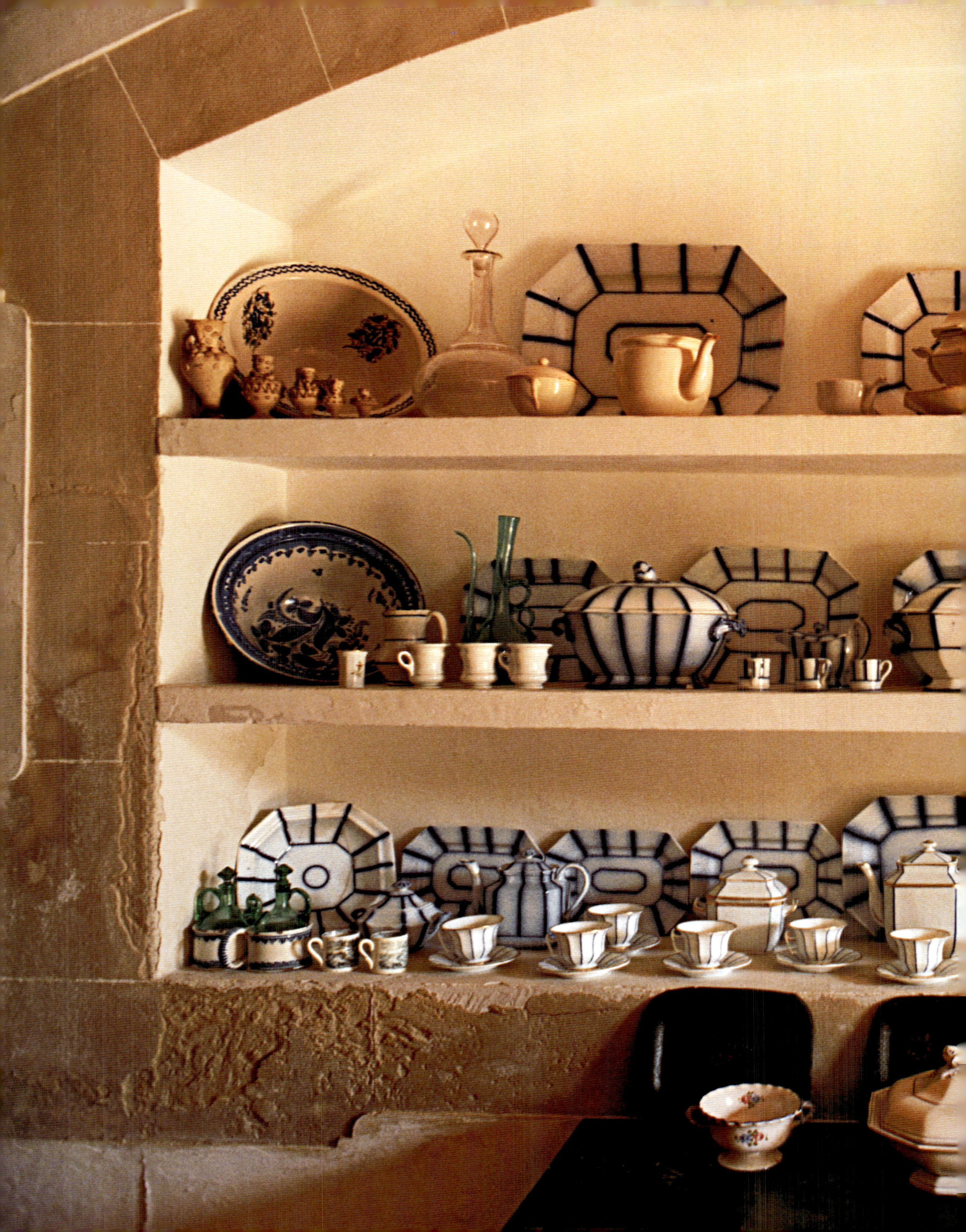

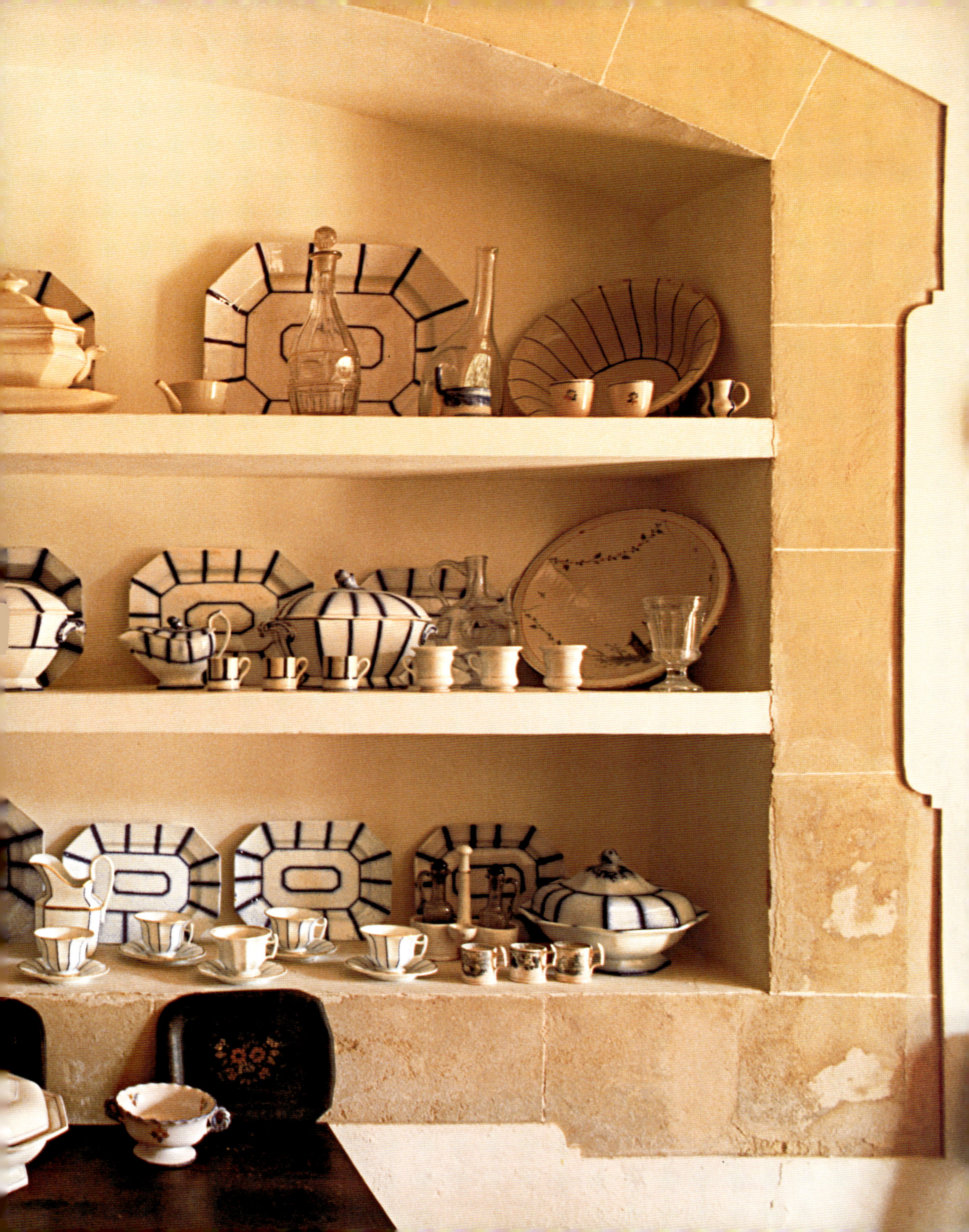

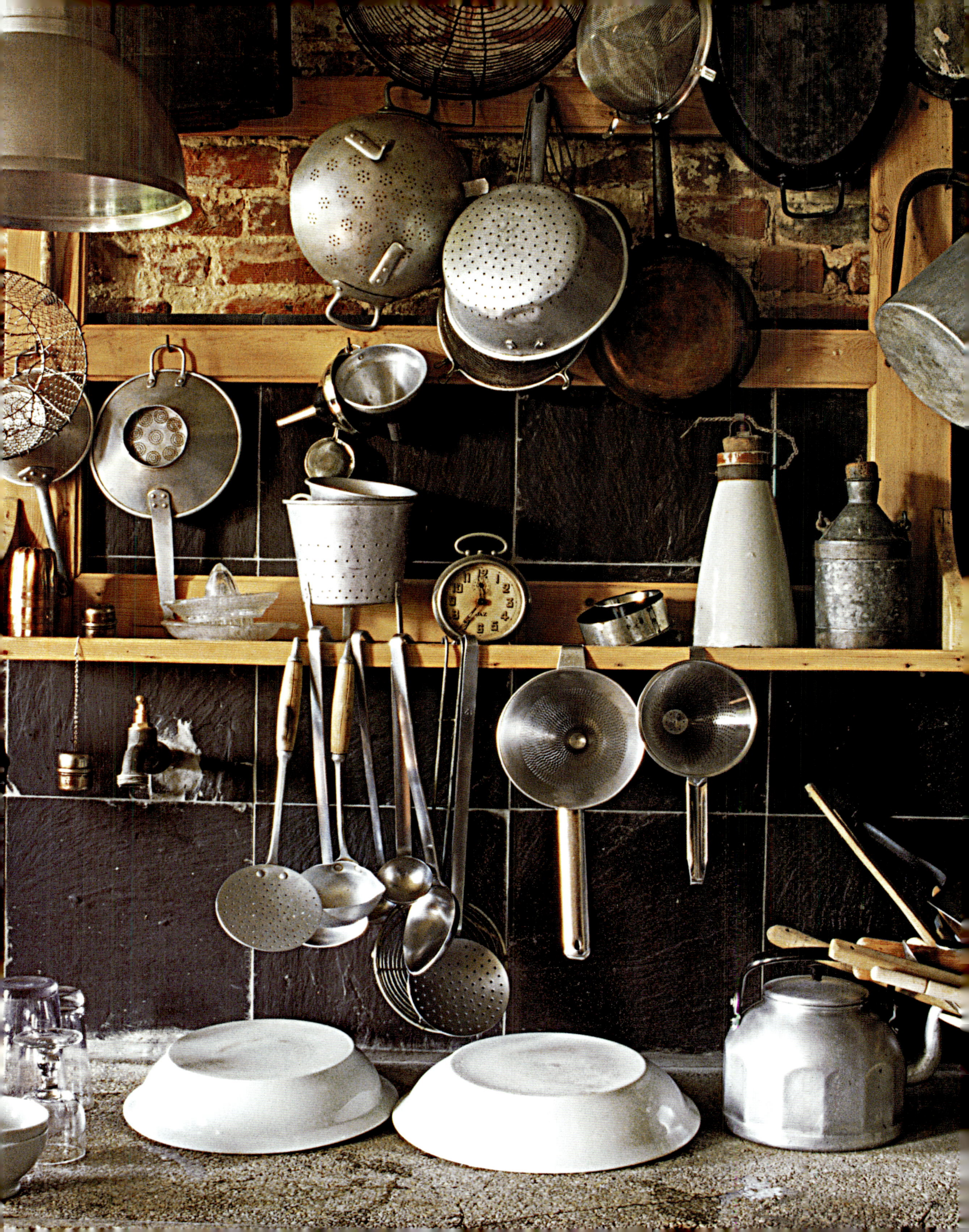

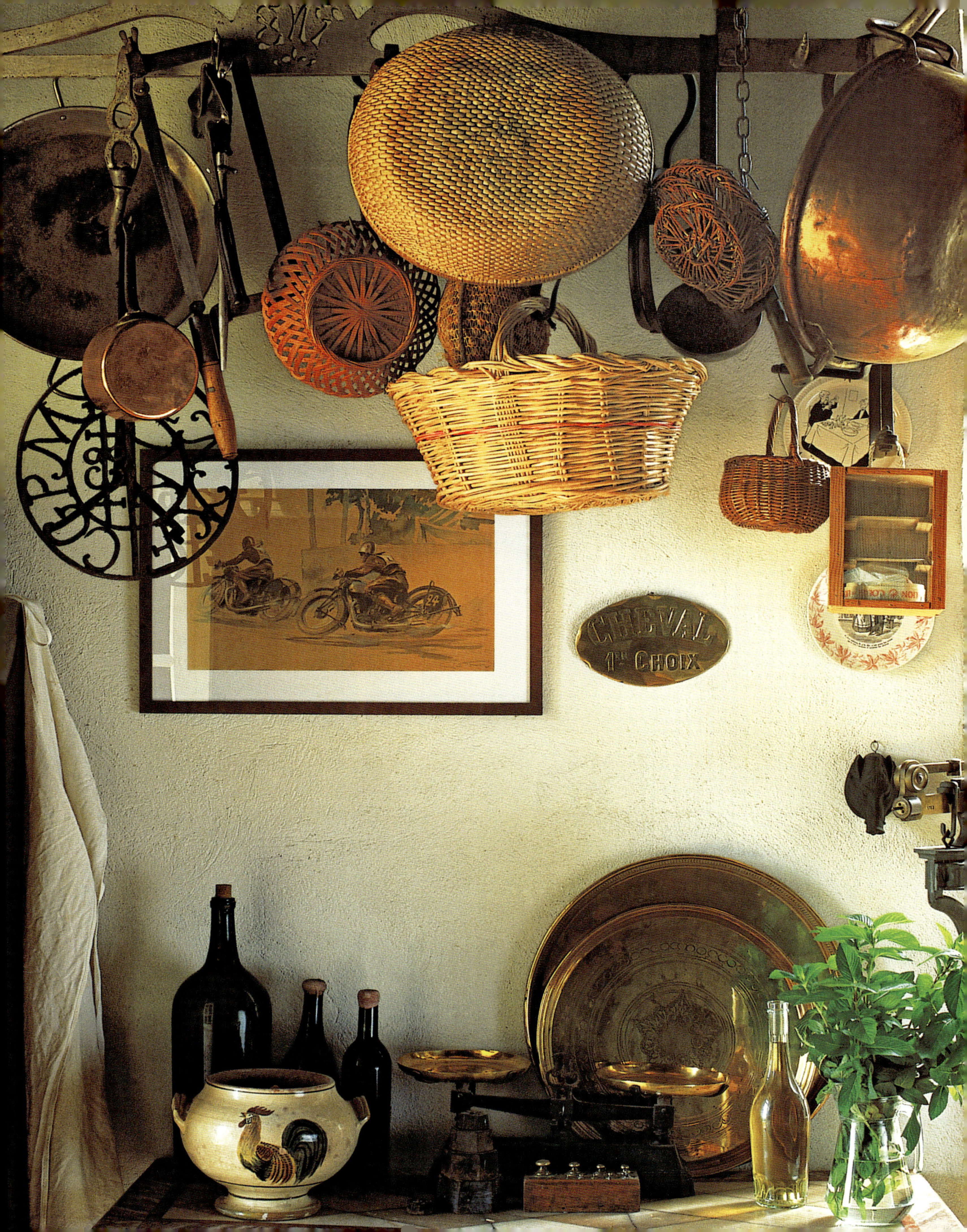
CHEVAL
1er CHOIX

見せる収納

見せる収納

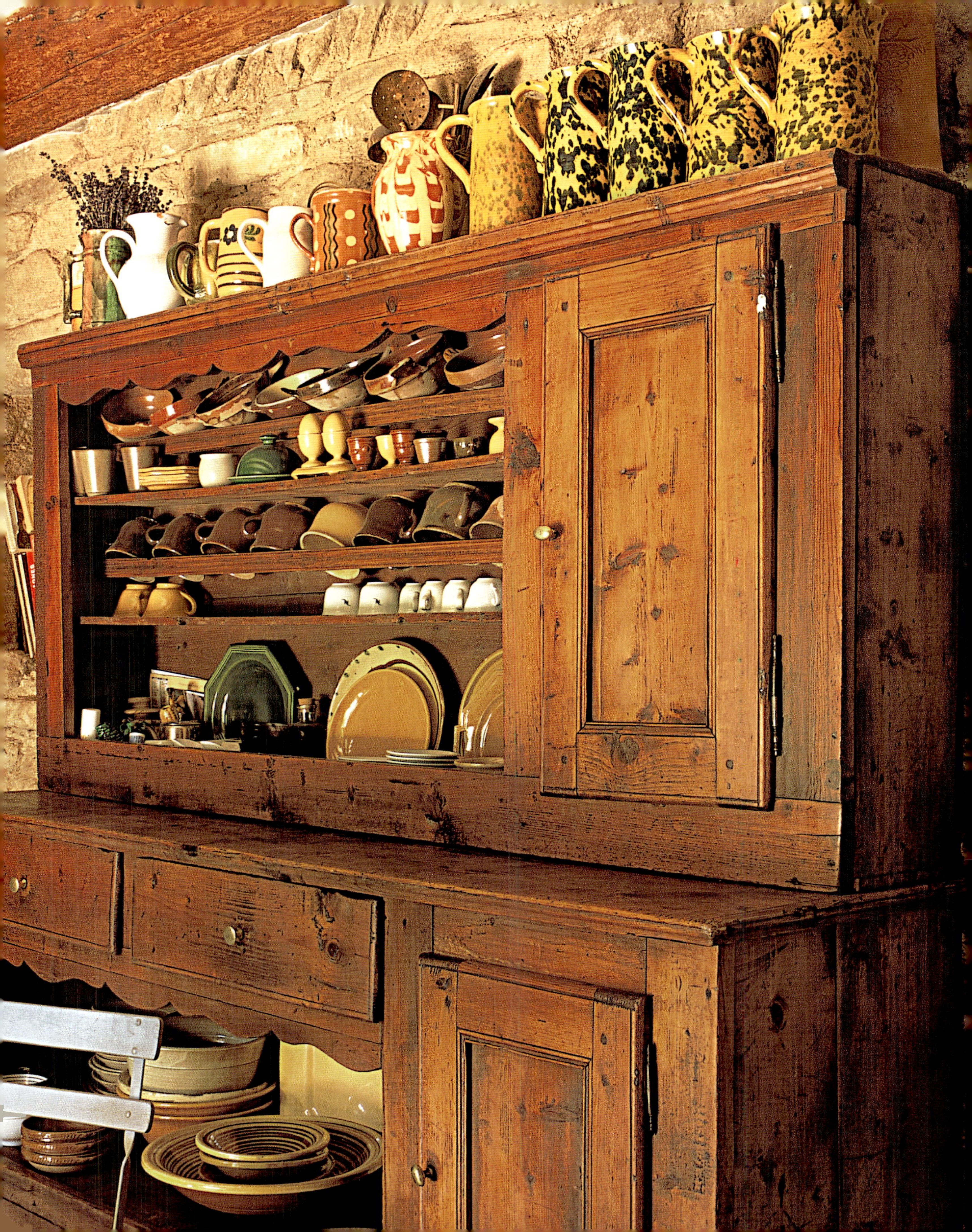

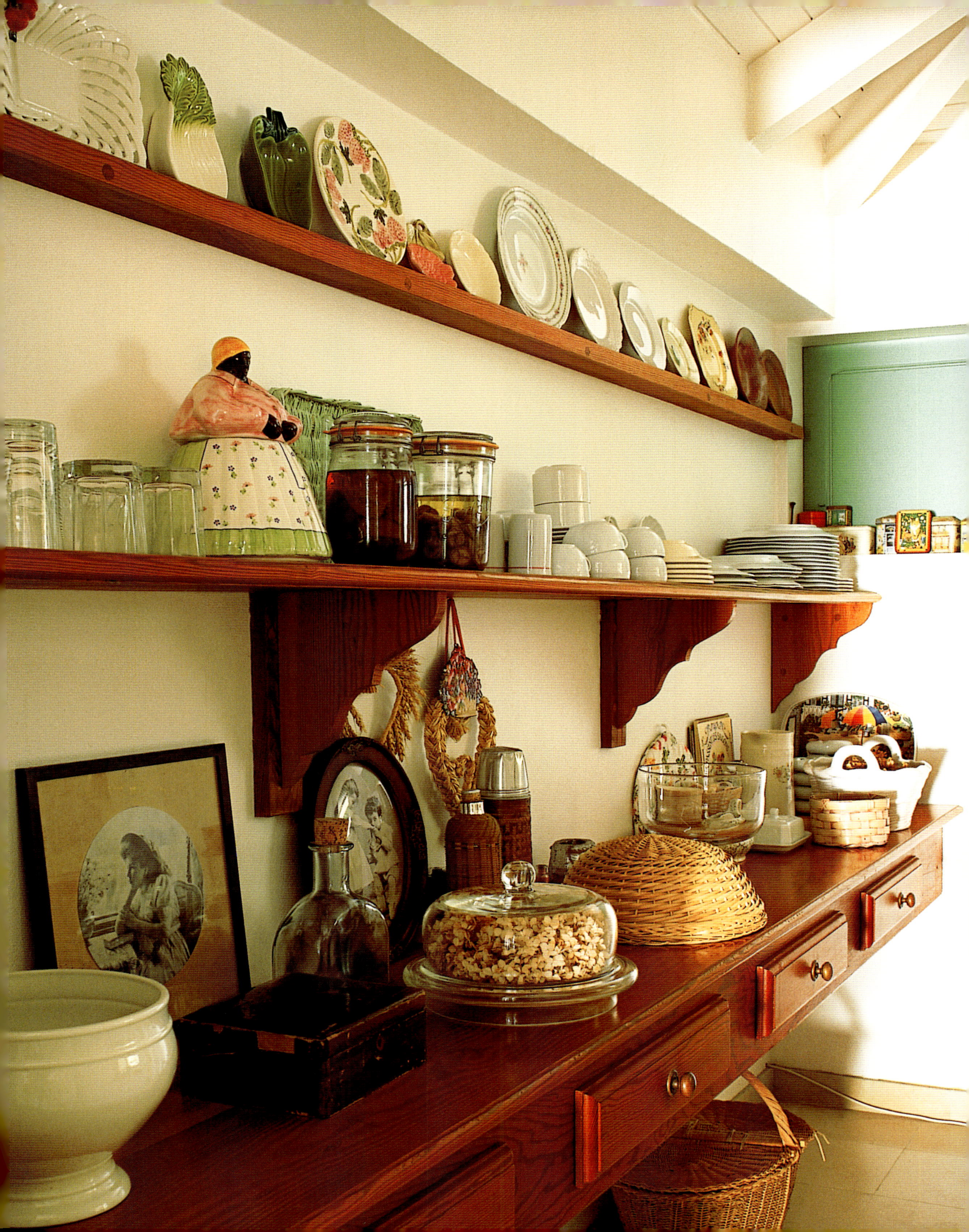

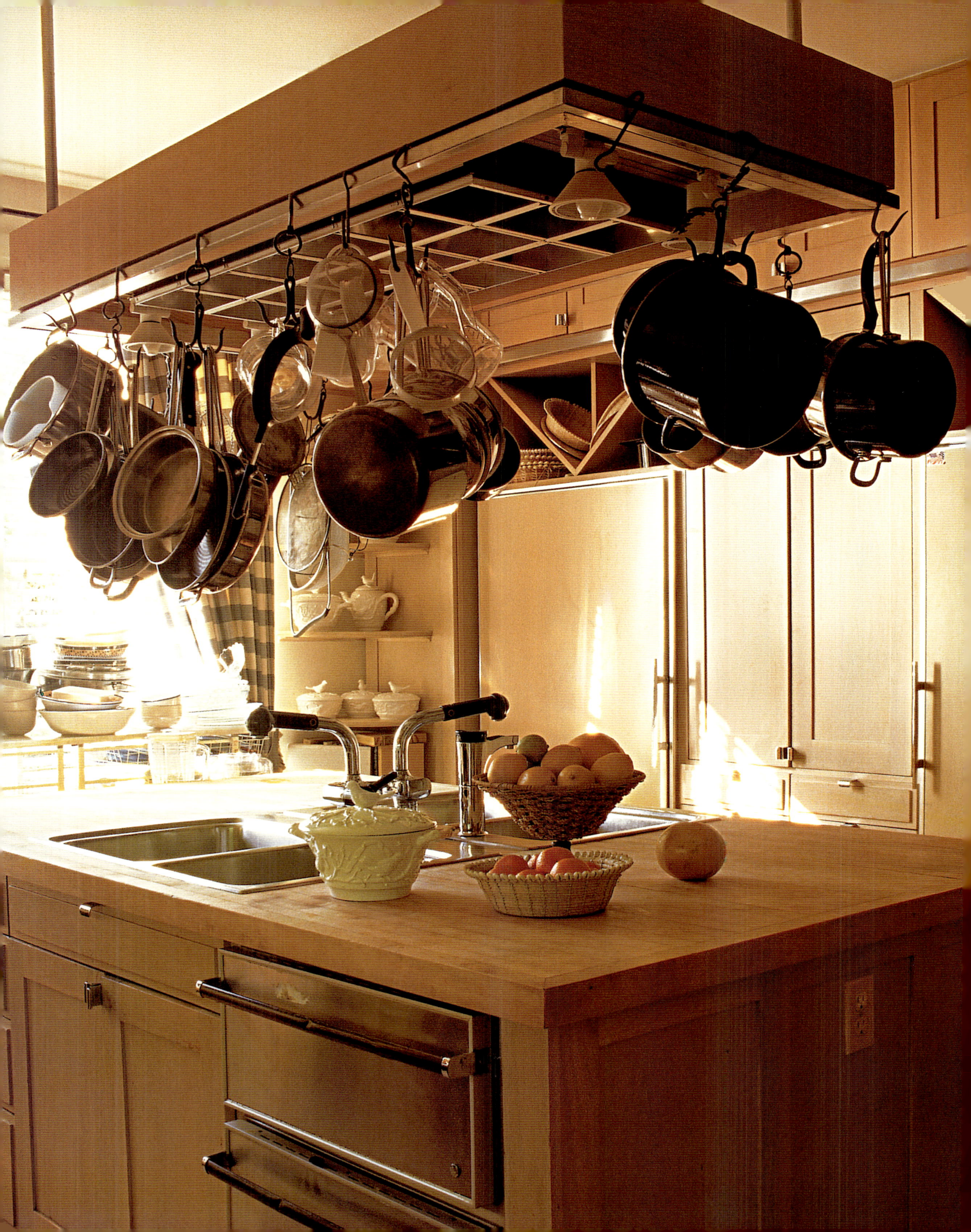

見せる収納

見せる収納

見せる収納

見せる収納

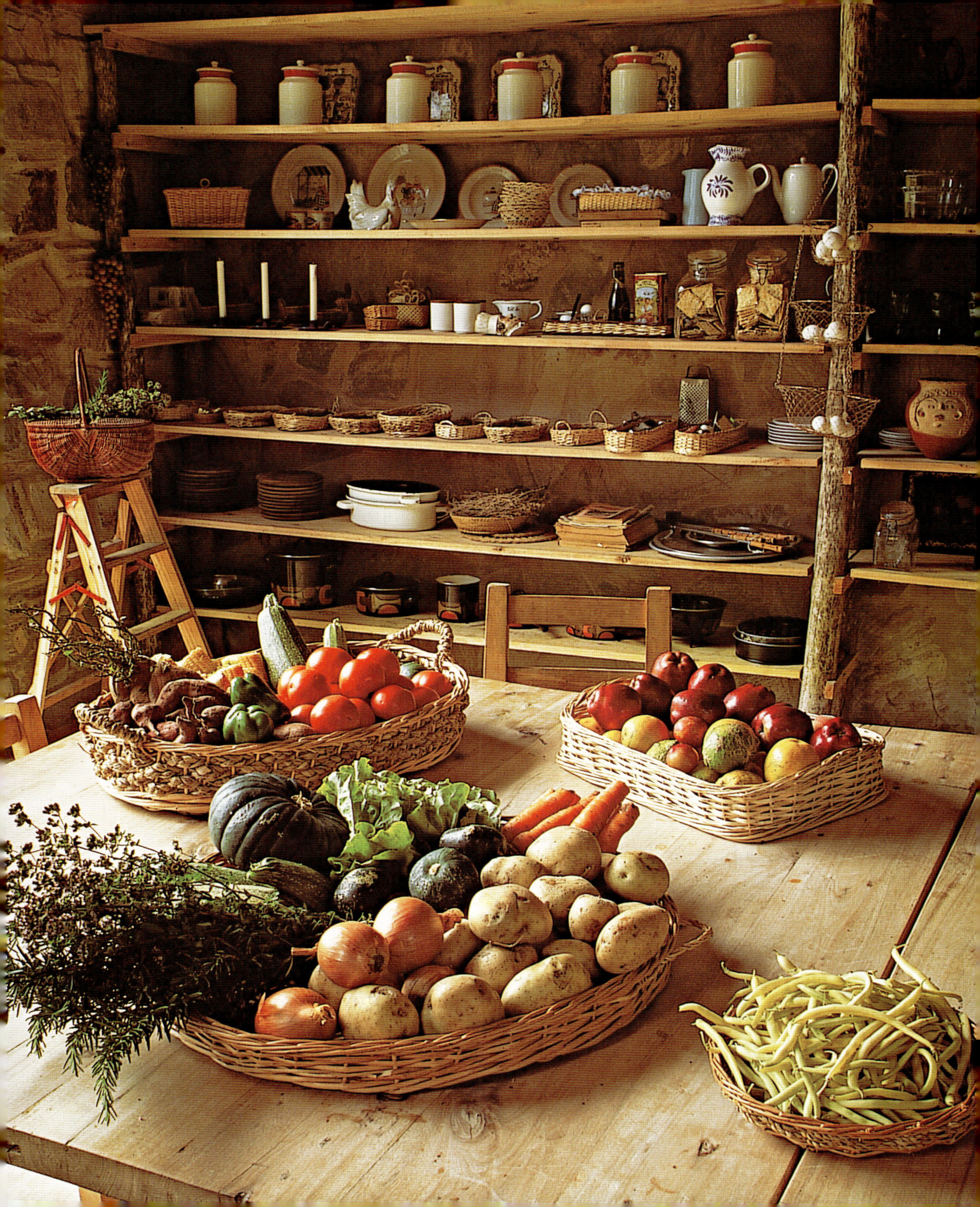

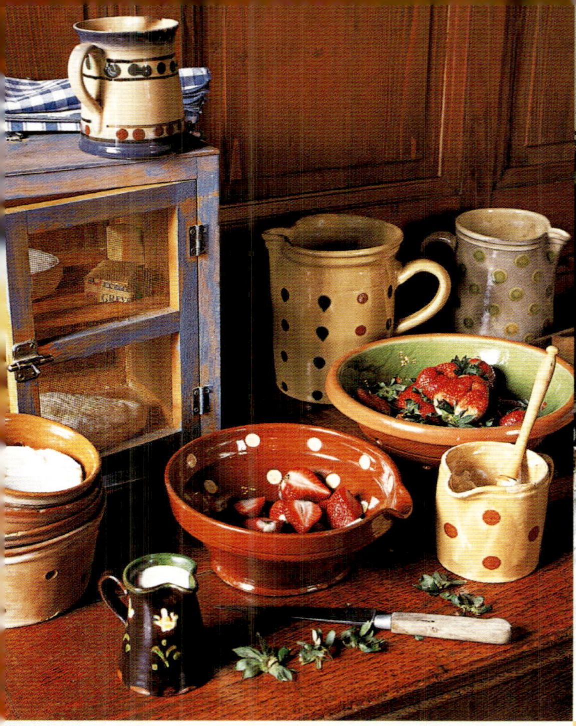
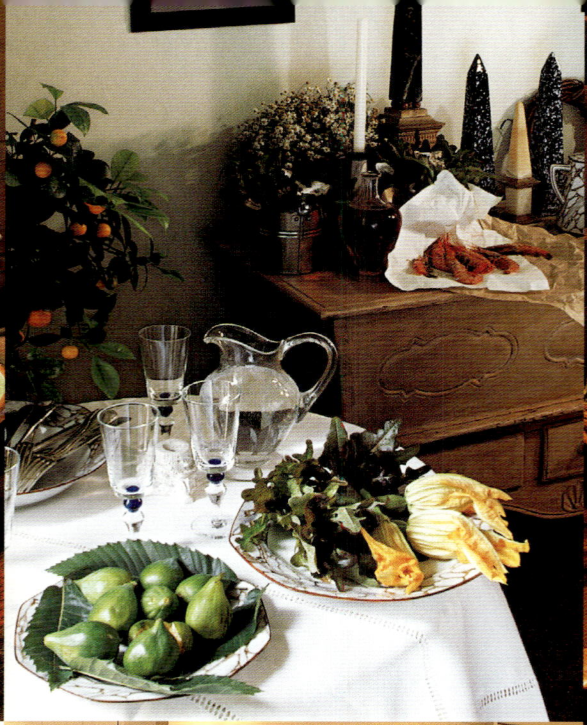
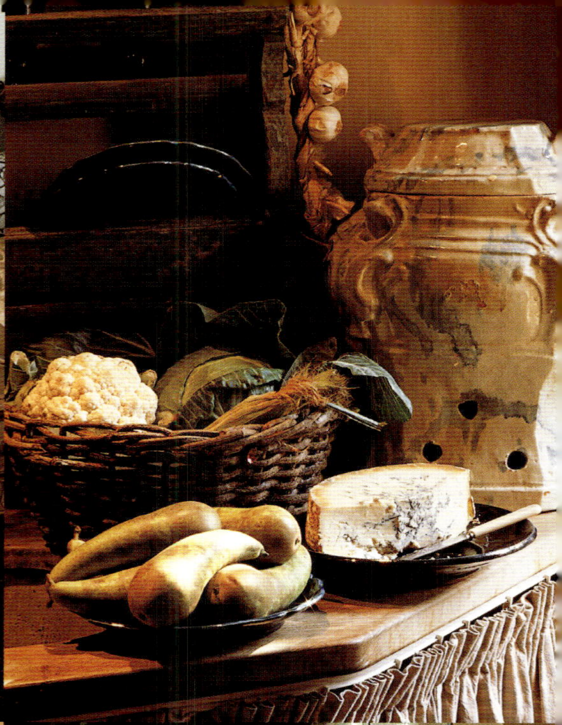
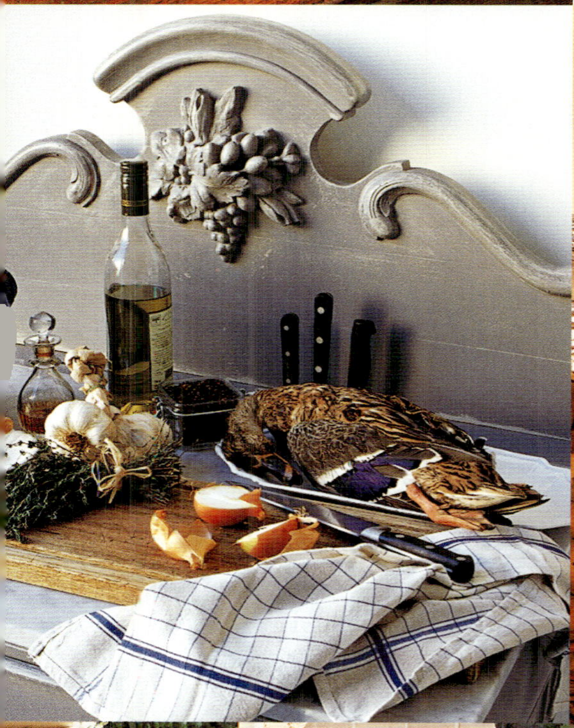
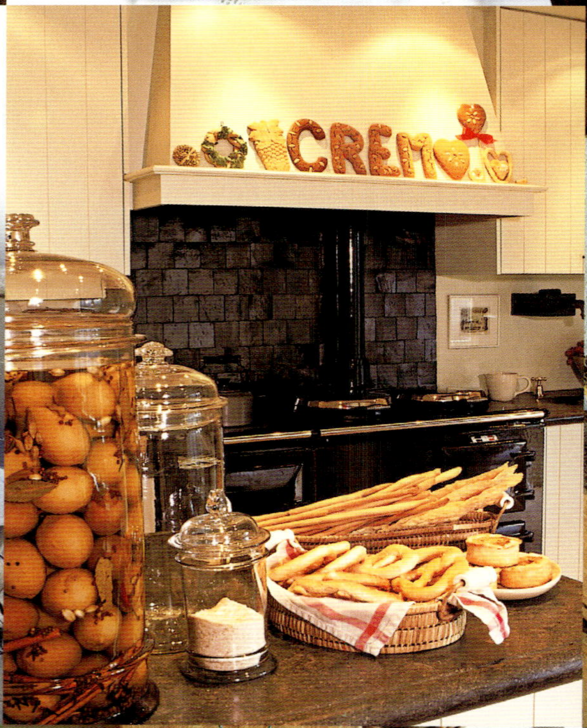
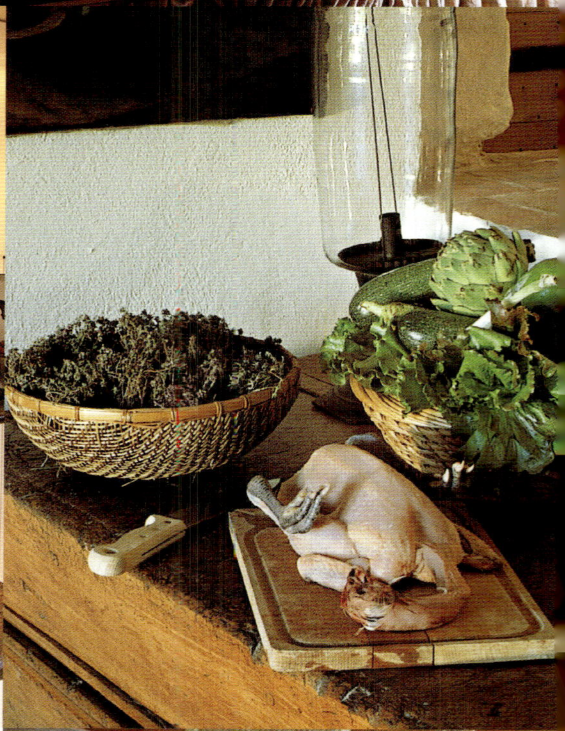
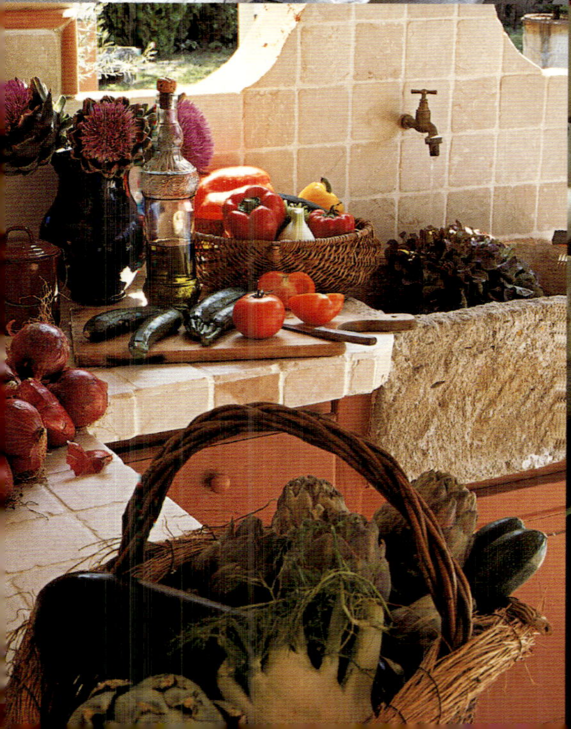
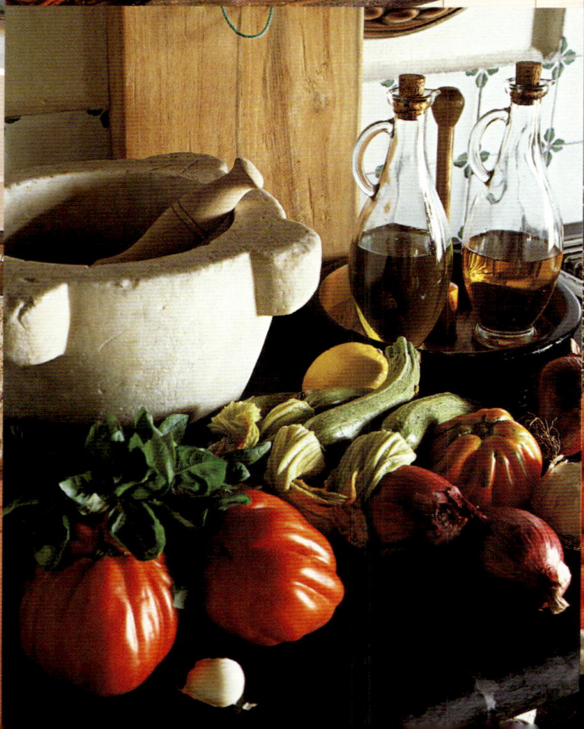
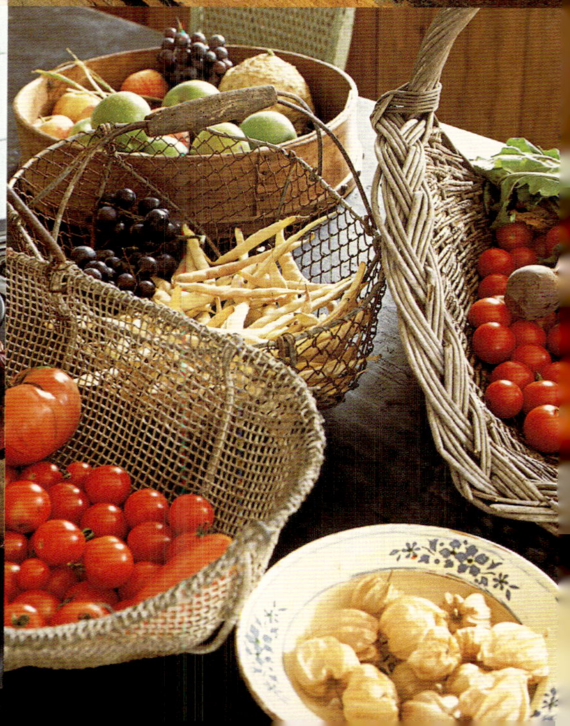

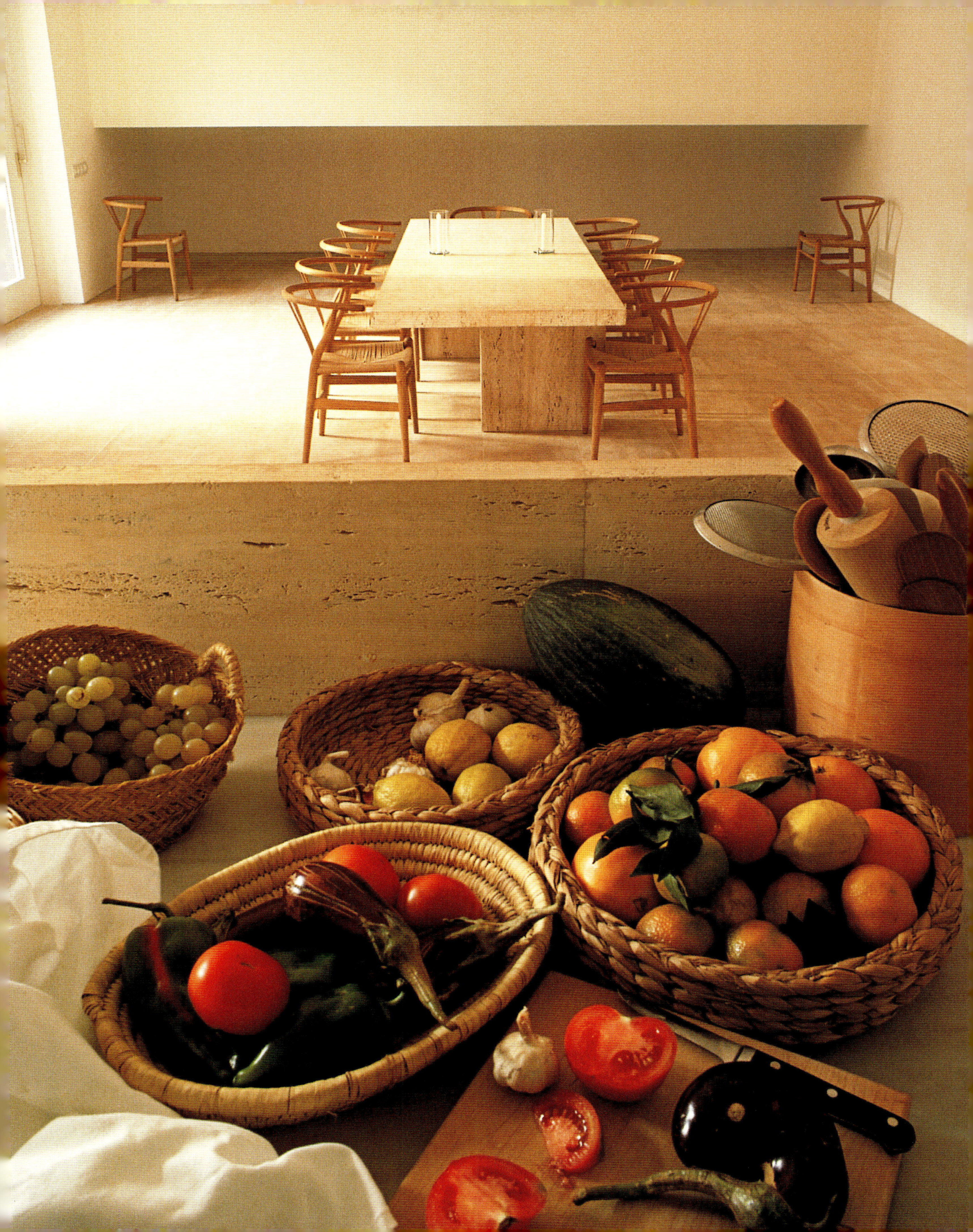

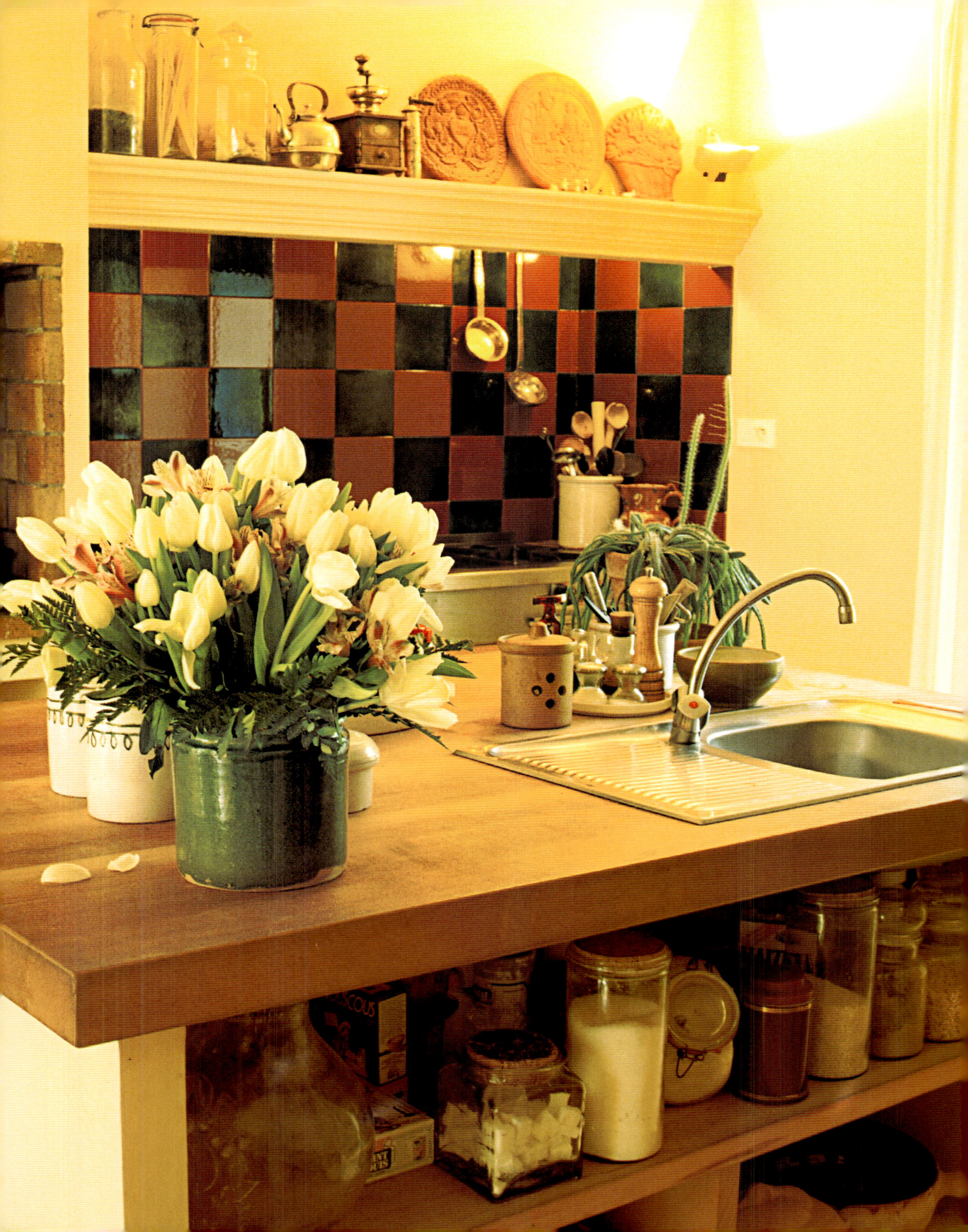

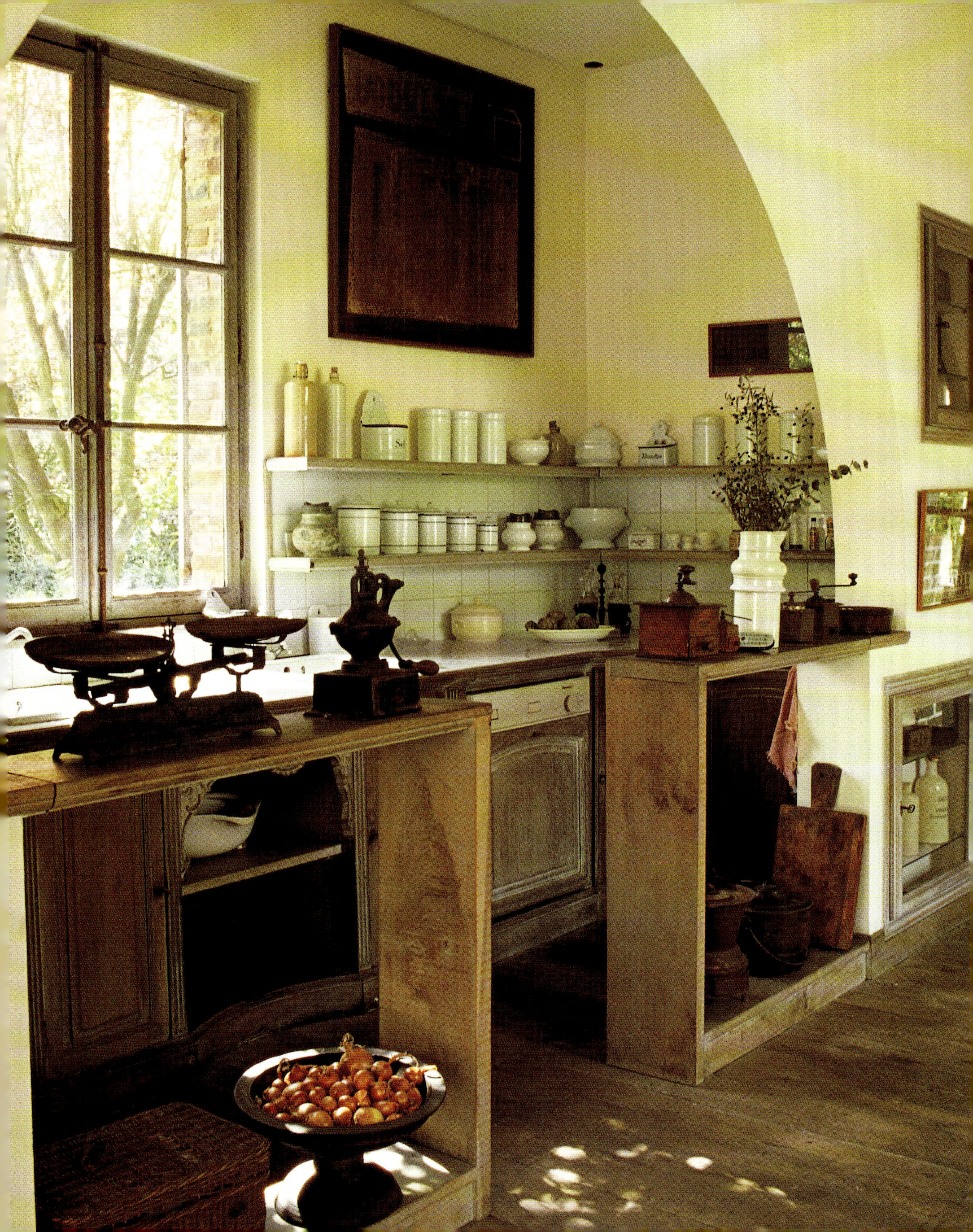
Sel

床と壁

Walls and Floors

キッチンは、伝統的な素材が、好んで使われる部屋です。概して、耐久性のある素材は、もっとも人気があると同時に、もっとも高価なものです。ご自宅の床は、古い敷石、テラコッタのタイル、レンガ、小石などが使われている、伝統ある見事な物かもしれません。しかし、これらの床は、長い間立ち仕事をすると、決して足に優しくはないものです。一方、コルク、ラバー、リノリウム、木の床は、少ない費用で、簡単に敷くことができます。足への当たりが優しく、足音も静かですし、子どもさんがケガをしにくいという利点があります。住んでいる場所、家のタイプ、置こうと考えているキッチンの家具のスタイルで、床も決まってくるでしょう。伝統的な床材は、伝統的なキッチンに、またスレート、タイル、金属板といった「モダンな」素材は、モダンなキッチンに向きます。色も重要です。ナチュラルなアースカラーと、対照をなすのは、グレー、シルバー、ホワイト、ブラックです。カラフルな模様があると、楽しいムードになりますが、しばらくすると飽きてしまうことのないよう、慎重に柄を選んでください。カーテン、ブラインド、テーブルクロスには、お金をかけすぎないほうがいいでしょう。壁に関しては、タイルにするのが実用的です。特に、加熱調理機器やシンクの回りには、タイルがおすすめです。しかも、タイルは、サイズ、色、柄とも、とても豊富です。最後に、すでに部屋に使われている素材を見て、さらに何か付け加えることよりも、全部取り払うことを考えてみましょう。むきだしになったレンガ、プラスターボード、さね継ぎの木材が、キッチンに驚きの要素をもたらしてくれる、思いがけない材料になる場合もあります。

These are the aspects of the kitchen where most people prefer to use materials that are of a traditional nature. Generally speaking, the most permanent materials are the most desirable and the most expensive. You might be lucky enough to inherit a wonderful floor of old flagstones, terracotta tiles, brick or pebbles. On the other hand, these surfaces can be pretty unforgiving on the feet if you spend a long time standing, whereas cork, rubber, linoleum and various types of wood can be cheaper and easier to lay, as well as being softer and quieter to pad about on, and more child friendly too. A lot will depend on where you live, the type of house, and the style of the kitchen furniture you plan. Traditional floors suit traditional kitchens and 'modern' materials such as slate, tile, or sheet metal, suit modern schemes. Colour also plays a part – natural earth tones versus grey, silver, white or black. Colourful patterns can be fun, but take care not to choose something that you might grow tired of. Better to save extravagant excesses for curtains, roller blinds or tablecloths. When it comes to walls, tiled surfaces are practical, especially near the cooker or sink – and there are plenty of sizes, colours and patterns to choose from. Finally, look at what you have already and consider taking away, rather than adding. Exposed brickwork, raw plaster or tongue-and-groove timber can sometimes be the unexpected solution for adding the wow factor.

床 と 壁

床 と 壁

床 と 壁

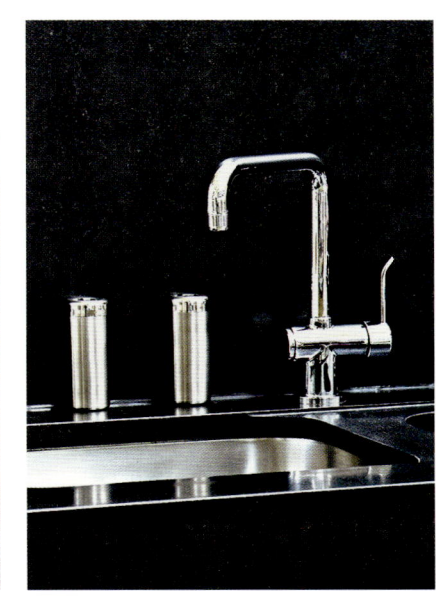

床 と 壁

床 と 壁

床 と 壁

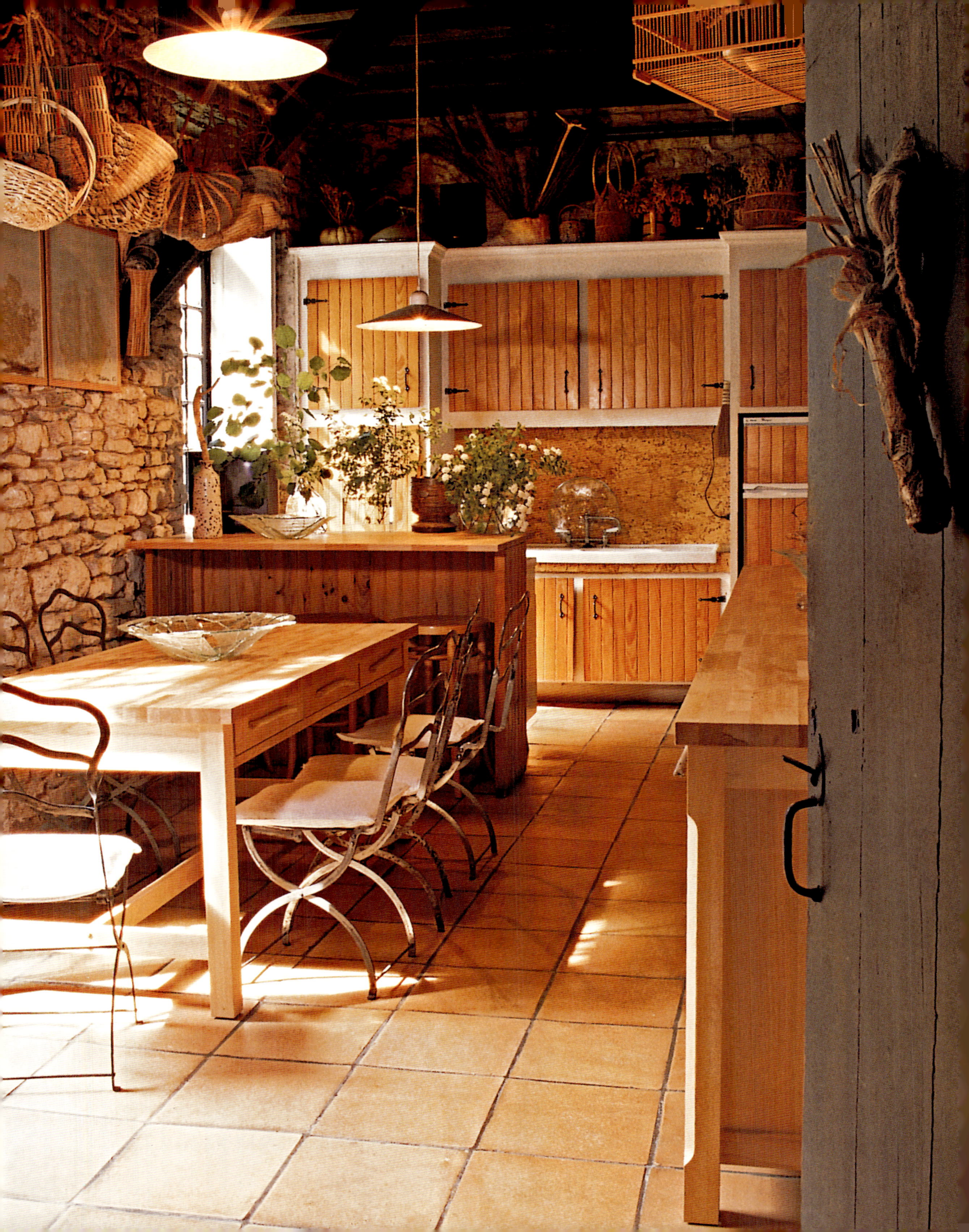

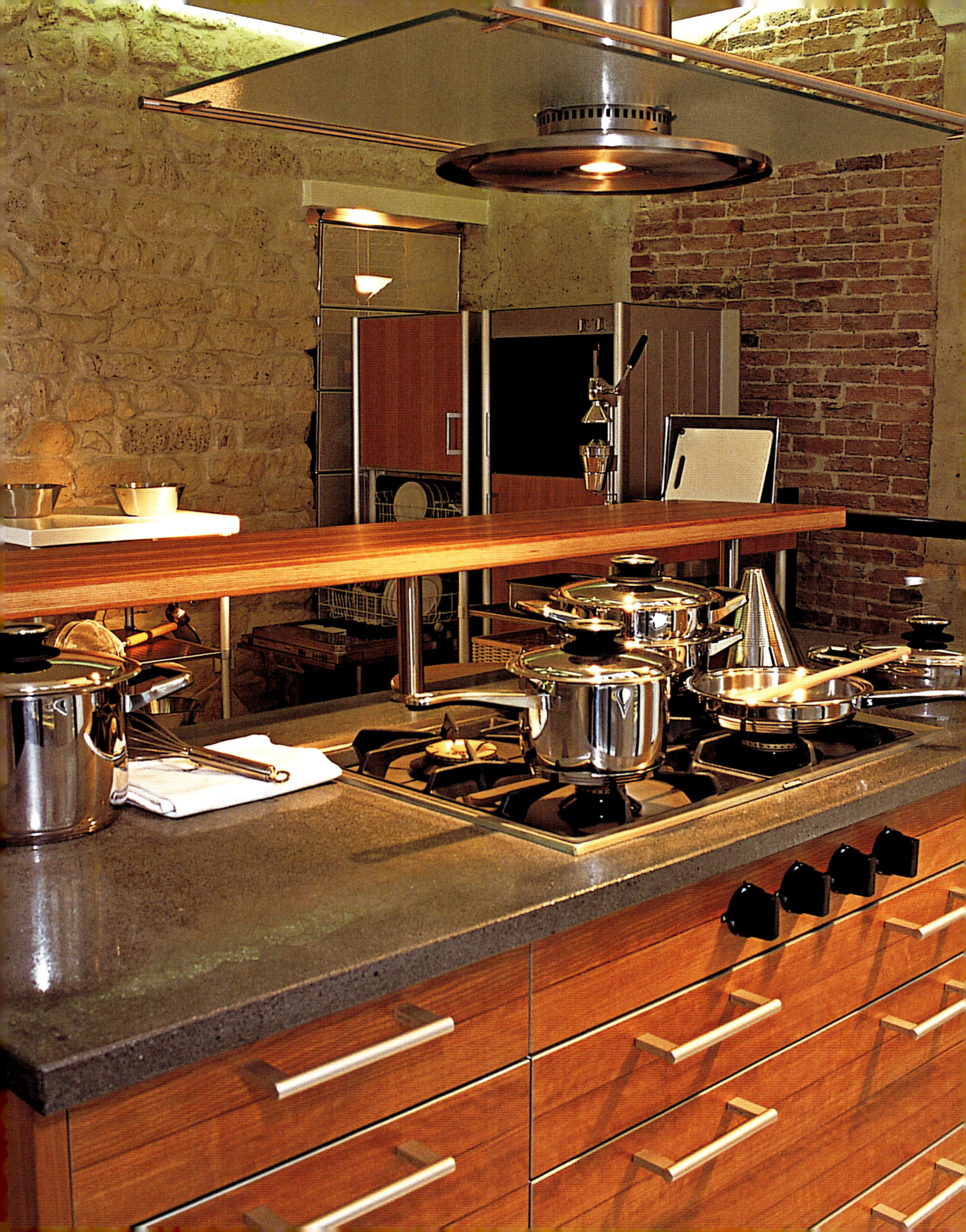

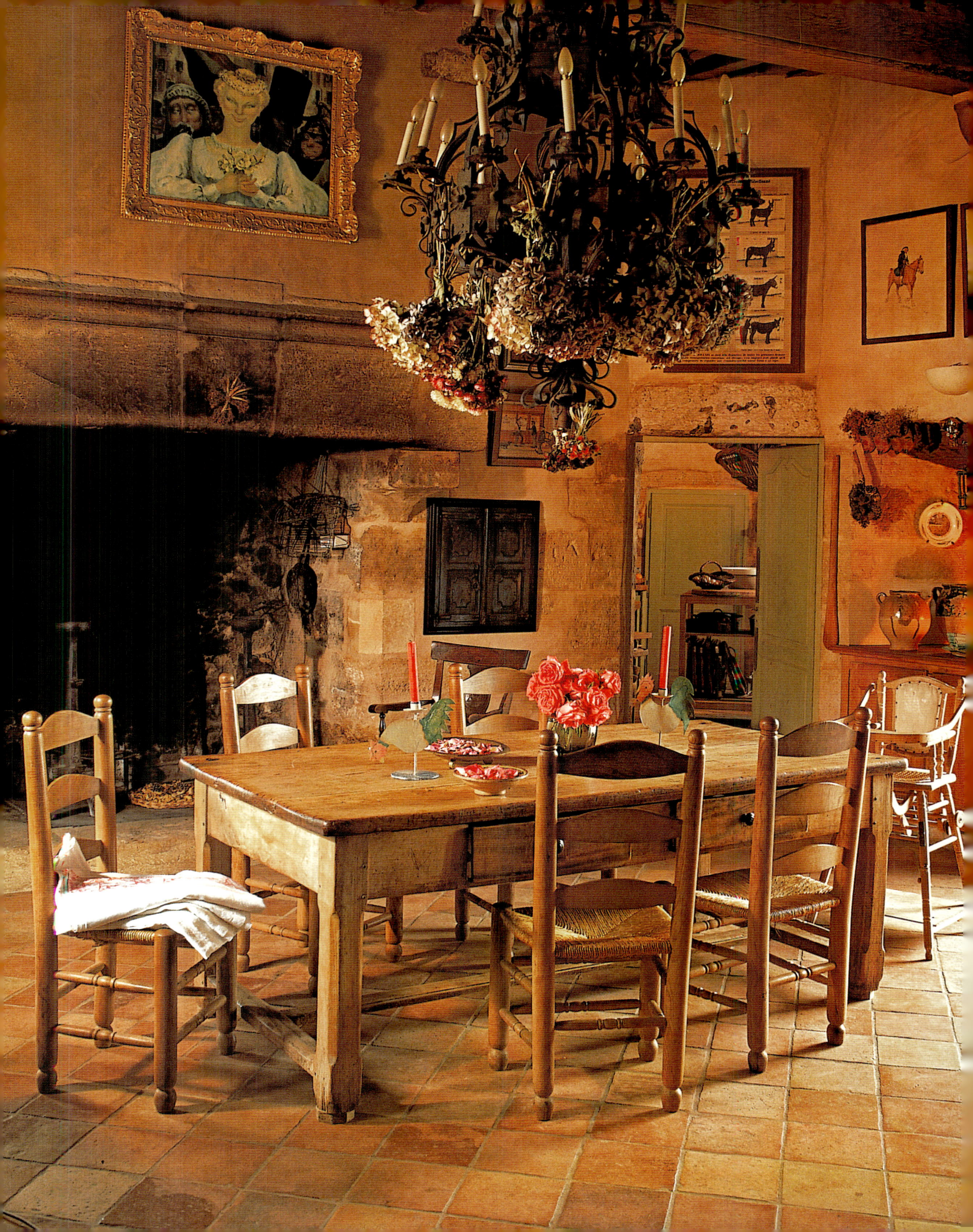

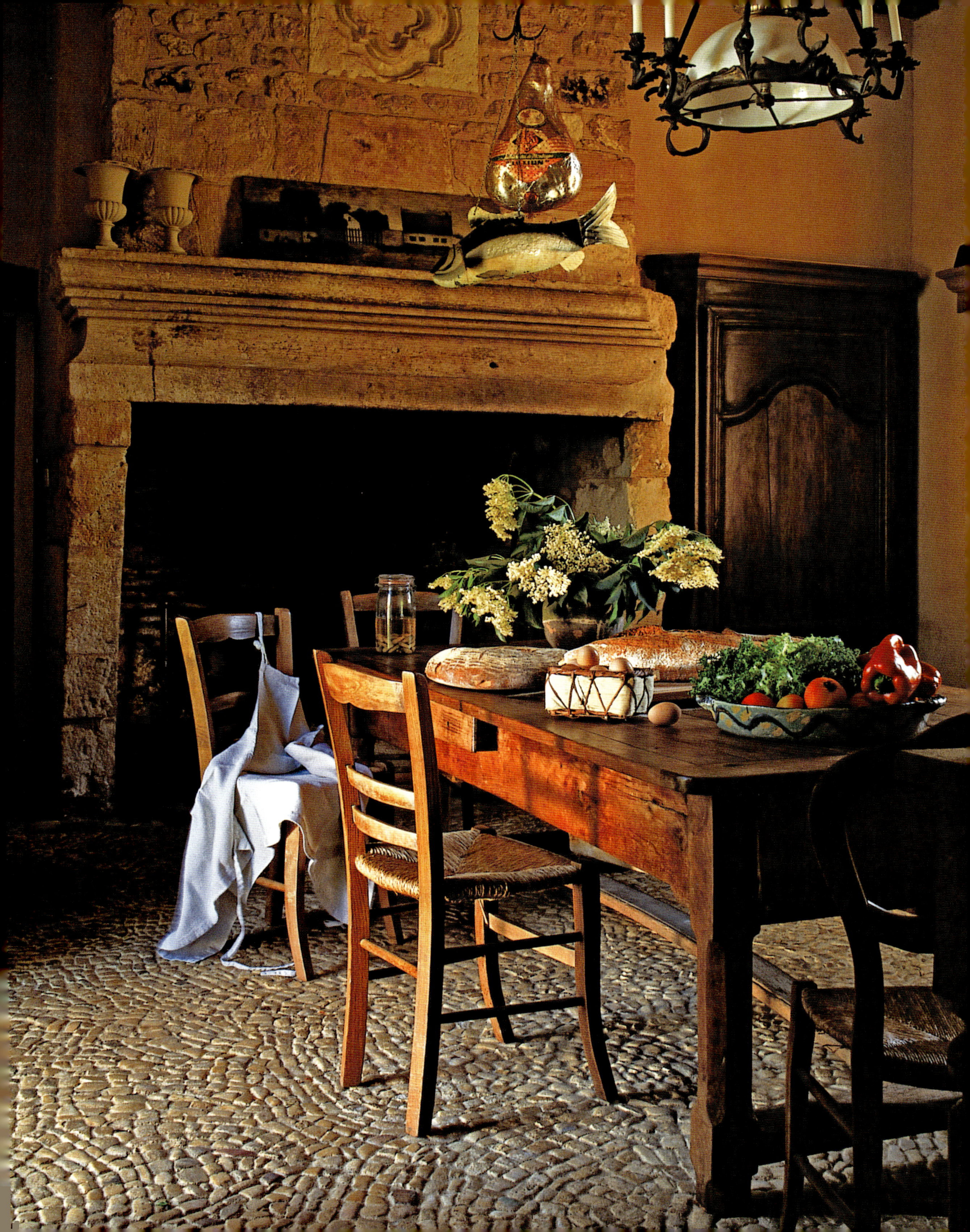

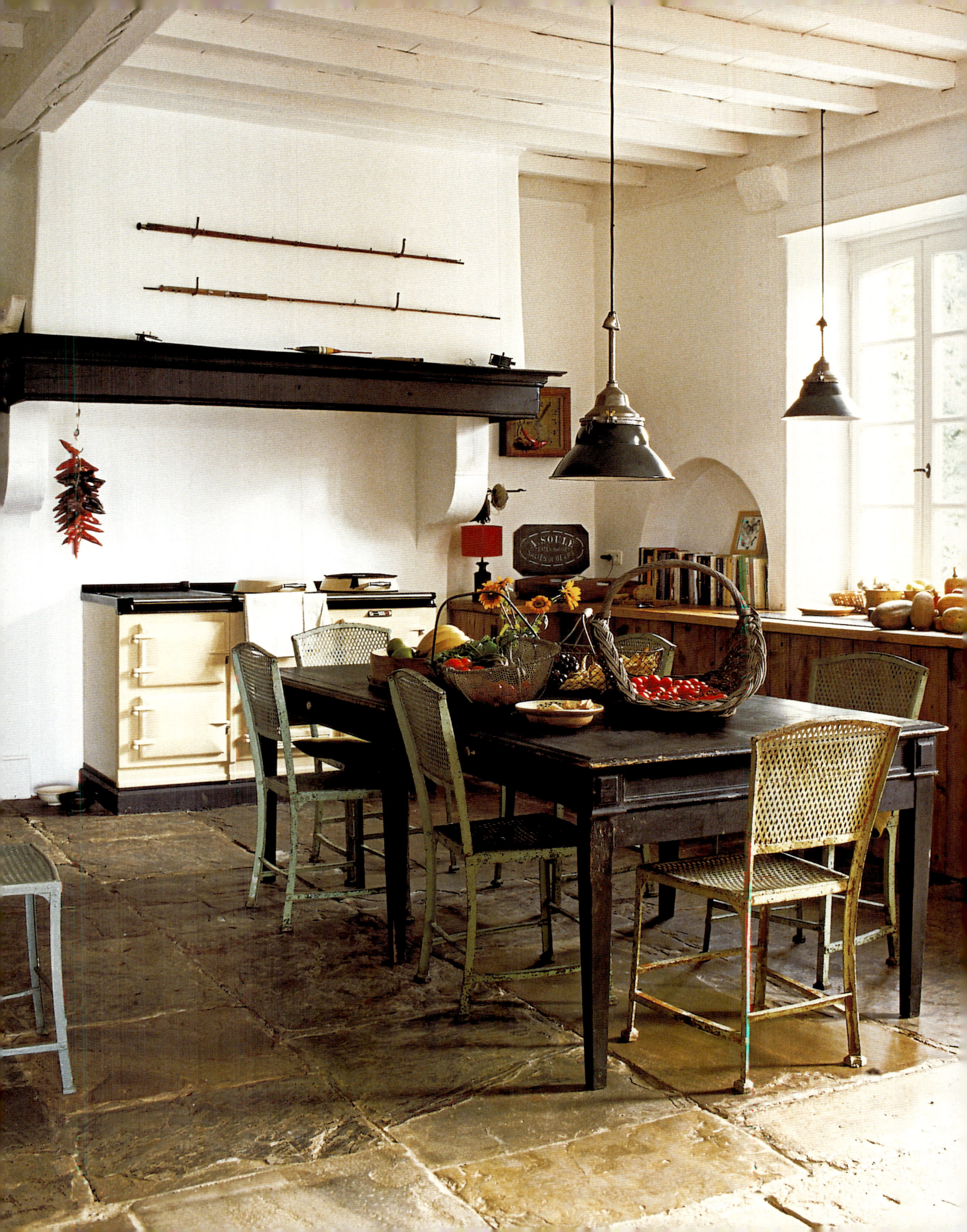
A. SOULE

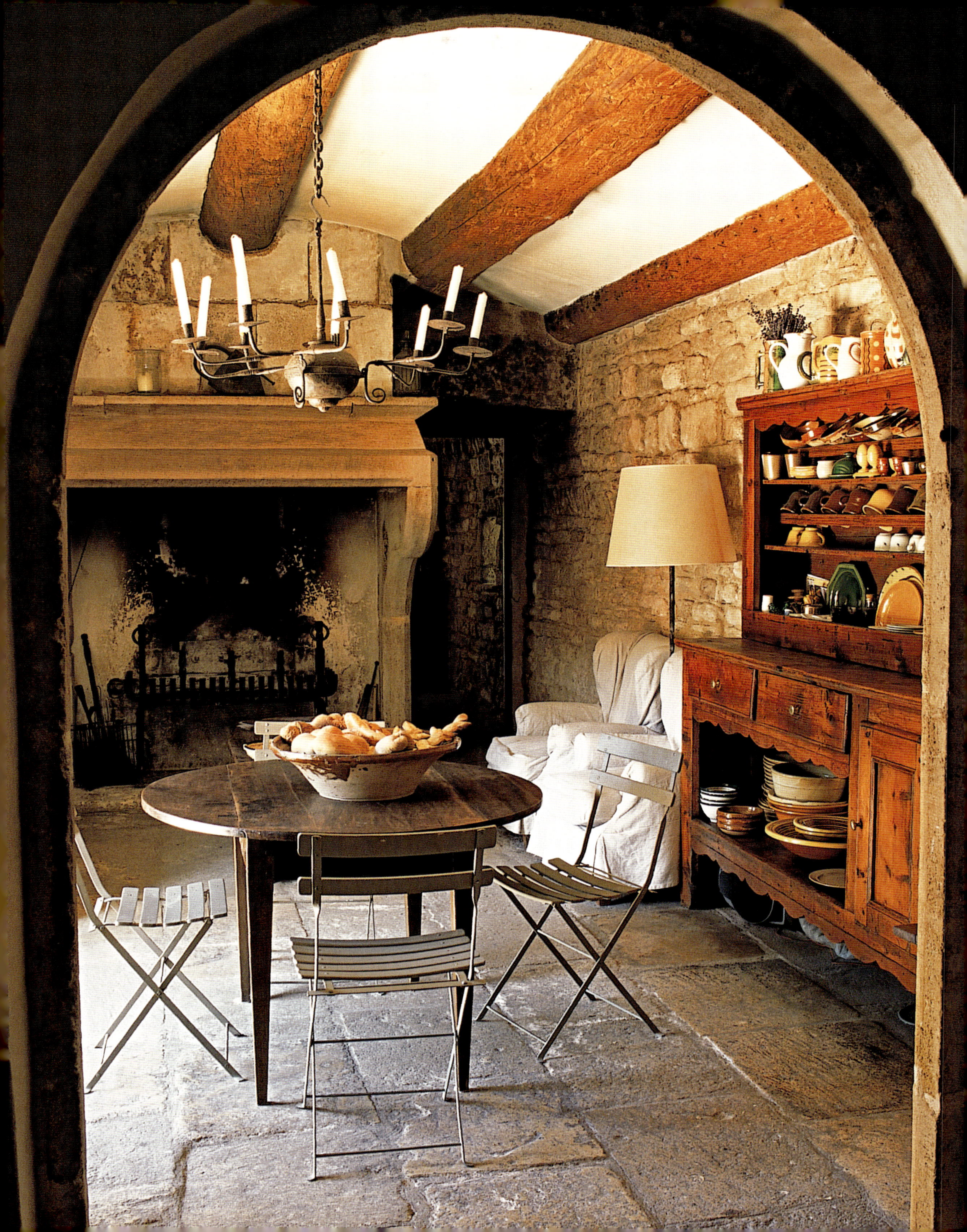

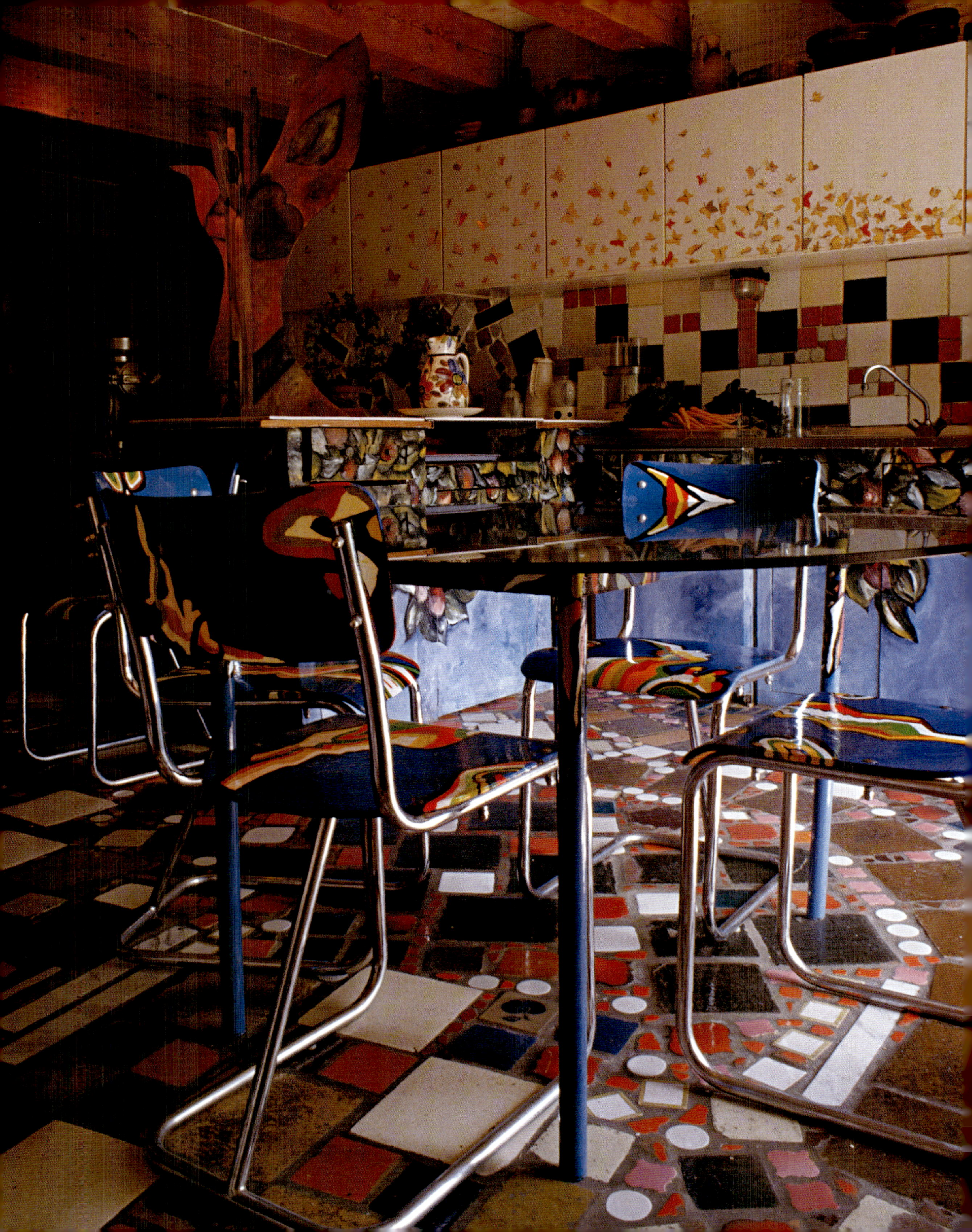

床 と 壁

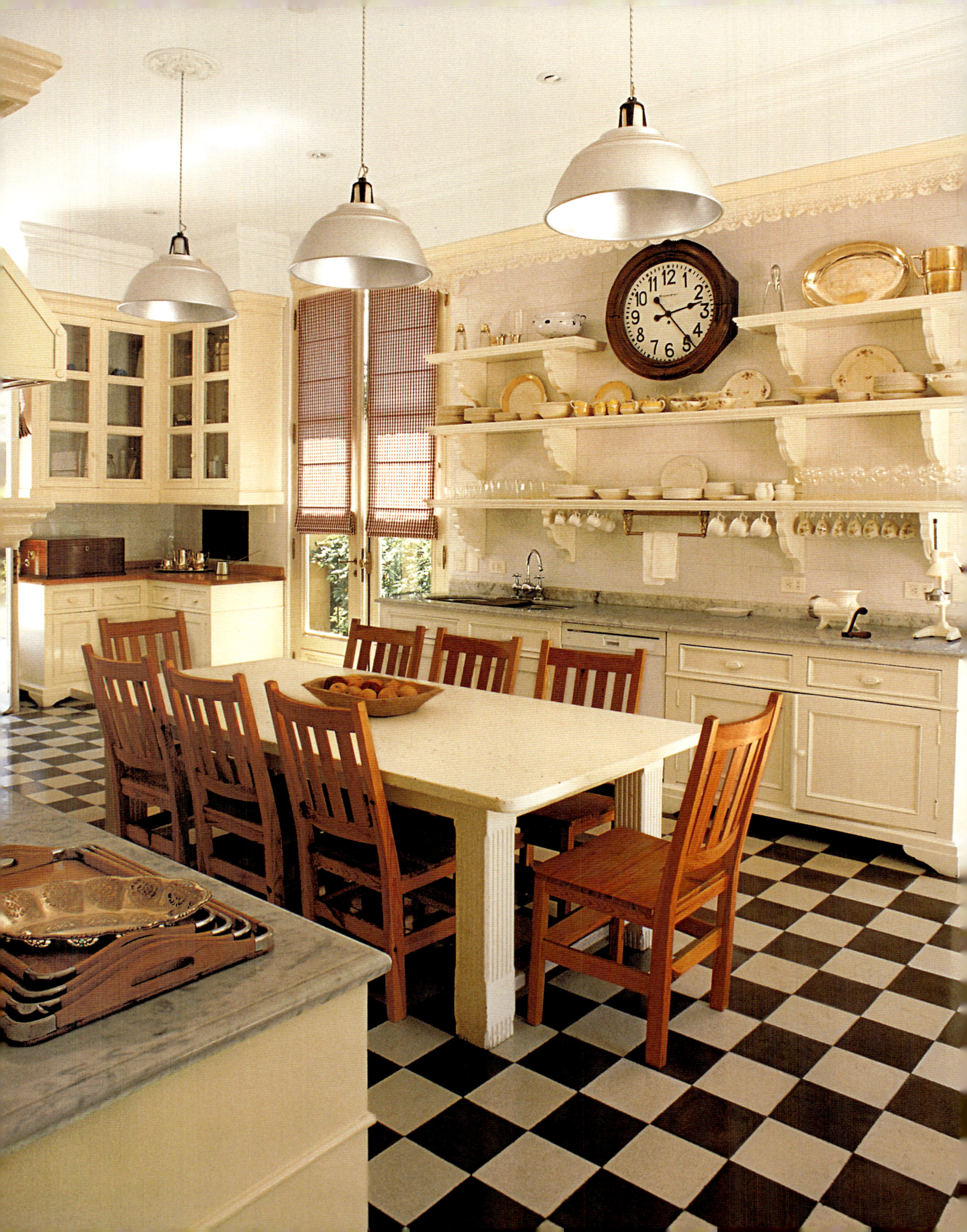

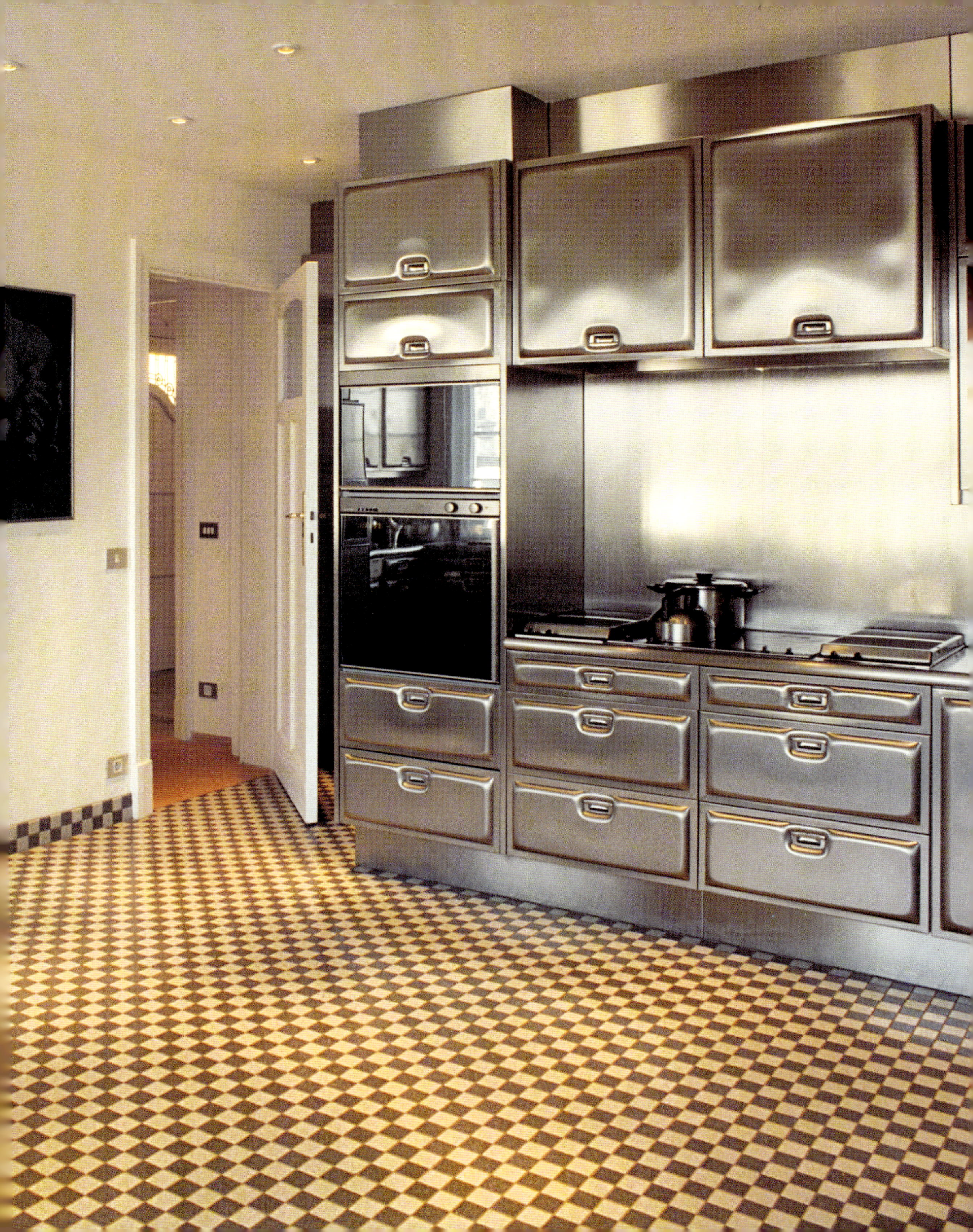

床と壁

床 と 壁

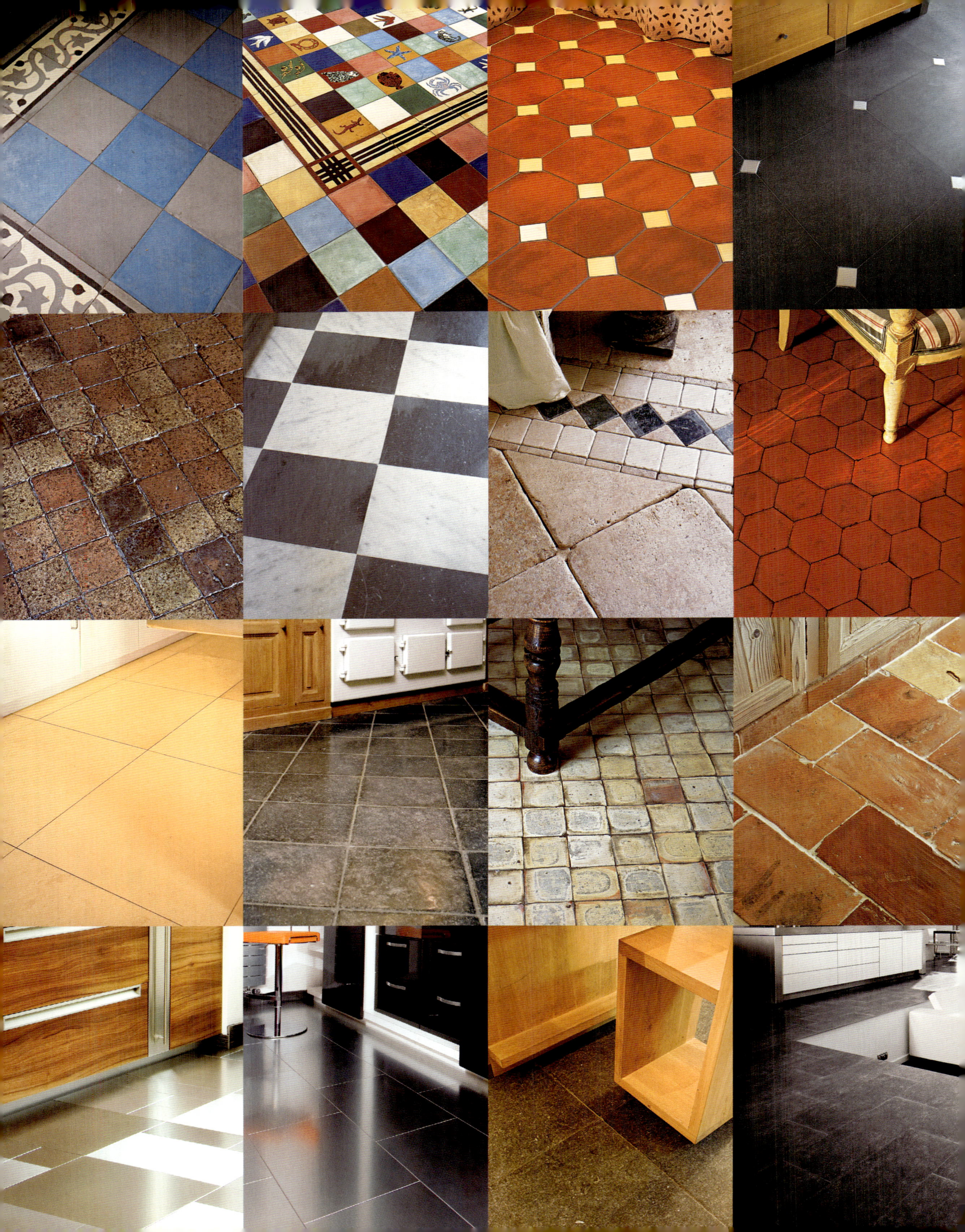

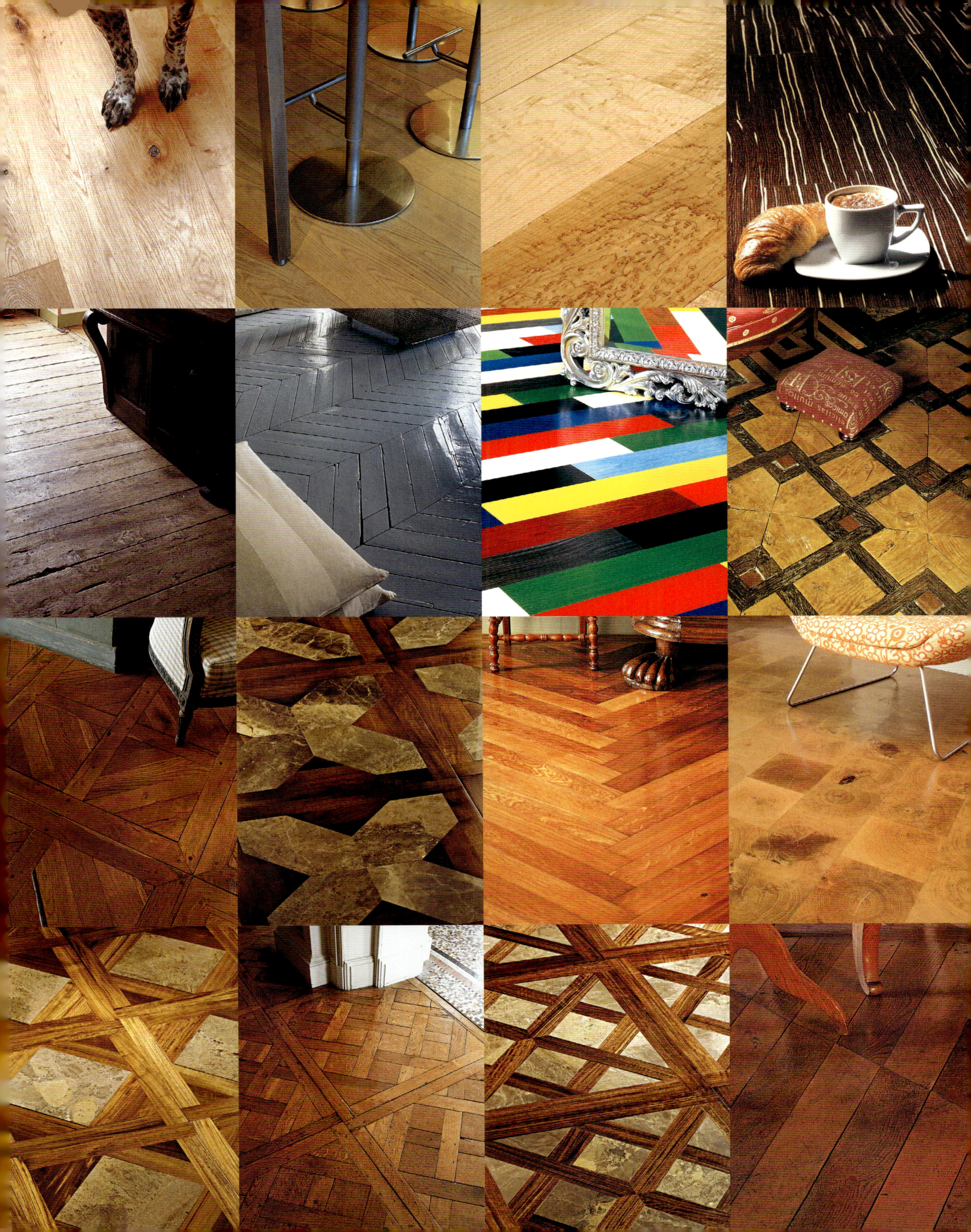

色と素材感

Texture and Colour

ムードのある照明、ピカピカに光った鍋、コポコポと音を立てるコーヒーメーカー、スムーズに閉まる引き出しの次に、感覚を刺激するキッチンの要素といえば、色と素材感です——少なくとも、この2つは、そうなり得る要素です。金属製冷蔵庫やワークトップの、鏡のように光る表面、無垢のチークやオーク材の外観や手触り、陶器タイルの光沢に、目を向けてみましょう。ここから始まるのです。ワークトップのメーカーは、様々な複合材を製造しています。御影石から、ガラス、コンクリート、ステンレス、そしてココナツの外皮や、貝殻から作った素材もあります。人造大理石なら、どのようなサイズ、形、色にも加工することができ、継ぎ目もありません。また、強光沢、または、つやなしのラッカー仕上げなら、7層塗り重ねるため、光沢に深みがあります。また、合板なら種類も多いうえ、熱帯雨林を材料にしないので、環境破壊につながりません。地元の職人さんに頼んで、自分だけの収納家具を作ってもらうのもいいでしょう。キッチンの色はとても大切です。ワークトップ選びは、新しい食器を選ぶのと同じです。まず、その場所で、食品がどのように見えるか、考えなければなりません。素材感に関してもっとも革新的なのは、最近手に入るようになった、3次元素材でしょう。壁や天井に向くこの素材は、どんな壁面でも、立体感のある幾何学模様にし、砂丘のように波立たせてくれます。フォーチュニー社のファブリックのようにセクシーでもあります。この3次元素材を、MDFボードに張り込んで金属箔で覆えば、時代の最先端のイメージや、アートの世界、ファッションショーの張り出し舞台を、そのままキッチンの中心に持ち込むことができます。

After the moody lighting, gleaming pans, gurgling coffee maker and smoothly closing drawers, the next really sensual aspects of the kitchen are colour and texture – or at least they can be. Consider the semi-reflective finish of metal fridges or worktops, the look and touch of natural teak or oak; the gloss of ceramic tiles. This is just the beginning. Manufacturers of worktops are producing dozens of man-made composite surfaces – from granite to glass, concrete to stainless steel, and even some made out of coconut husks and seashells. A number, like corian, can be seamlessly moulded into any size, shape or colour, while others, like high gloss or matt lacquer, have the deep sheen of seven coats. There are also lots of sustainable wood veneers to choose from, without destroying any rainforests in the process, or you could commission a local craftsman or cabinet maker to create something uniquely for you. Colour in the kitchen is not forgotten, but choosing a work surface is like choosing new china – you need to think first about how food will look on it. Perhaps most remarkable of all are the three-dimensional textures now available. Suitable for walls or ceilings, they transform any surface into a folding geometric or rippling cascade as sinuous as a sand dune or as slinky as a Fortuny fabric. Etched into MDF board and coated with a foil membrane, they bring the computer age, art world and fashion catwalk right into the heart of the kitchen.

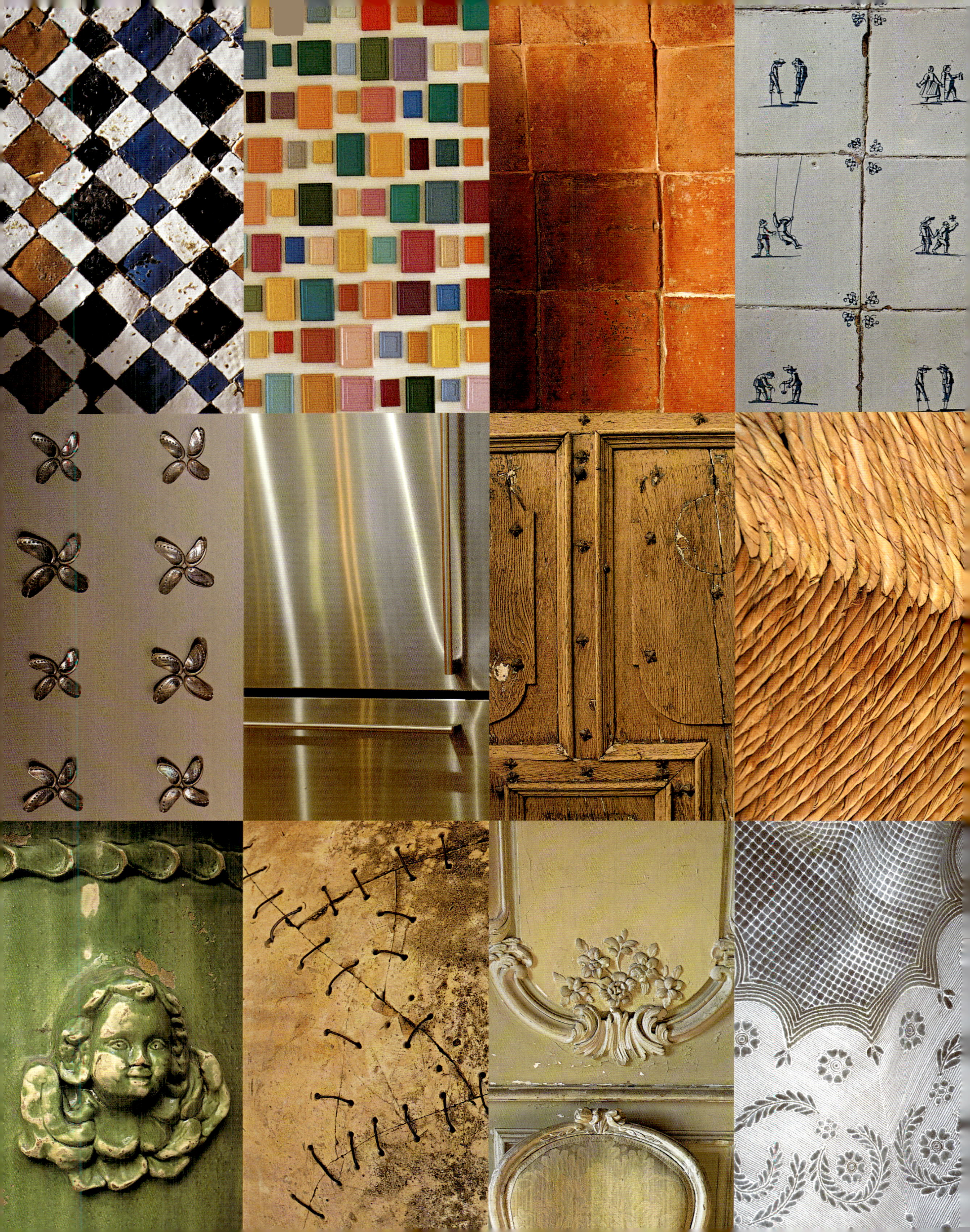

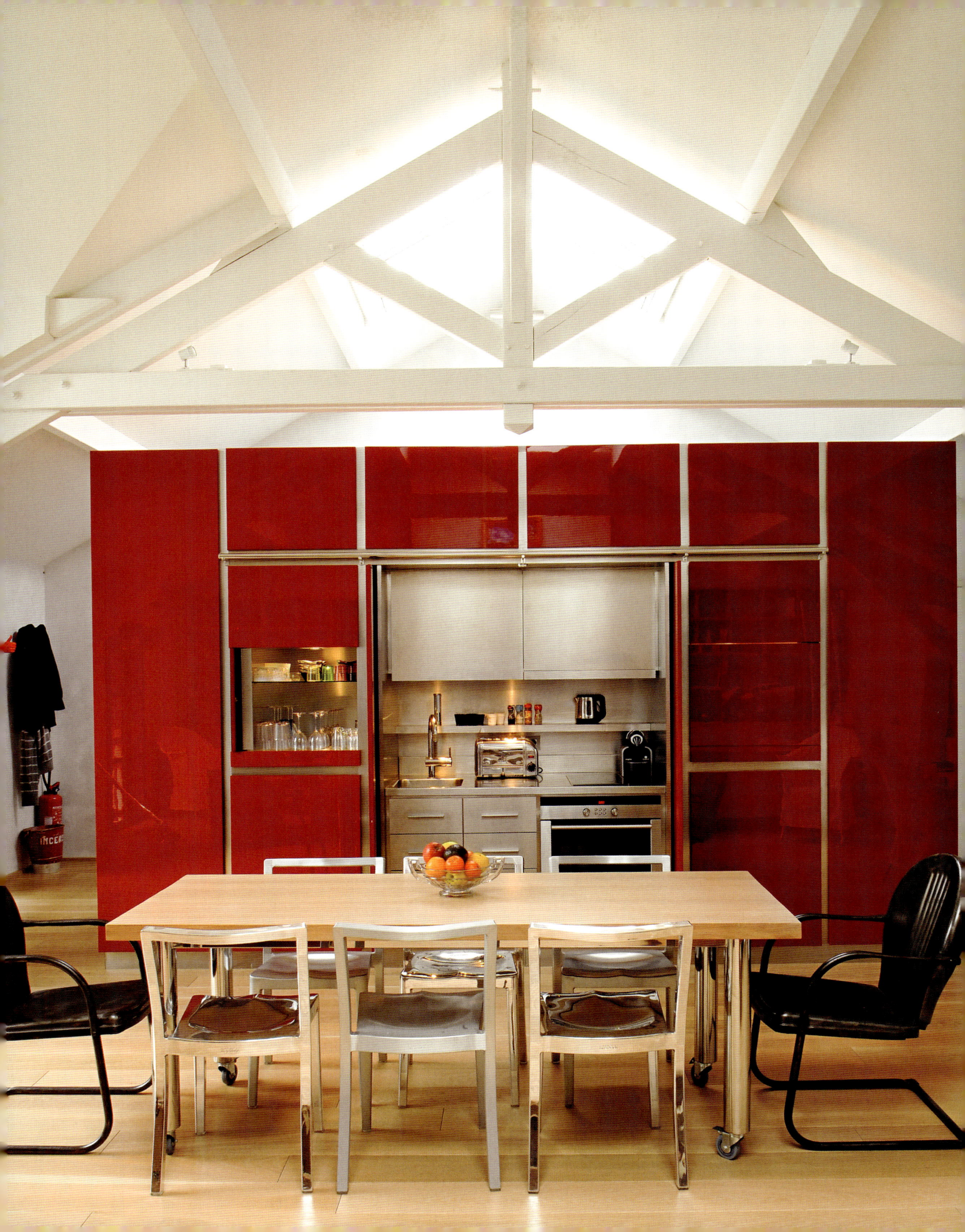

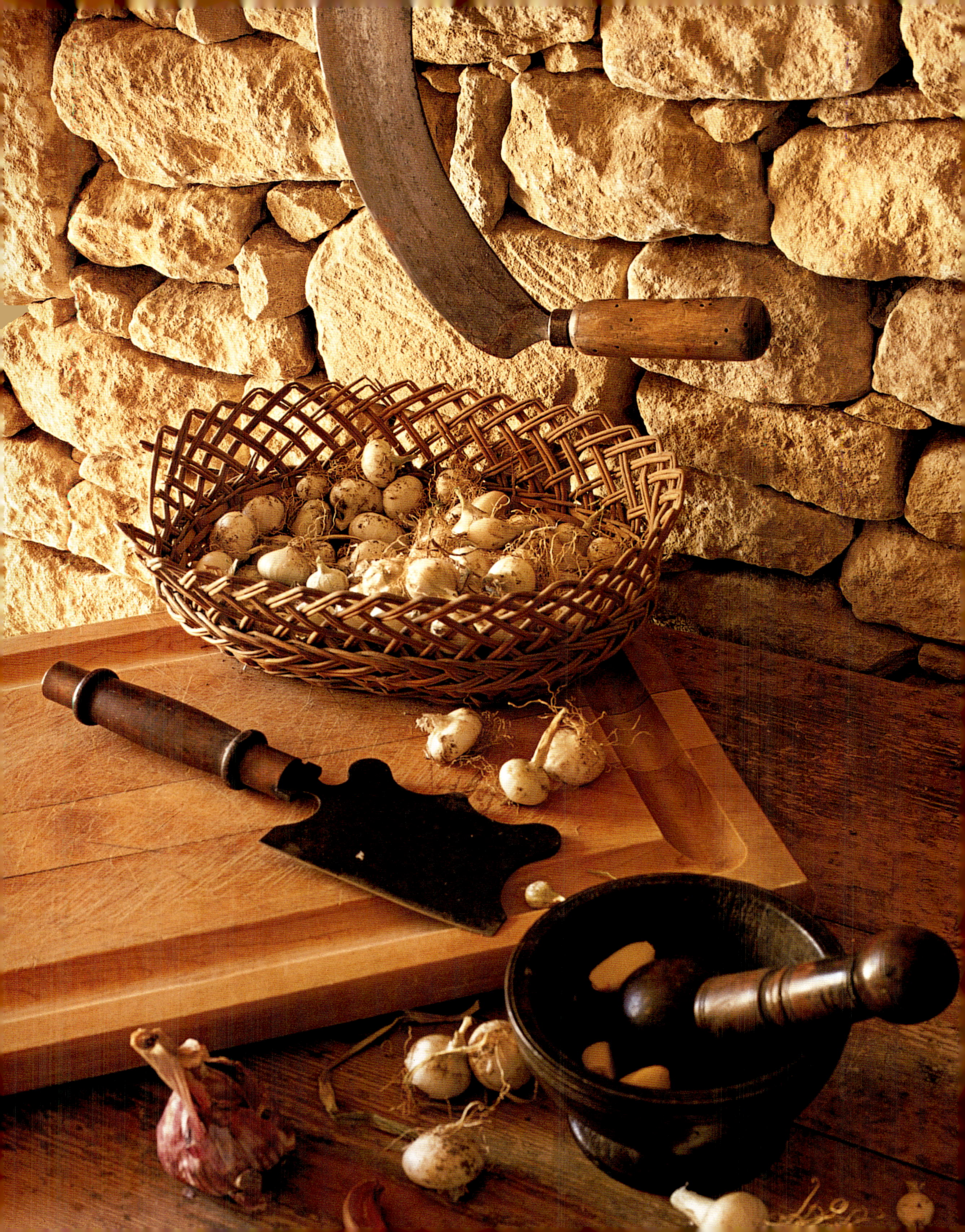

色と素材感

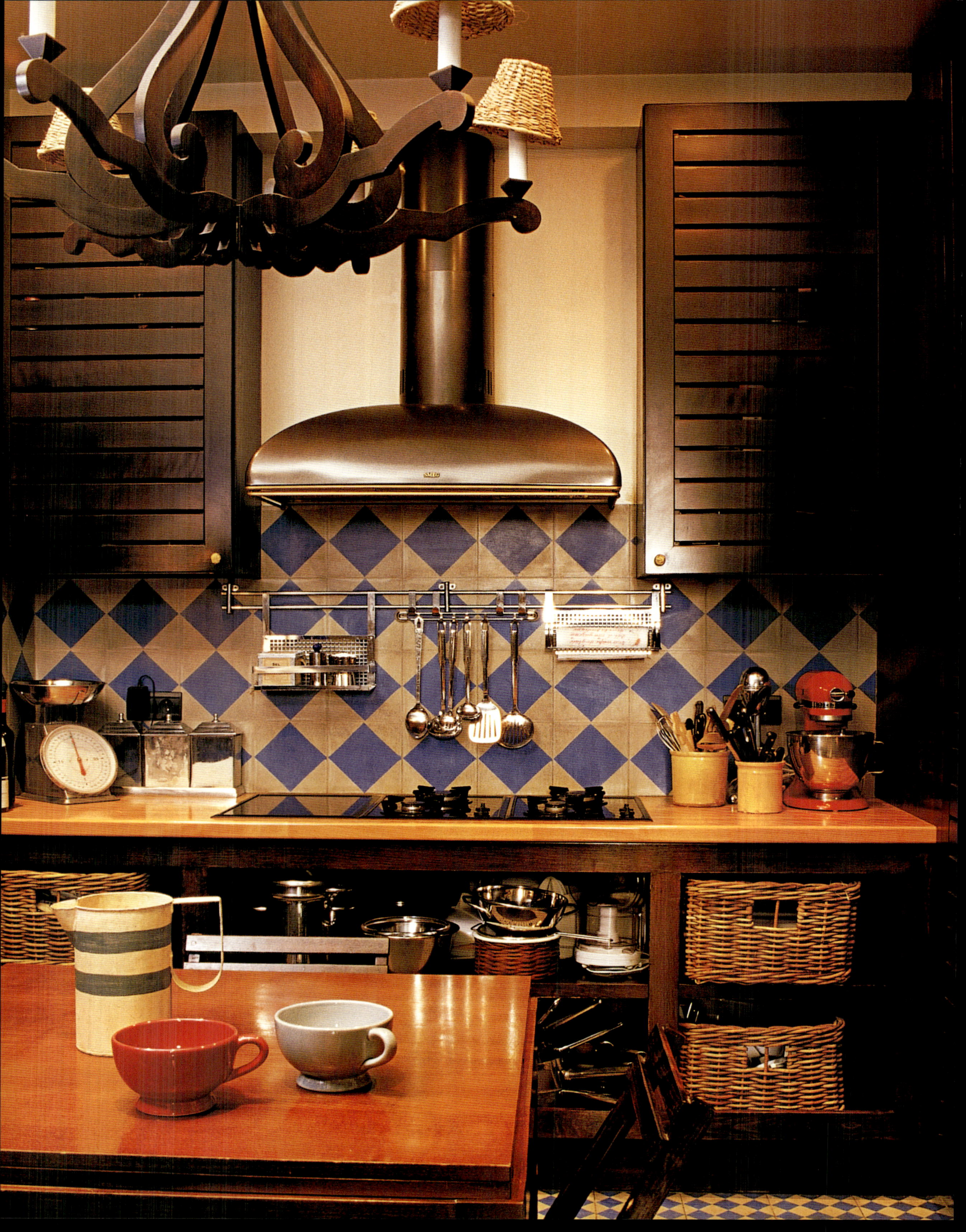
SMEG

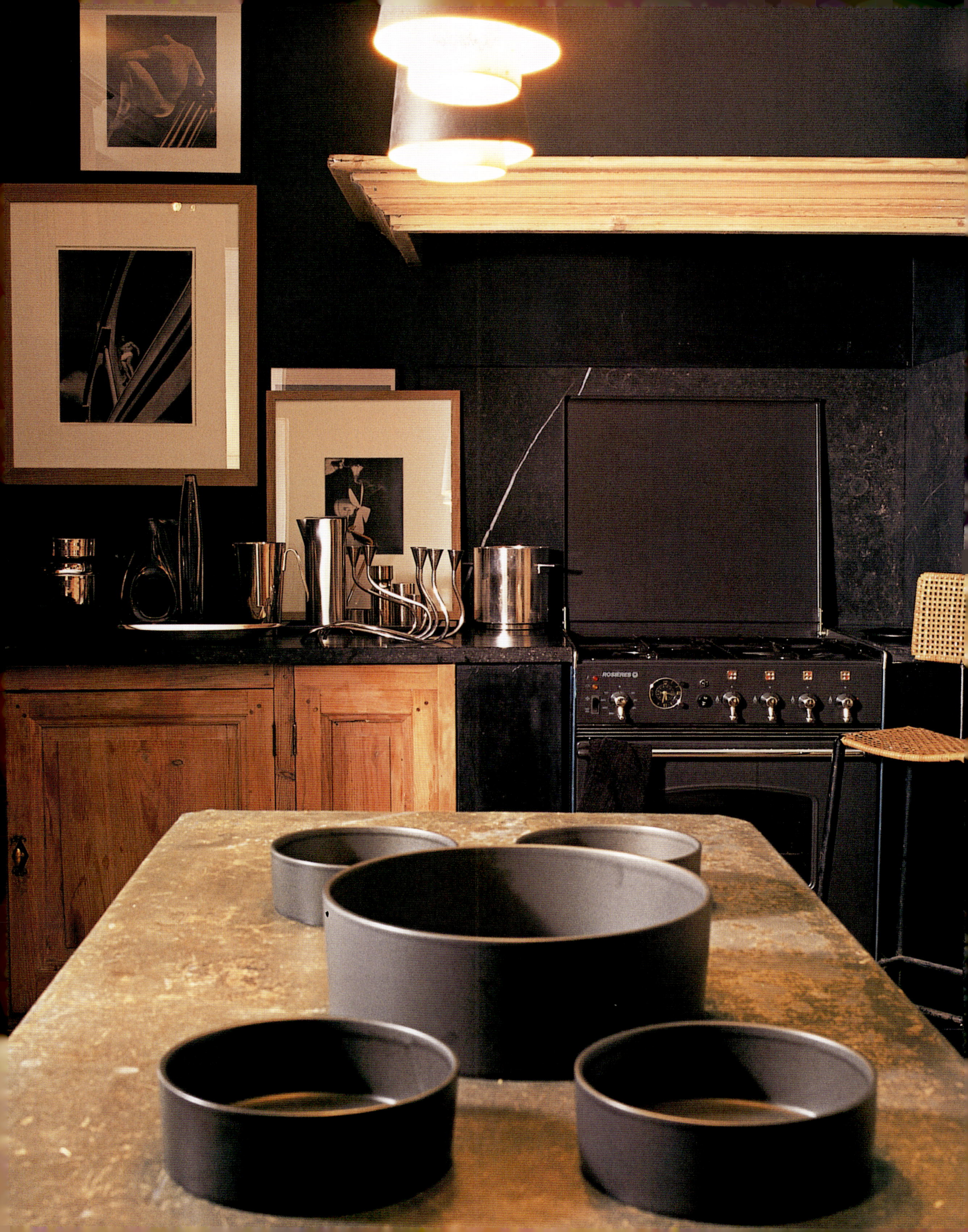
ROSIERES

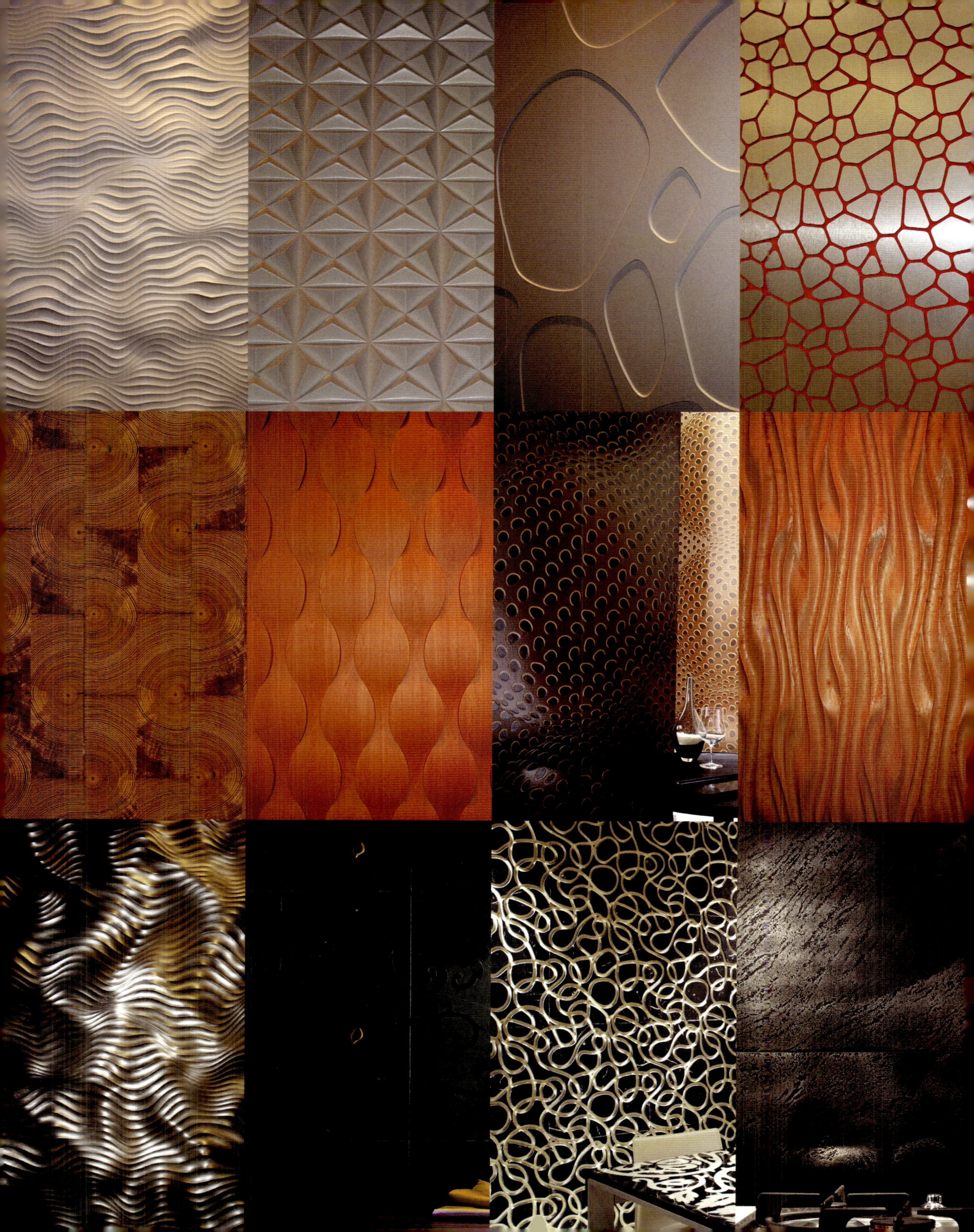

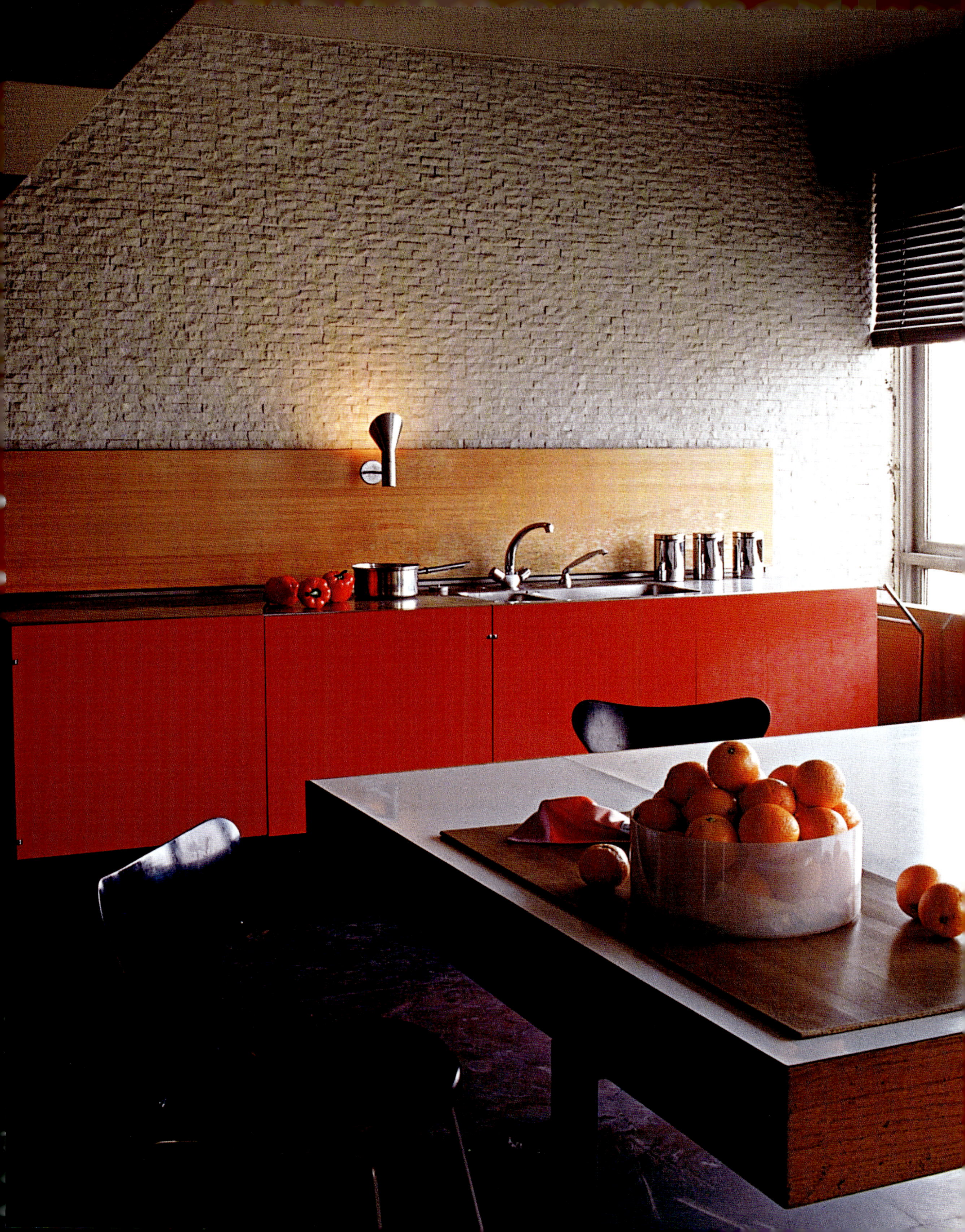

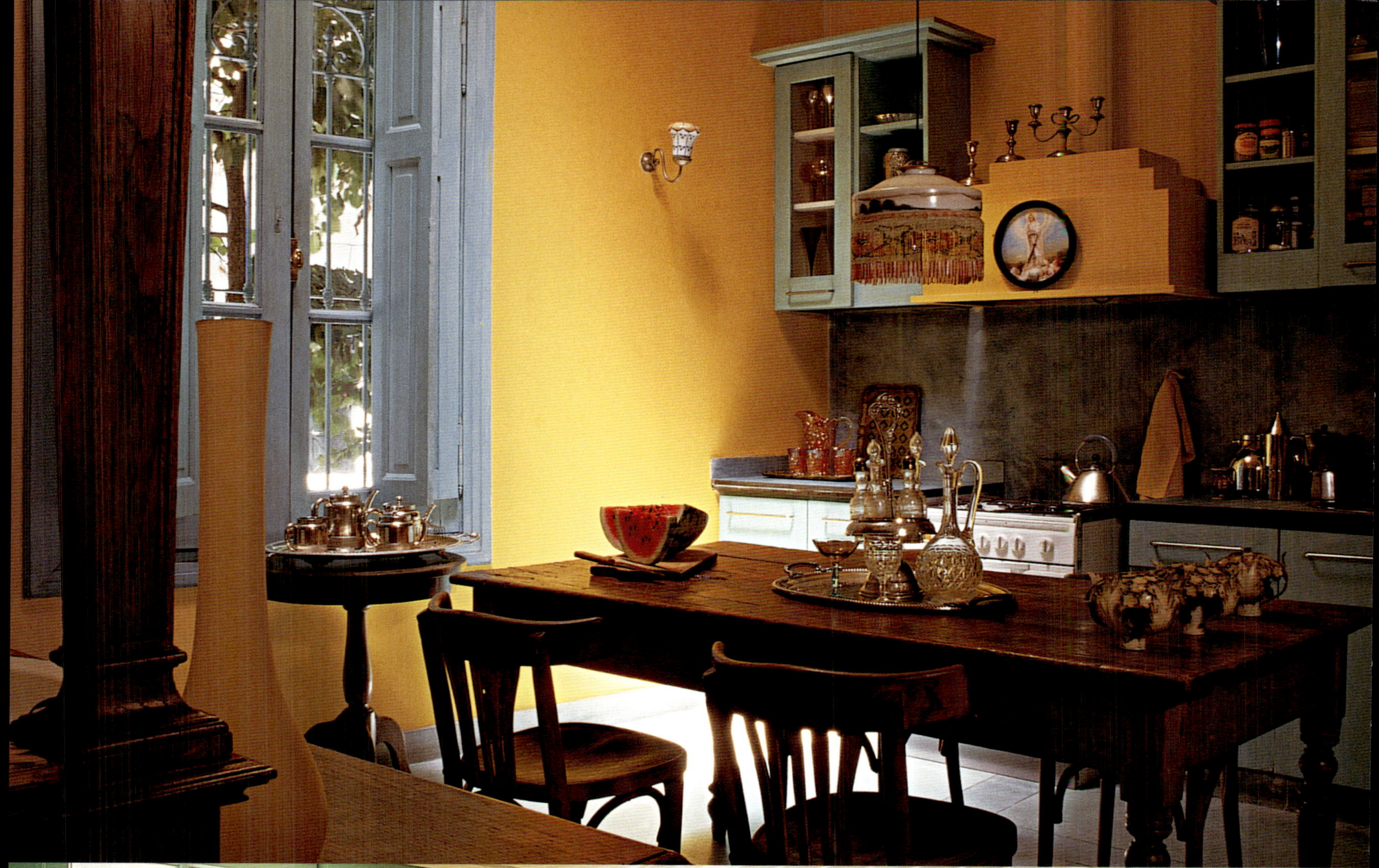
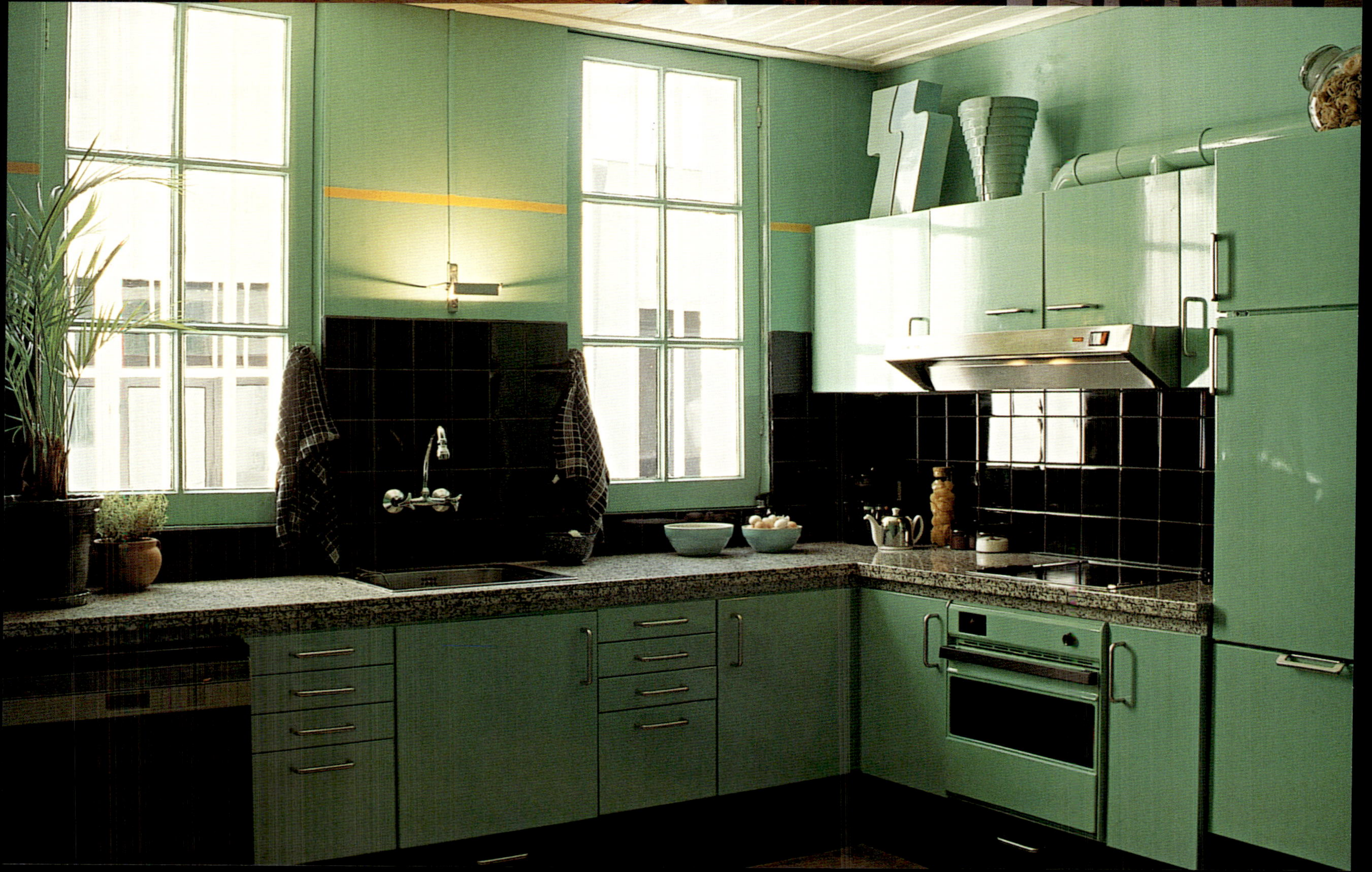

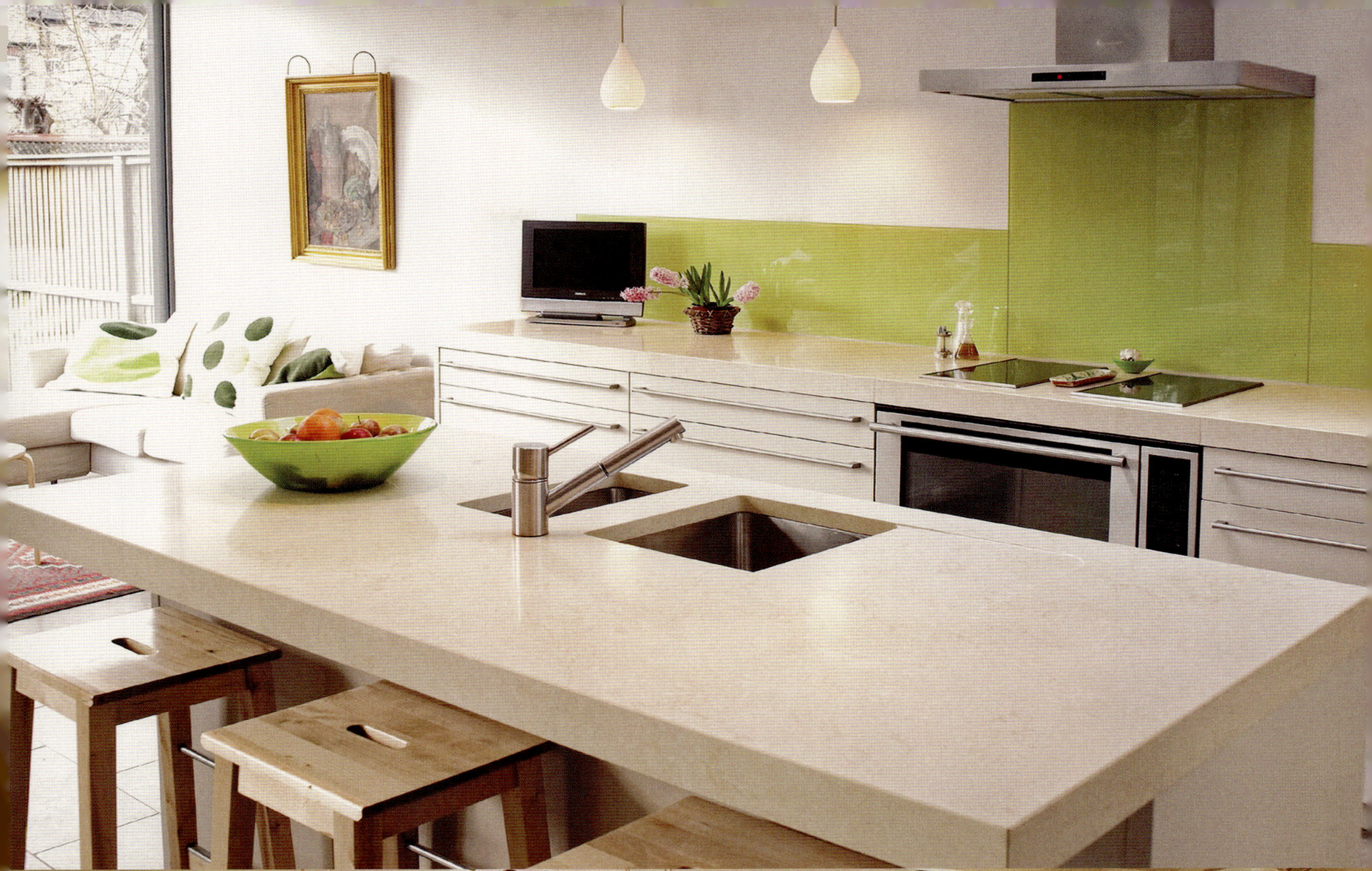

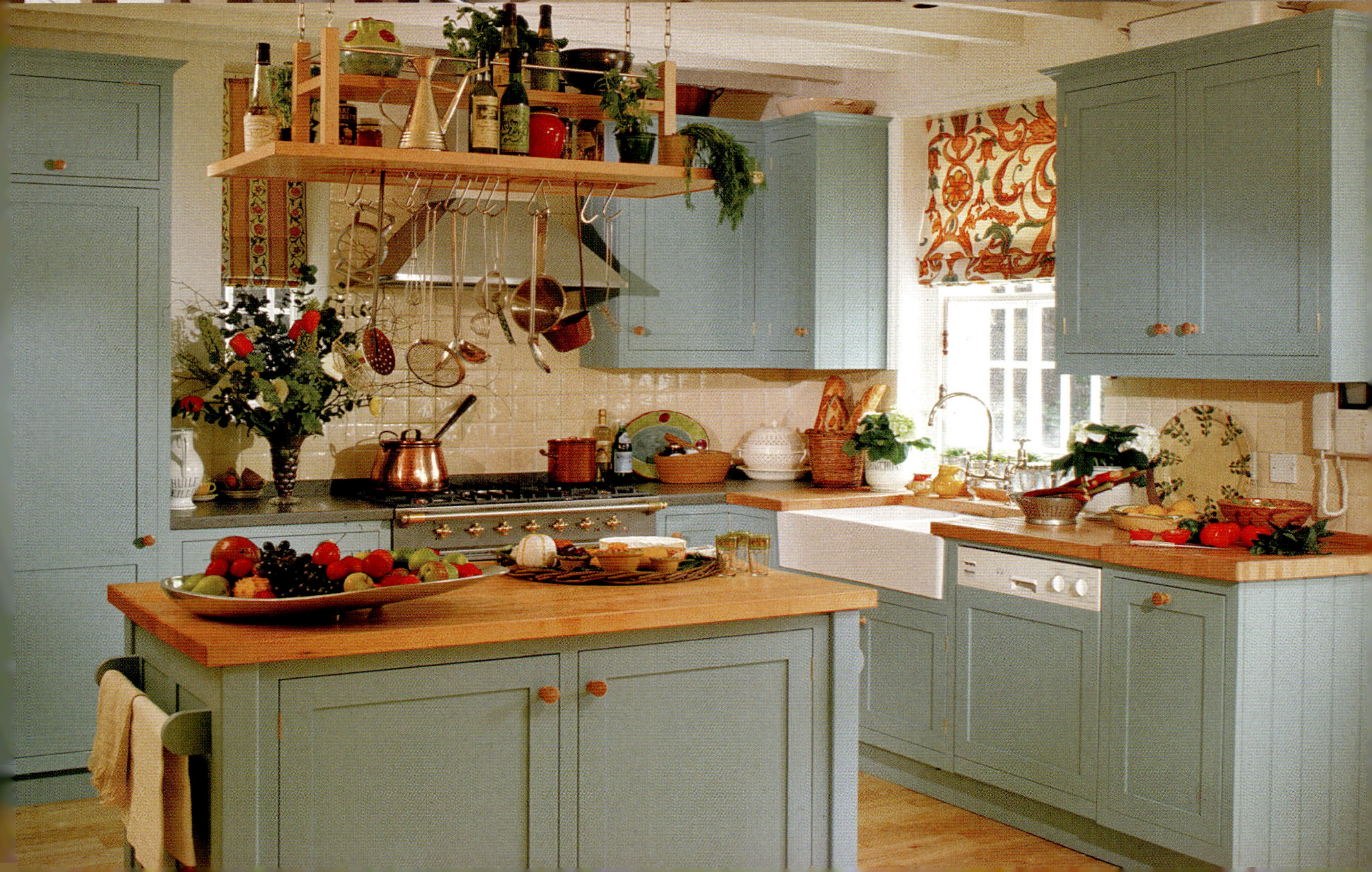

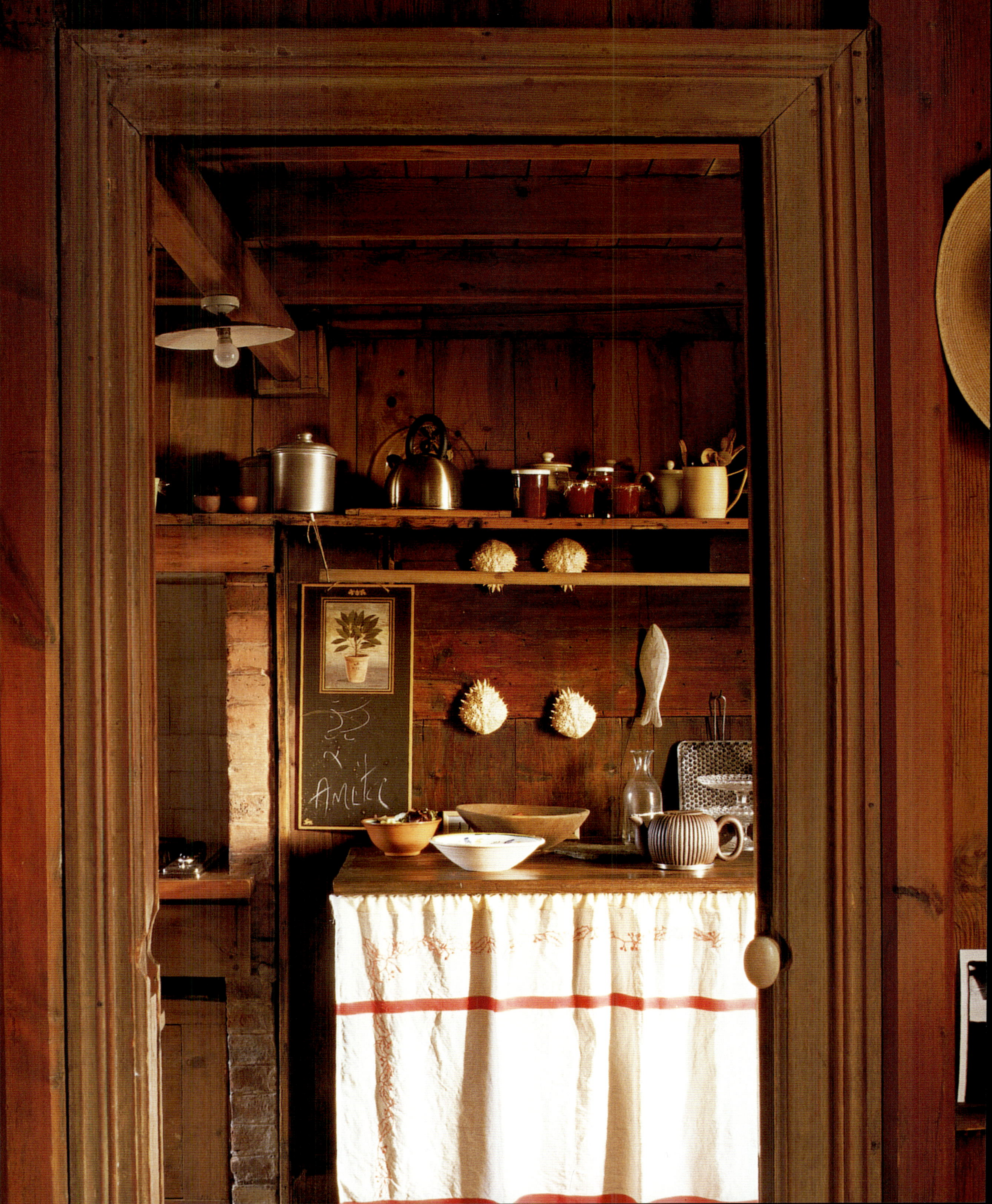

色と素材感

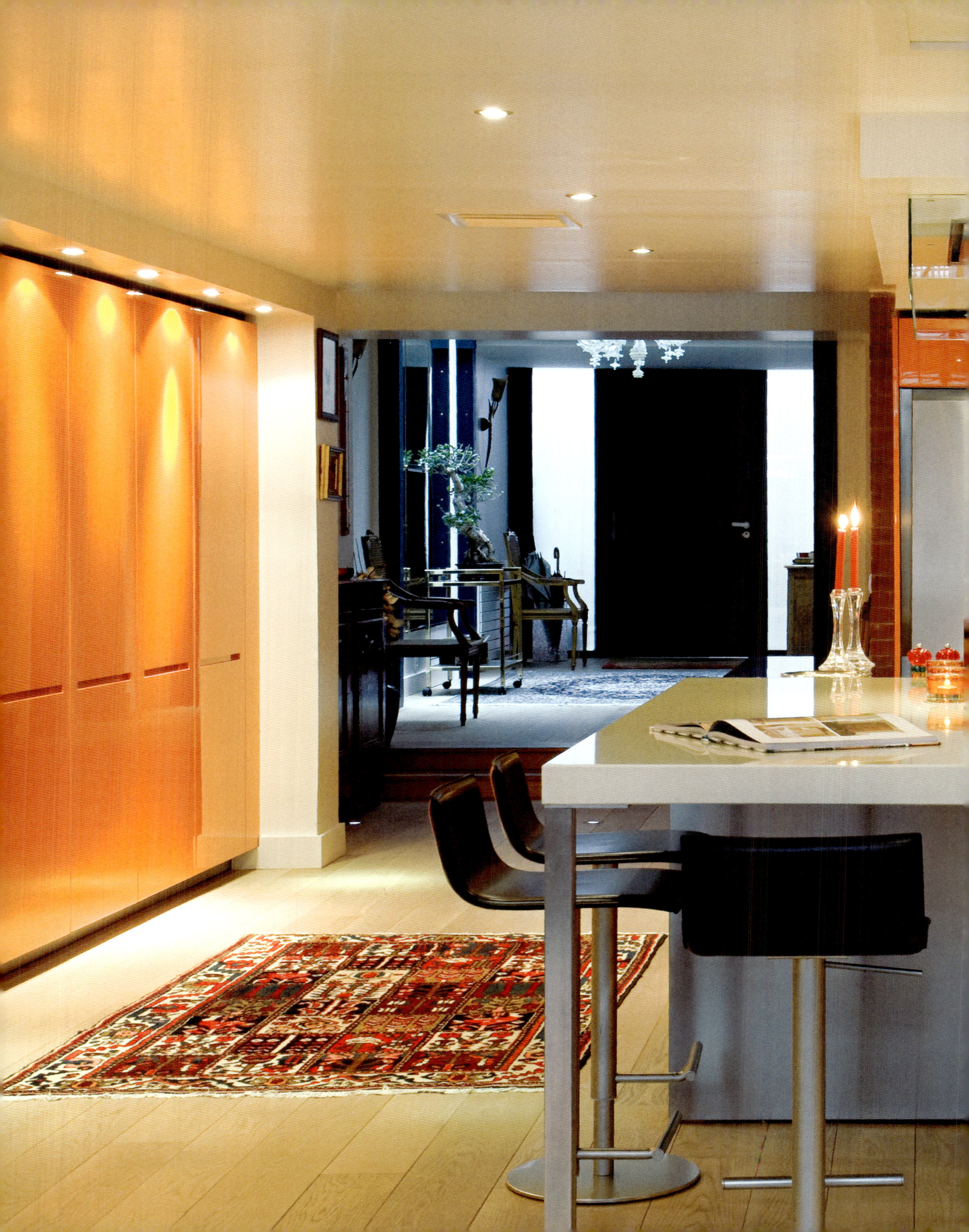

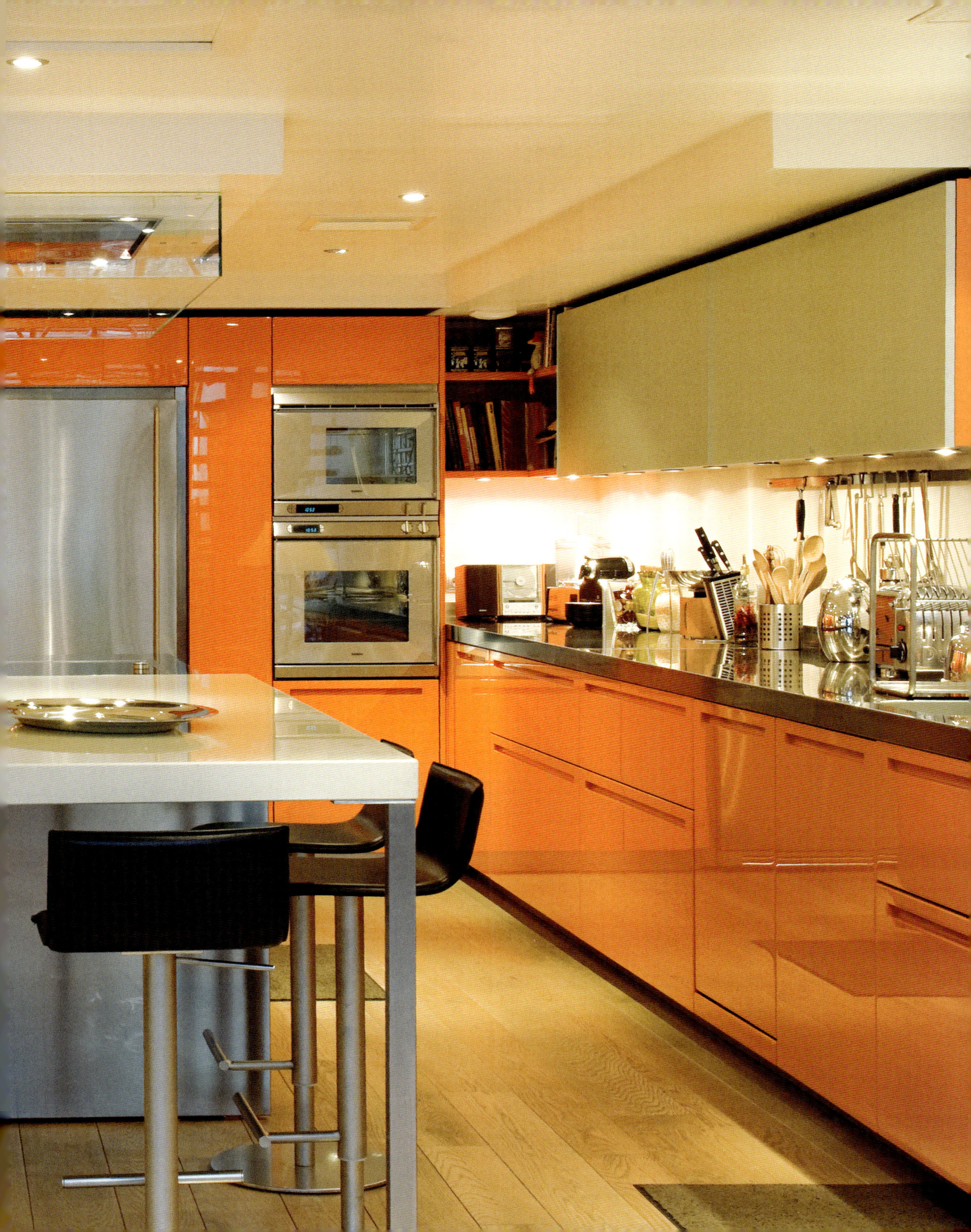

調理設備

Fully Equipped

もし、キッチンのショールームに最近足を運んでいないのなら、キッチン設備の進化を知って、仰天するかもしれません。もちろん今でも、ガス台やシンクはありますが、その技術水準の高さは、以前と比べものになりません。ガスや電気オーブンと同様に、今では、スチームオーブンというものがあります。そして、オーブンの棚に、チキンやターキーを入れてボタンを押せば、自動的に重さを量って、正確な調理時間を計算してくれます。IH調理器のガラストップの色は、ブラックとホワイトから選べます。表面に触れても、熱くありません。それは、鍋のような金属だけに熱を伝える仕組みになっているからです。また、「鉄板焼き」は、調理台にセットされた平らな金属プレートで、その上で混ぜながら、炒めることができます。今日のキッチンでは、コーヒーメーカーですら、キッチンの一部として組み込まれています。シャンデリアに隠されている換気装置もあります。また、水栓のノズルにも様々な工夫が凝らしてあり、吐水口に小さなLEDが組み込まれている商品まであります。1つの水栓でよく冷えた水を飲み、もう1つの水栓で、100度の熱湯を出すことも、即座にできます。引き出しには、どんな物でも収納できます。温かいお皿や、食器洗い機や、冷凍庫も組み込めるのです。引き出し用の引き出しすらあり、たいがい、心地よく、ゆっくりと閉まる仕組みになっています。最後に、あるキッチンメーカーのマーケティング戦略によれば、冷蔵庫は、もはや姿を消しつつある存在だとか。温度調整機能のついた、最新鋭の「鮮度保存庫」に取って代わりつつあるそうです。

If you haven't been to visit a kitchen showroom recently, you might be surprised to discover that some amazing things have been happening. Of course, they still sell cookers, hobs and sinks, but the technology has changed. As well as gas or electric, you can now get steam ovens, and even ovens with shelves which – when you put in your chicken or turkey and press 'roast', 'bake' or 'broil' – automatically weigh the bird and calculate the correct cooking time. Available in black or white glass, flush-mounted induction hobs feel cool to the touch and only transfer heat to metal objects like cooking pans, whilst a teppanyaki is a heated flat metal plate set into the work surface, on which you can stir- or pan-fry. Everything in today's kitchen, even the coffee machine, can come fully-integrated. Extractors can be found concealed in various designs of chandelier, while taps are available with all sorts of flexible nozzles, including one that hides a tiny LED light inside the spout. You can, if you wish, have ice-cold filtered drinking water in one tap, and instant 100°C boiling water in another. Drawers are available for everything, including warming plates, dishwashers and freezers. You can even have drawers within drawers, most with sensual, soft-closing mechanisms. Finally, according to one manufacturer's marketing ploy – fridges have now 'disappeared' and have been replaced by state-of-the-art climate-controlled 'freshness centres'!

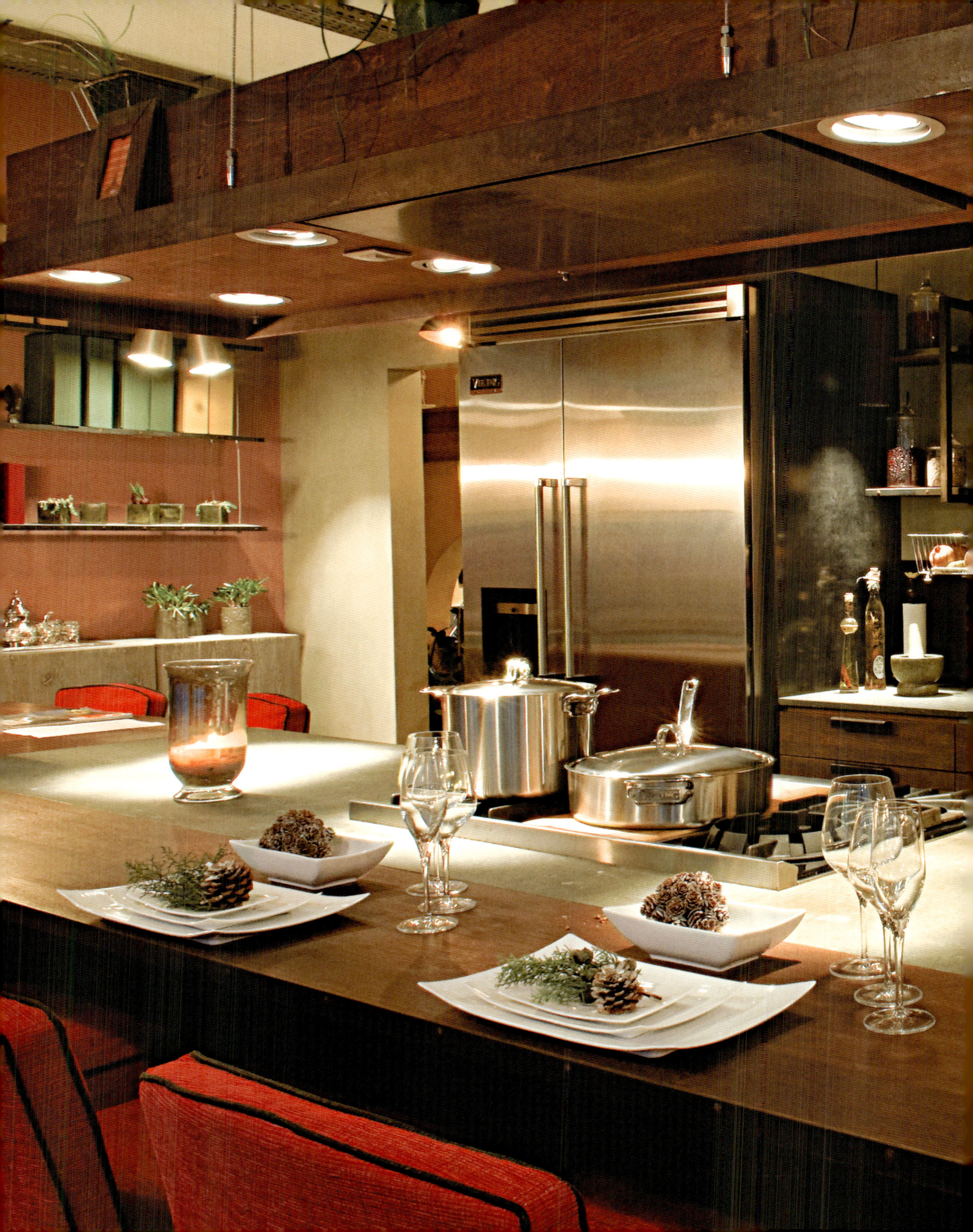

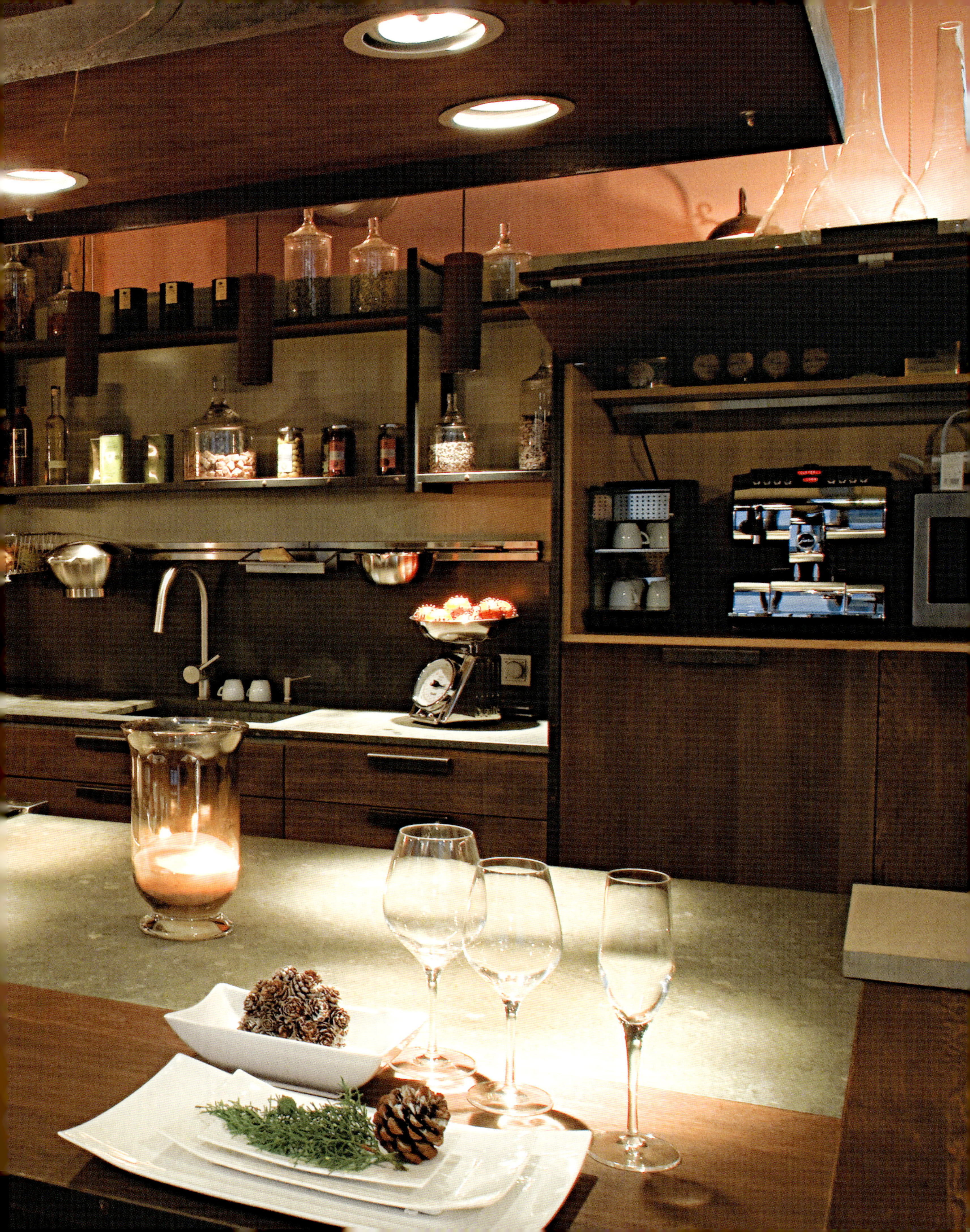

調 理 設 備

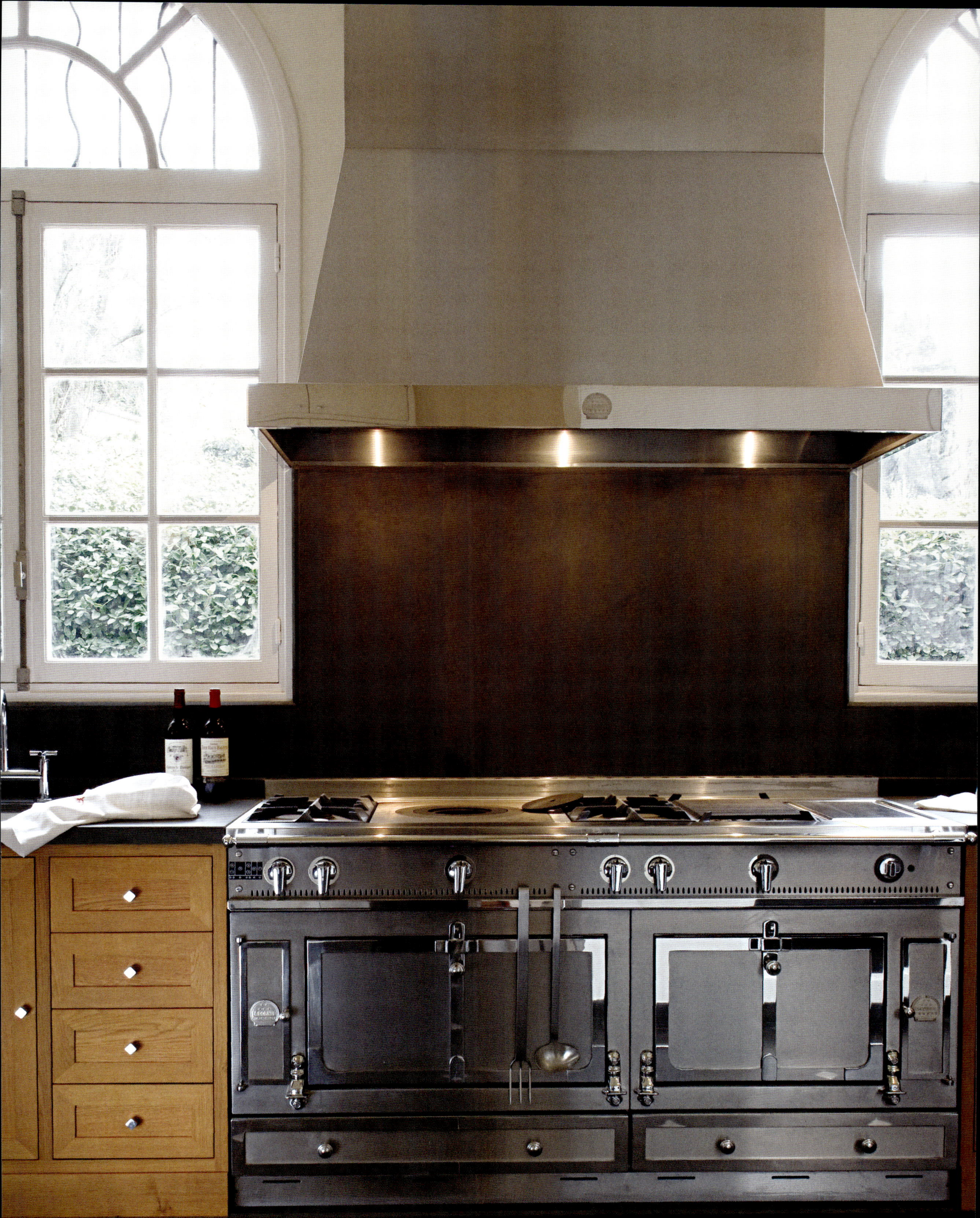

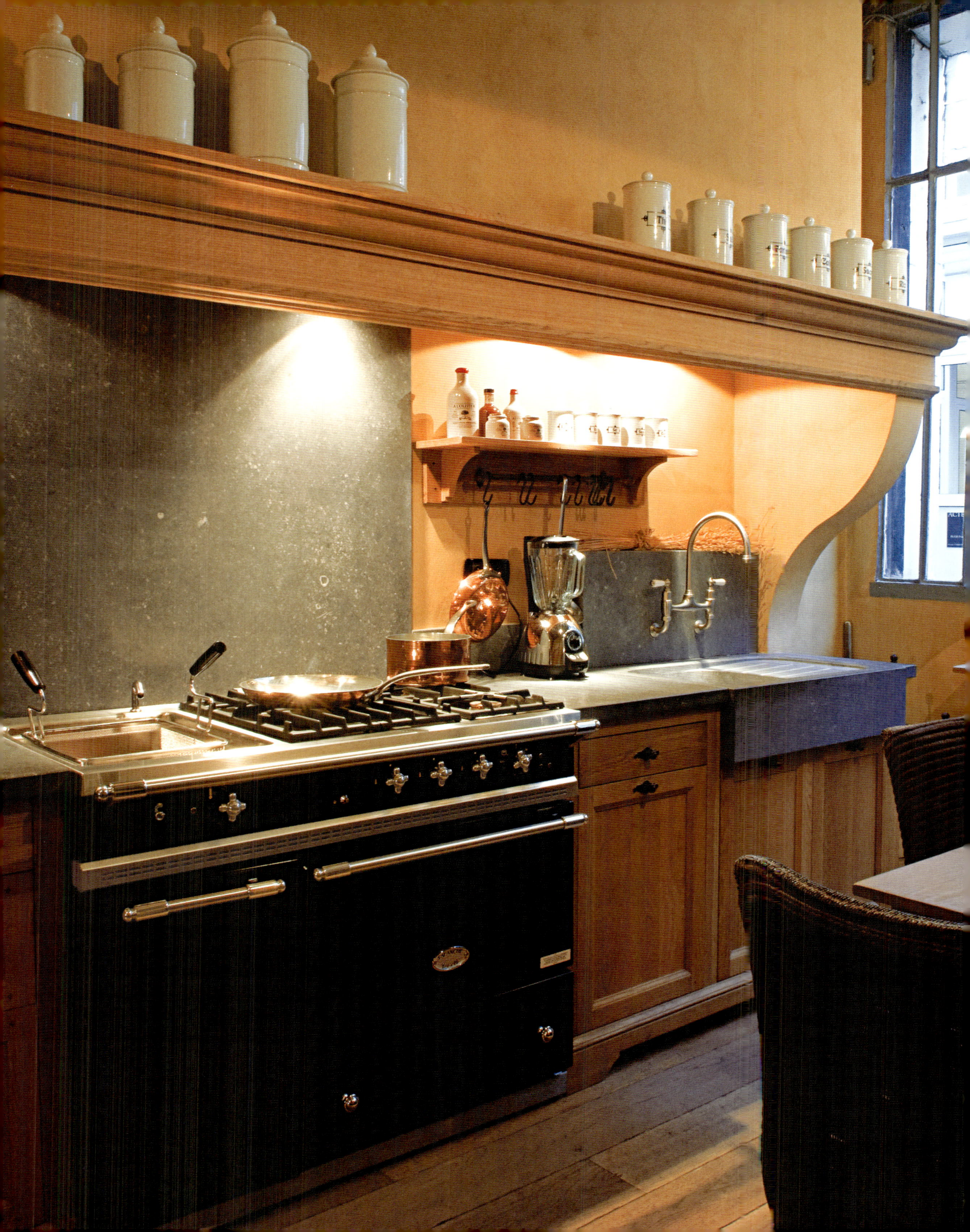

調 理 設 備

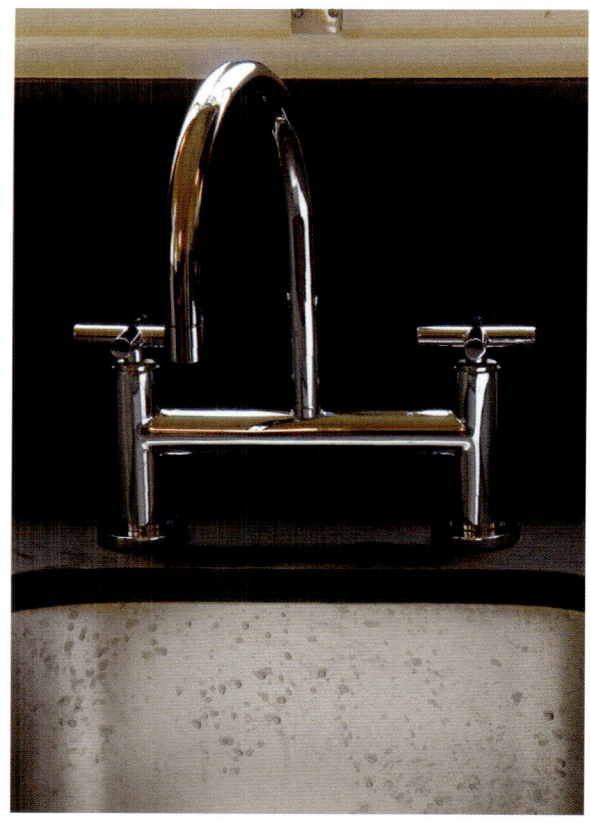

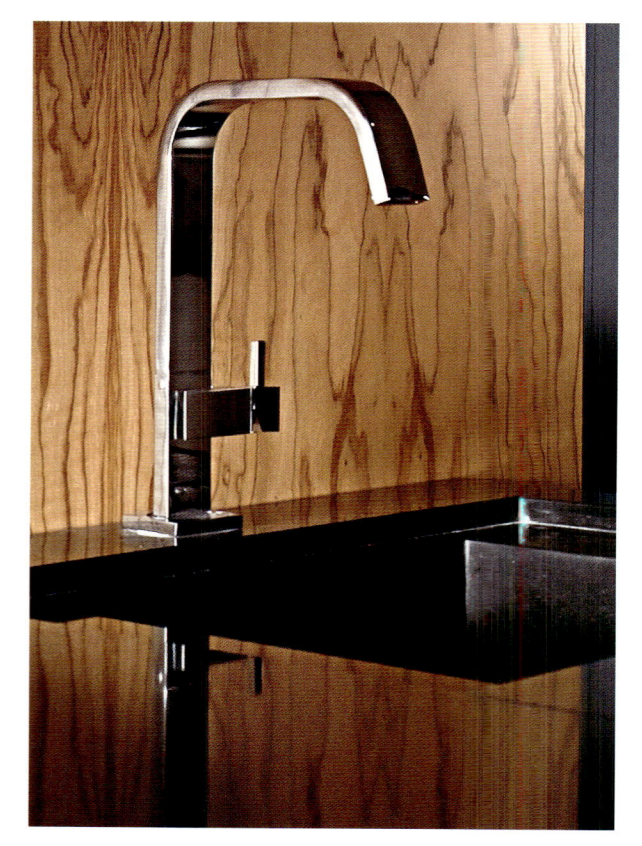

調 理 設 備

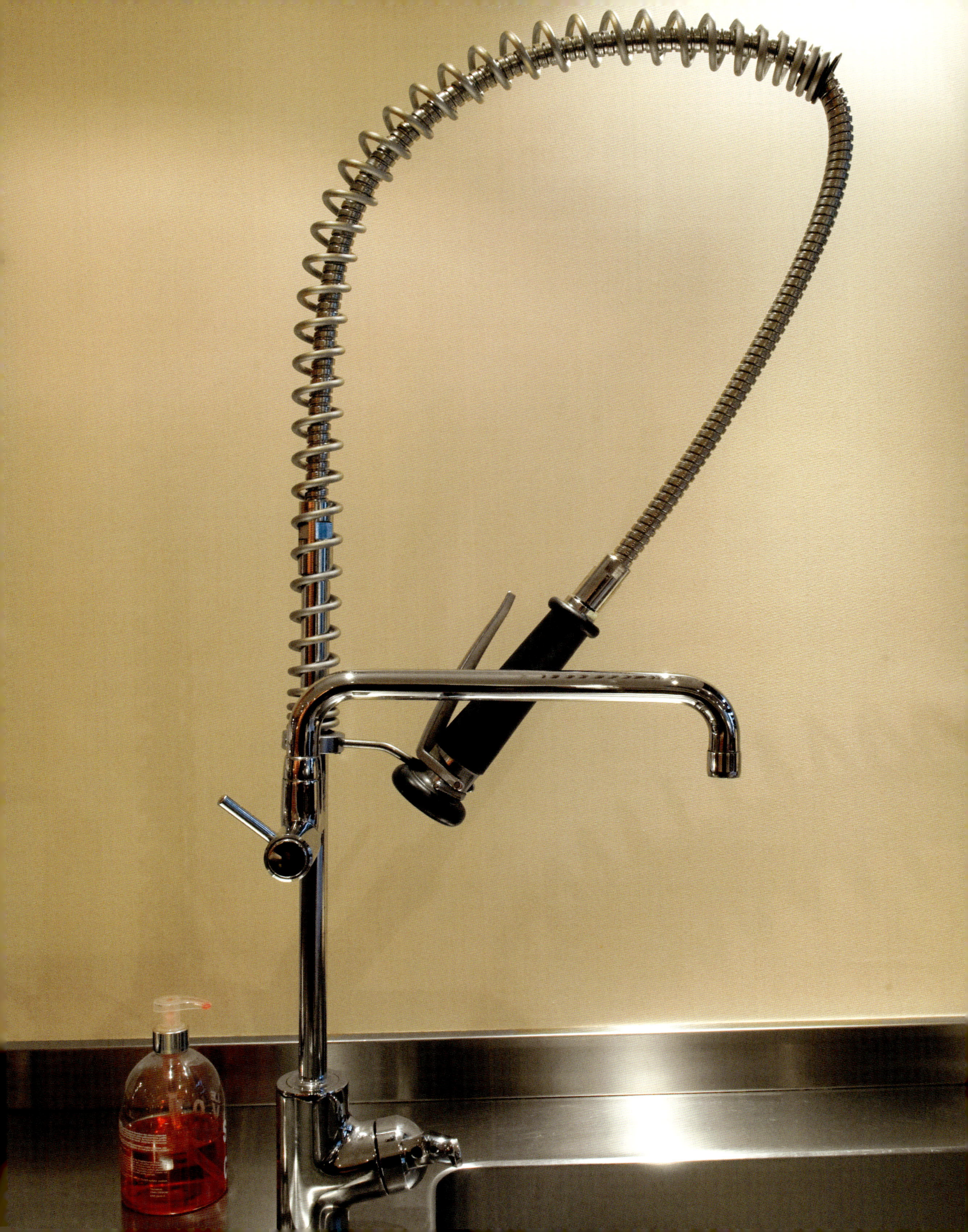

個性的な演出

Quirks and Details

この最終章で紹介しているキッチンの装飾や、収納アイデアは、一見悪ふざけに見えるかもしれませんし、確かに、そう思われても仕方ないかもしれません。鳥かご、剝製の動物、郷愁を誘うポスター、額に入れた版画や絵——物をまとめて置いたり、並べたり、集めたりしています。この本の他の章のページに散りばめられている物たちが、種類別にまとめてあります。しかし、キッチンを個性的に演出し、住む人の独自性を見せてくれるのが、こういった物たちなのです。初めて部屋に入ってきた時に、視線を引き付け、物語を感じさせ、情熱や、歴史や愛を表現してくれます。調理器具や、キッチンの小道具も、目を楽しませる装飾になります——とりわけ、アンティークの陶器、装飾的なホーローの器、モダンなデザインの調理器具類は、見映えがよいものです。キッチンは、調理や食事だけでなく、家族にとって、仕事や遊びの場にもなります。ですから、子どもたちの絵や、コラージュ、厚紙で作った建物、スポーツ大会のメダルや、休日に集めた宝物だって、絵はがきや写真同様に、キッチンに飾っても、おかしくありません。最近では、実用的でありながらも、こまごまとしていて、一癖ある物たちが、キッチンであまり目に触れなくなっています。こういった物をしまう専用のスペースを、キャビネットの中に作るようになったからです。ナイフやフォーク専用の引き出し、パンの保管庫、ハーブやスパイス入れ、野菜専用の収納庫、皿用のラック、鍋用の引き出し、分別用のごみ箱などがセットされています。最先端のキッチンでは、カウンターのドアの下は、なめらかに開閉する引き出しになっているものがほとんどです。身をかがめて、カウンターの奥の暗がりで物を探した経験は、過去のできごとになってしまいました。たくさんの物を集めて、飾ることは、悪ふざけなんかではないんです！

At first glance, you might think that many of the ingredients and the ideas in this last chapter are pretty frivolous and, to an extent, you would be right. Bird cages, stuffed animals, nostalgic posters, framed prints, paintings and drawings – clusters, arrangements and collections of objects. The sort of things that are scattered throughout the other pages of this book. And yet, it is these objects that make your kitchen unique and personal. These are the things that attract your eye when you first walk into a room. They tell stories. They show passion, history and love. Even kitchen utensils and cooking equipment can be interesting to look at – particularly if they are antique pottery, decorative enamelware or modern design icons. The kitchen is a room full of activity that involves the whole family – so children's drawings, collages, cardboard constructions, sports awards or holiday-collected treasures can all be found here, as can postcards and photographs. Less visible are the many practical quirks and details that make up the storage components inside the kitchen's cupboards: the cutlery drawers, bread bins, herb and spice containers, vegetable trays, plate racks, saucepan drawers and segregated waste disposal bins. In the super-modern kitchen, most below-counter doors have been replaced by smoothly-sliding drawers, which make stooping and searching in dark recesses a thing of the past. Not so frivolous after all!

個性的な演出

個性的な演出

個性的な演出

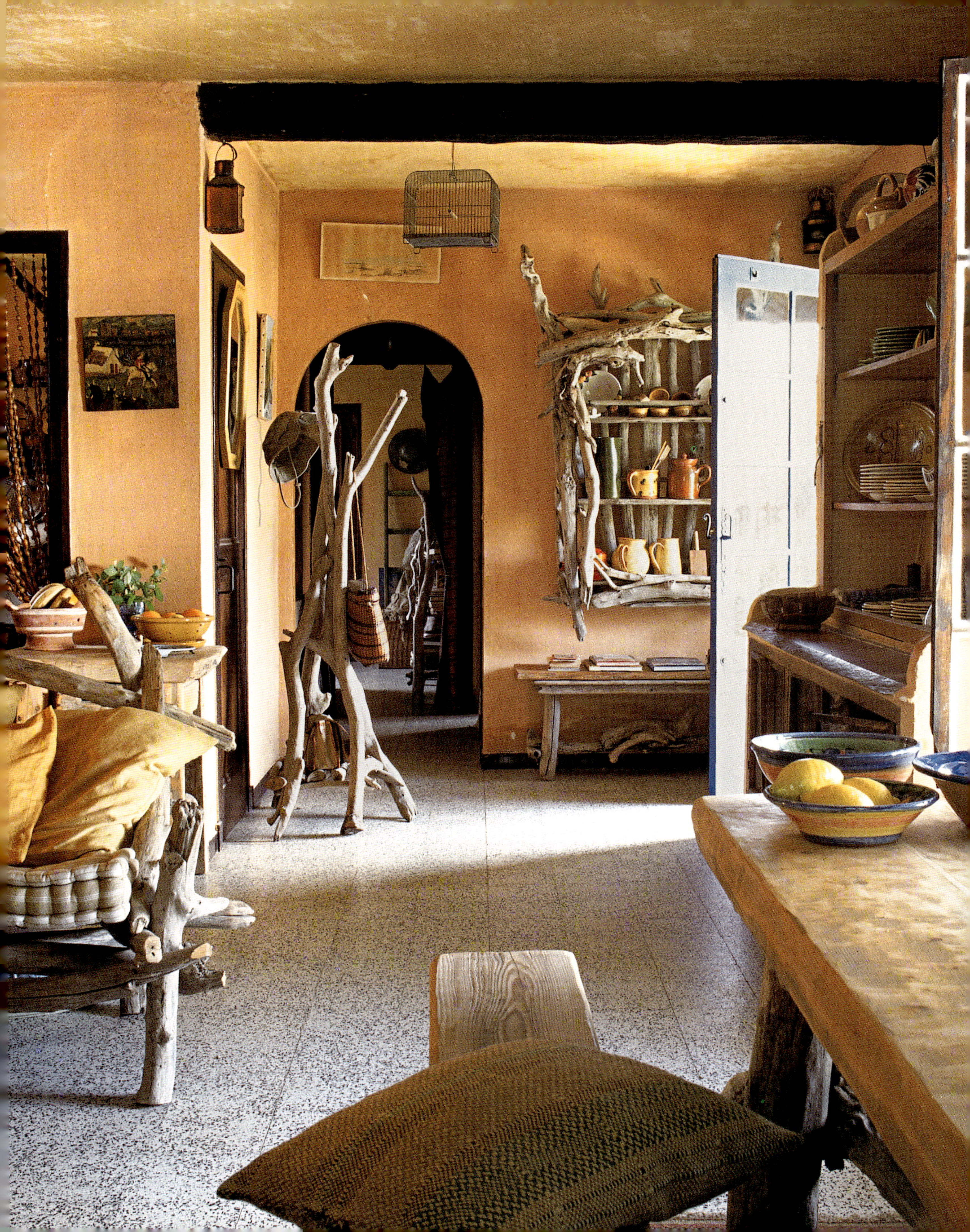

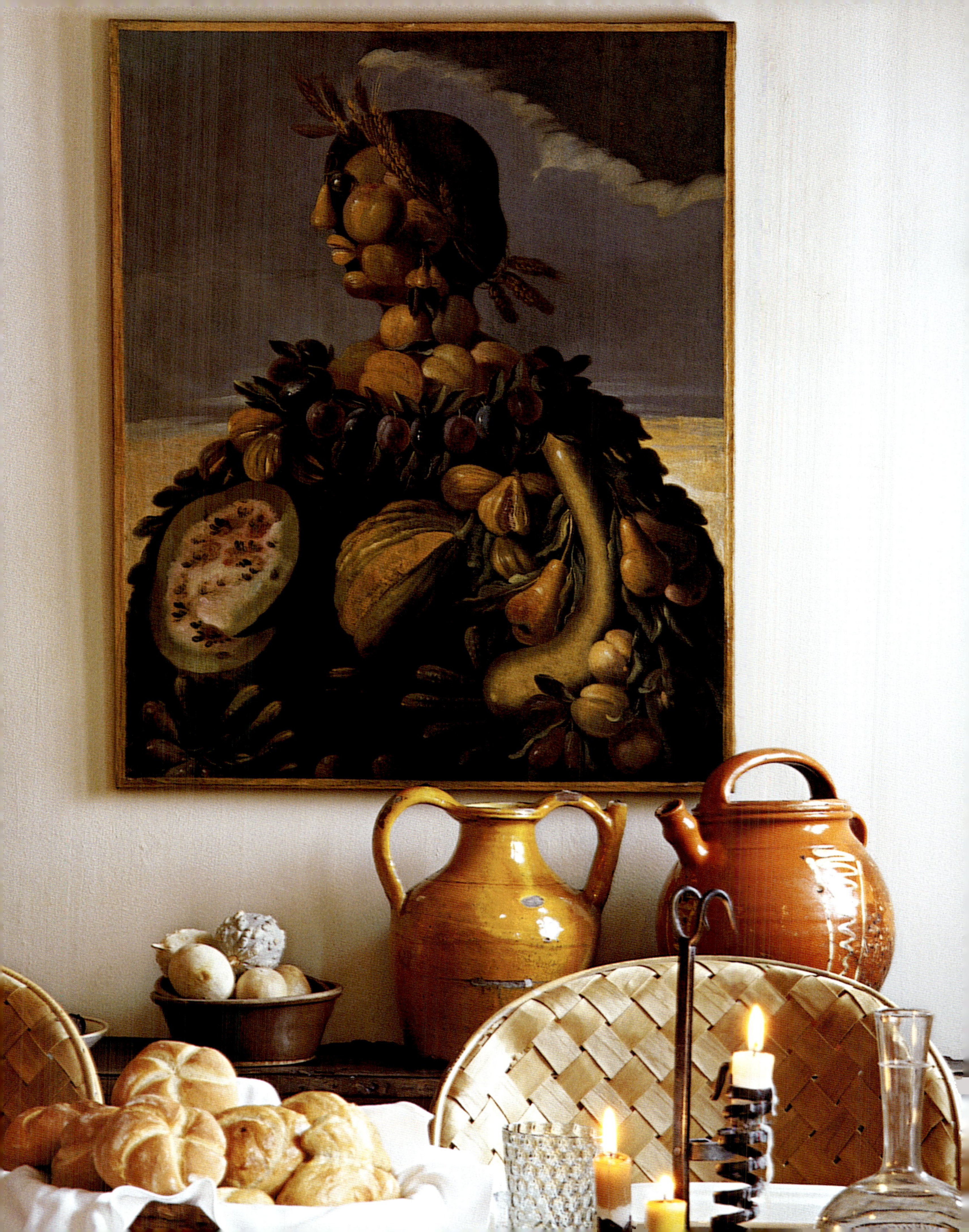

個性的な演出

個性的な演出

個性的な演出

個性的な演出

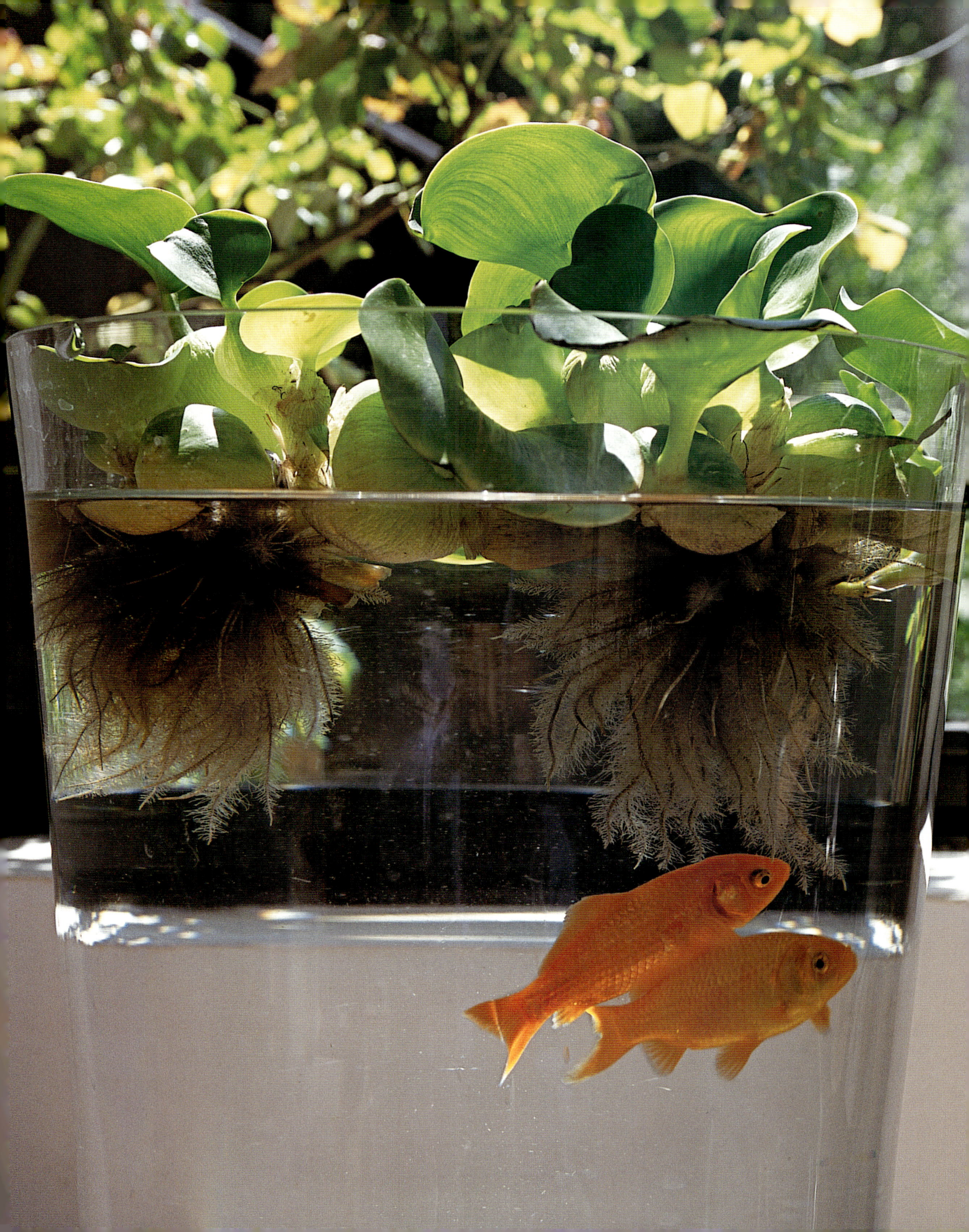

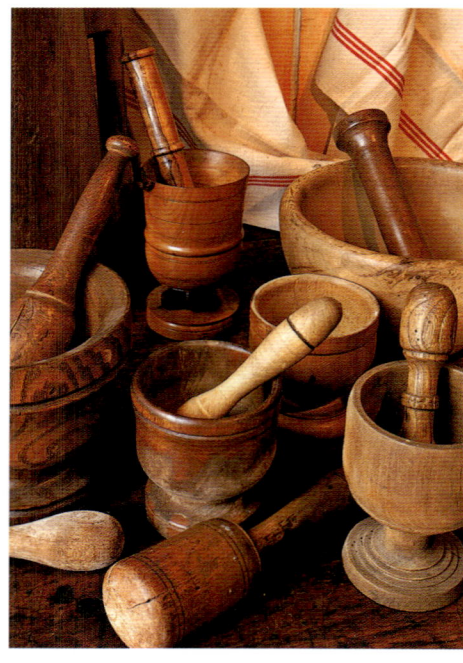

個性的な演出

個性的な演出

もし、キッチンが住まいの中枢だとしたら、キッチンという車輪の中心部から伸びるスポークは、私たちの暮らしのあらゆる部分につながっています。料理と同じように、思い出もまた、キッチンで生まれるのです。ご存じのとおり、キッチンにとってもっとも重要なのは機能ですが、その機能を充分役立てるためには、外観を整えて、美しさを感じる喜びを、味わえるキッチンにしなければなりません。本書では、1000を越えるキッチンのアイデアを提供していますが、どんなキッチンが自分に最適かという判断は、ご自身の直感にまかせてください。小鳥が巣を作るように、お好みのパーツを選び、自分らしさを加味しましょう。親から子へと料理のレシピが受け継がれるように、これからの長い年月、キッチンは、あなたに大きな喜びをもたらしてくれるでしょう。

スタッフォード・クリフ
ロンドンにて

Manufacturers' details

Page 40 bottom right; page 41 top centre and right, bottom left; page 82 bottom left; page 90 top left and top middle left; page 175 bottom left; page 179 bottom; page 188 top left; page 202 top left, centre four; page 203 top right, centre four pictures: **Newcastle Furniture**
www.newcastlefurniture.com

Page 81 top; page 118 top; page 202 top right and bottom right: **Harvey Jones**
www.harveyjones.com

Page 120 top row, centre row left and centre, bottom row centre and right; page 202 bottom left: **Sycamore Lighting**
www.sycamorelightingltd.co.uk

Page 120 middle row far right, bottom row left; page 168 bottom row left and second left: **THG Stainless Steel systems**
www.thginternational.co.uk

Page 168 bottom row far right; page 169 third row centre, bottom row nos 1 2 & 4 from left; page 176 bottom row nos 2 3 & 4 from left: **Byrock**
www.byrock.co.uk

Page 169 top row left and third from left, third row far right; page 176 middle row far left: **Ted Todd and Sons**
www.tedtodd.co.uk

Page 169 top row far right, second row second from right: **Tabu**
www.tabu.it

Page 151 far right; page 168 third row far left and second left; page 179 top; page 192 top right: **Stone Age**
www.stone-age.co.uk

Page 176 top row, second row second and fourth from left, bottom row far left: Art Diffusion Panels by **Interlam**
www.naa.ie

Page 176 middle row second from the right: **Elitis**
www.elitis.fr

Page 192 bottom right; page 203 top left, bottom row right and left: **Simply Italian UK Ltd**
www.simply-italian.co.uk

Editorial Director Jane O'Shea
Designer Stafford Cliff
Photographer Christian Sarramon
Design Assistant Katherine Case
Editor Simon Davis
Production Vincent Smith, Marina Asenjo

First published in 2009 by Quadrille Publishing Limited
www.quadrille.co.uk

Design and layout © 2009 Quadrille Publishing Limited
Photography © 2009 Christian Sarramon
Text © 2009 Stafford Cliff

The rights of the author have been asserted.
All rights reserved. No part of this book may be reproduced, stored in a retrieval system or transmitted in any form or by any means, electronic, electrostatic, magnetic tape, mechanical, photocopying, recording or otherwise, without the prior permission in writing of the publisher.

Printed in China

1000 kitchen ideas
ダイニングキッチンブック

発　　行　2010年2月1日
発 行 者　平野　陽三
発 行 元　**ガイアブックス**
　　　　　〒169-0074 東京都新宿区北新宿3-14-8
　　　　　TEL.03(3366)1411　FAX.03(3366)3503
　　　　　http://www.gaiajapan.co.jp
発 売 元　産調出版株式会社

Copyright SUNCHOH SHUPPAN INC. JAPAN2010
ISBN978-4-88282-729-0 C3052

落丁本・乱丁本はお取り替えいたします。
本書を許可なく複製することは、かたくお断わりします。
Printed in China

著　者：スタッフォード・クリフ (Stafford Cliff)
　　　デザイン・コンサルタント、アート・ディレクター、ライター。長年、住宅関連のパンフレットやカタログ、雑誌のデザインと執筆を行ってきた。テレンス・コンラン卿との、住宅カタログの制作を経て、1974年『The House Book』のデザインを担当。ロングセラーとなる。以降、デザインや住宅関連書を60冊以上制作。主な作品に、世界中で行った住宅の調査結果を、480ページにまとめた『The Way We live』、住む人の意識をテーマに取り上げた草分け的な書『Home』『1000 Garden Ideas』がある。近著の『1000 Home Ideas』は、10ヶ国語に翻訳されている。

写　真：クリスチャン・サラモン (Christian Sarramon)
　　　フランスの写真家。30年以上にわたり、世界をめぐって、目を見張るようなアイデア豊富なキッチンを、カメラに収め続けている。

翻　訳：今井由美子（いまい　ゆみこ）
　　　広島女学院大学英米文学科卒業。訳書に『実用カラーの癒し』『アロマセラピー活用百科』『自宅の緑化インテリア』『自宅の書棚』(いずれも産調出版)など多数。